Not Lost Forever

My Story of Survival

CARMINA SALCIDO
WITH Steve Jackson

HARPER

An Imprint of HarperCollinsPublishers

HARPER

An Imprint of HarperCollins*Publishers*
10 East 53rd Street
New York, New York 10022-5299

Copyright © 2009 by Carmina Salcido
ISBN 978-0-06-204494-5

First Harper mass market printing: July 2011
First William Morrow hardcover printing: October 2009

HarperCollins ® and Harper ® are registered trademarks of Harper-Collins Publishers.

Printed in the United States of America

Visit Harper paperbacks on the World Wide Web at
www.harpercollins.com

10 9 8 7 6 5 4 3 2 1

"Oh my God!"

That afternoon, a young man had been poking around the Petaluma dump as he waited for a friend to get off work at the quarry. When he wandered over by an embankment and looked down, the man saw three large dolls lying at the bottom. At least he thought they were dolls—a bit worse for wear, unwanted, discarded with the rest of the trash. He started to walk away, but something about the dolls made him look back.

That's when I moved my leg.

"Oh my God!" I heard him yell, and he took off running up the road to the quarry.

The young man, Mike Mikesell, found the quarry superintendent, Tim Smith, and told him what he'd seen. Tim ran to the road above the embankment and looked down, where he saw three little girls lying in the grass below him. Two of us were dead. But I was sitting up.

I remember Tim trying to comfort me. And I remember when the helicopter arrived. The light and the noise terrified me. When they put me on the stretcher to load me into the helicopter, I started screaming and kicking, flailing my arms so wildly that they had to send the copter away and wait for a regular ambulance.

Strapped to the stretcher, surrounded by strangers poking me with needles, I started to cry. I didn't want to be hurt anymore.

On the way to the hospital, the paramedics asked me what happened. "Daddy cut me," I said. "Please don't hurt me."

By Steve Jackson

True Crime

MONSTER
ROUGH TRADE
NO STONE UNTURNED
PARTNERS IN EVIL
NOT LOST FOREVER
LOVE ME TO DEATH

Biography/History

LUCKY LADY
TO THE EDGE AND BACK

I dedicate this book in loving memory of my dear mom, Angela, who only wanted freedom, love, and happiness. Also, to my grandma Louise, my sisters, Sofia and Teresa, and my dear aunties Maria and Ruth. All of you are forever in my heart and mind, a part of my soul until we are together again.

Carmina Salcido

Prologue

---

*C*armina Salcido sits *in the front passenger seat of the sedan gazing out the window as the car races along the serpentine highway between the towns of Sonoma and Petaluma, California. The hills on either side of the road rise and fall, rolling toward the horizon like giant swells on a straw-colored ocean. Remnants of the morning fog drift over the brush-filled gullies between the hills, lingering briefly on the shadowed side of their peaks, ghosts reluctant to leave a favorite haunting.*

The grass on the nearby hills is short, grazed to parklike uniformity and guarded by lonely umbrella-shaped oak trees. Other hills and bottomlands next to the highway have been given over to neat, terraced rows of grapevines. It is September 2007, and the wine-grape harvest in this beautiful country north of the Bay Area was early this year. Most of the fruit has been picked, largely by Mexican farmworkers, and is going through the process of crushing, fermentation, and storage in oak barrels that will turn it to wine. A few dark blue bunches still hang heavy on the vines, but autumnal yellows, reds, and oranges are coming to light as well.

Sean Kingston's "There's Nothing" comes on the radio. Hopeful about love, it's one of Carmina's favorites.

There's nothing in this world
There's not another boy that could make me feel so sweet

Like her mother, Carmina is a strikingly pretty young woman. She has large, topaz-colored eyes, a wide, engaging smile, and a delicate, upturned nose. She laughs a lot—a surprisingly big, unself-conscious sound. Considering what she's been through since she was not yet three, it's a wonder she laughs at all.

The sound is incongruous with a thick white scar that circles her throat from just below her right ear to just below her left. Another round scar marks the spot at the bottom of her throat where the surgeons placed a tracheotomy tube.

That was over eighteen years ago. Today she is revisiting the landscape of that horrific past—a tour that takes her to Boyes Hot Springs, a run-down working-class community on the northwest edge of Sonoma; to the house on Baines Avenue where she spent the first three years of her life; then out the two-lane, tree-shrouded Sonoma Highway, otherwise known as Highway 12, to the vineyards and winery at the Kunde Estate and the Dunbar Elementary School and what was once the Grand Cru winery near Glen Ellen.

Each stop is another chapter of what a local newspaper once breathlessly labeled "the Rampage in Sonoma." As Carmina tells the story, some of her memories are as vivid as yesterday; some are fuzzy and dreamlike yet nonetheless real to her. Certain experiences, even painful ones, she recalls with a shake of her head, as if they had happened to someone else. "Can you believe that?" she'll say. Others bring tears to her eyes and a hitch to her voice.

Much of what Carmina knows about April 14, 1989, and what happened afterward comes from reading old newspaper and magazine clippings at the library, and from the documents, letters, and photographs that occupy twenty-six boxes of evidentiary material in the possession of the Sonoma County District Attorney's Office. She has filled in some of the blanks with the recollections of other people who were living in Sonoma at that time. Some of these stories are real and reliable; some are exaggerated; some are pure fiction. She knows all that. Still, she is trying to piece together their memories and explanations into something true.

Even the self-serving excuses of her father, Ramón Salcido, who still waits for the executioner on death row at San Quentin State Prison.

Up ahead, Carmina spots the turnoff she's looking for. Later the tour will move on to the Calvary Catholic Cemetery in Petaluma, then to the house of horrors in Cotati, and finally to the Santa Rosa home of Mike Brown, the Sonoma County detective who headed the investigation of the murders. But now, first, the car pulls onto a gravel road and up a hill near a rock quarry.

As the car crunches to a halt at the entrance to the Petaluma dump, Carmina is finally overwhelmed. In the years since she returned to California to learn the truth about her family, she has visited each of the other sites, some of them many times. But never here. Her grandfather pointed it out, but he couldn't bring himself to take her.

"Every time I drive past this place," she says, "I can feel this almost magnetic pull trying to get me to stop. You could blindfold me and I would still know when we were going by."

The view hasn't changed much in the intervening years; only the seasons, her age, and the circumstances are different. In April 1989 the leaves on the grapevines along the highway were the freshly minted color of lima beans. The wild grasses at the dump were as tall as the almost-three-year-old girl who sat among them, waiting for rescue.

For a moment now, she seems to have second thoughts. She hesitates to leave the safety of the car. Then, with a sigh, Carmina gathers her courage and steps out. Glancing at the nearby ravine, she takes note of the embankment, then quickly looks away, swaying unsteadily in the sunlight.

"This is the last place I was with my sisters. This is where I saw their faces for the last time . . . the last time we were all together."

It is a lonely spot and somber despite the bright blue sky and beauty of the surrounding hills. "I know this place," she says as her head drops and her eyes fix on the gravel road beneath her feet. Her shoulders sag and tears spill one at a time onto her cheeks, rolling off and splashing to the ground. "This is difficult," she says.

Everything comes back to her in these moments: Fear. Hate. Love. Longing. And guilt. "Survivor's guilt, yes," she acknowledges, stealing a look toward a barely discernible shed on the quarry grounds above. "I remember standing up and looking at a shed. I was only three years old, but why couldn't I have made more of an effort? Why didn't I walk up there and cry for help?" She shakes her head slowly. "I know I probably couldn't have saved them, that they were already dead. But another part of me says I just lay there watching them die. I didn't know—I still don't know—the extent of their injuries, if theirs were any worse than mine. And look at me. Everybody says I should have died. Maybe if . . ."

It's too big a cross. She stops and leans against the car. "I've had to live with that for a long time."

Ahead and toward the right, across sheer ridges of the mountains, separated by deep green canyons and broadening lower down into rolling orchards and vineyards, they caught their first sight of Sonoma Valley and the wild mountains that rimmed its eastern side.

JACK LONDON, *The Valley of the Moon*

One

S onoma County, where I was raised for the first three years of my life and where I returned in 2005, lies about an hour's drive north of San Francisco. Its geography includes seventy-six miles of Pacific coastline and plains and an interior marked by rounded hills and steep-sided mountains. It was created when ancient tectonic plates crashed into one another, shoving those mountains into the sky, and by volcanic activity that spewed rolling rivers of molten rock across the valley floors. That violence was later tempered by the beauty of primordial forests, grass-covered meadows, and clear streams, when the original inhabitants wandered in and stayed thousands of years ago. Their descendants were the Pomo, Miwok, and Wintun tribes, who were living there when the Europeans first arrived.

To make sense of what they couldn't otherwise explain, these native peoples relied on shamans to communicate with the spirit world, which harbored animal spirits both good and evil—the one helpful to mankind, the other casting dark shadows across his path. The natives lived a simple life, hunting and gathering in the game-filled, fertile valleys. And when they died, they believed, their spirits jumped into the ocean at Point Reyes—a finger of land jutting into the Pacific—and made their way west beyond the breaking waves, where they remained with Coyote, the creator, in an afterworld known as Dead Home.

For two hundred years the Europeans in that part of California stayed close to the coast. They began moving inland after the arrival of Padre José Altimira, a Franciscan priest who established the Mission San Francisco Solano in July 1823 in a lovely, stream-fed valley between two mountain ranges.

San Francisco Solano was the northernmost of twenty-one missions connected by El Camino Real, or "the Royal Road." It was the first and only California mission Mexico established after gaining its independence from Spain. The Franciscans forced the natives to convert to Catholicism, but of course the priests, too, communicated with spirits—their saints and demons, who involved themselves in human affairs for both good and evil. Except that now when people died their spirits went to heaven, hell, or that place in between they called purgatory.

The Indians had called the valley Sonoma. I'm told that the exact translation of the word isn't known for certain. Some say it meant "many moons," others "where the moon rises." But the name that stuck was Valley of the Moon.

In the 1830s, Mexico founded a small town at the site of Altimira's mission. Pueblo de Sonoma was a military outpost, but in many ways it was also a typical Mexican town, with a central plaza across from the mission. The military was there to protect the Mexicans from the native population, but they were never really a threat, and in 1837 a smallpox epidemic wiped out most of the Pomo, Miwok, and Wintun people living in the area.

In 1846, American settlers—who were living in California under permission of the Mexican government—attacked the garrison. They raised the Bear Flag over the plaza. It was the first act of the so-called Bear Flag Revolt, which seized the land from the Mexicans and established the Republic of California. Four years later, California became the thirty-first state in the United States. Now it was the Mexicans who were illegal immigrants when they crossed the border.

Sonoma County was a lovely and fertile valley, and it attracted people from many races and cultures—from the Italian quarrymen who came in to work the local quarries to the migrant farm laborers who rode the rails to follow the harvest. At first these itinerant farmworkers were "hoboes" from other parts of the United States, but eventually the landowners came to rely on immigrants who were willing to do the work.

Yet those workers from other lands weren't always welcomed with open arms. The late 1800s were a time of ugly anti-Chinese sentiment, and some of Sonoma County's most prominent residents banded together to chase the Chinese out. For a good part of the twentieth century, one of the main jobs of the sheriff's office was keeping immigrants in line during the harvest season—and making sure they left when it was over.

In 1903 the valley became home to the author Jack London. A champion of socialism and organized labor, he had grown disillusioned with both movements by the age of twenty-seven and was looking to leave the city for a quiet life in the country. He fell in love with its wildwood and rugged mountains, as well as its vineyards, orchards, and pastures. He and his second wife, Charmian, went on to purchase six bankrupt ranches to create the fourteen-hundred-acre Beauty Ranch in Glen Ellen, a small community just off the narrow, two-lane Sonoma Highway, which ran the length of the valley between the town of Sonoma and the county seat of Santa Rosa.

In August 1913 London published his sixteenth novel, *The Valley of the Moon*. The book chronicled the lives of a young couple from an impoverished neighborhood in Oakland who decided to break from their working-class environment and seek a peaceful life in the country. London had always defended the working class, and *The Valley of the Moon* was full of praise for the work ethic of the region's immigrant farmers. But he also shared the ethnic prejudices of that time, and the main character of *The Valley of the Moon* derides the local immigrants—Chinese, Japanese, Mexicans, Portuguese, and Italians alike—complaining that they were pushing aside "native-born," "old-stock" Anglo-Saxon Americans and driving them into low-paying jobs in the dirty cities.

Whatever his biases, London and his wife took to the Valley of the Moon. "I ride over my beautiful ranch," he wrote to friends. "Between my legs is a beautiful horse. The air is wine. The grapes on a score of rolling hills are red with autumn flame. Across Sonoma Mountain, wisps of sea fog are stealing. The afternoon sun smolders in the drowsy sky. I have everything to make me glad I am alive."

But his joy was short-lived. On November 18, 1916, the front page of the local paper, the Santa Rosa–based *Press Democrat,* was dominated by the headline:

JACK LONDON DIES IN
VALLEY OF THE MOON

The official reports say that London died of uremic poisoning—his kidneys shut down, probably as a result of drinking. But there were rumors that he had overdosed on a medicine containing arsenic prescribed to combat the pain of kidney disease, and some wondered if the overdose was accidental.

London's views on immigrants weren't unusual for the times, nor did they seem to have affected his friendship with local Sonoma residents. As time went on, Sonoma County would continue to offer a home to people from all over the world; it became as culturally diverse as any place in the country.

Even if not every immigrant dream ended well.

* * *

Some people—especially those who have lived here all their lives—tell me the Sonoma Valley is cursed. They say that something evil here causes men to lose their minds.

In 1910, as London was working on *The Valley of the Moon*, the *Press Democrat* reported what it called the "most atrocious crime in the history of Sonoma County." On August 4, readers were greeted by a two-inch tall headline:

ENTIRE KENDALL FAMILY
MURDERED AT CAZADERO

The story's subhead: "Father, Mother and Son Are Slain, Their Bodies Hacked to Pieces and Burned in Kitchen Stove."

The murders were blamed on a Japanese farmworker named Henry Yamaguchi, who'd recently been told to leave the ranch by one of the Kendall men. But suspicion later fell on Yamaguchi's boss, ranch owner Margaret Starbuck, the wife of a prominent Bay Area architect named Henry F. Starbuck.

Mrs. Starbuck claimed that Yamaguchi had come to her home in San Francisco and confessed the murders to her but disappeared before the authorities could be summoned. Then an anonymous person claimed to have seen Yamaguchi boarding a train for Mexico. But the police also had reports that Mrs. Starbuck wanted the Kendalls, who were tenants, off the ranch, and that she'd threatened them after they refused to terminate their lease. And her story of Yamaguchi's confession was inconsistent and full of holes.

The Japanese community in Sonoma County was sure that Yamaguchi was a victim, not a suspect. And they weren't the only ones who thought he couldn't have committed the murders. At five feet three and 120 pounds, he was much smaller than any of the victims, including Mrs. Kendall. It was hard to imagine that small man overcoming two men and an old woman, killing them in cold blood, dismembering them with axes, and then feeding the pieces to the kitchen stove and to the hogs. And he didn't seem like a mass murderer: He'd attended Oakland Polytechnic High School for a brief time after arriving in California from Japan, and was a faithful member of the Japanese Methodist Church. Friends and former employers described him as polite and intelligent.

The Kendall massacre made national headlines and sparked a massive manhunt. Across the country, Japanese men were arrested on suspicion that they might be the fugitive farmworker. Authorities worried that some vigilante might kill the wrong man. But Yamaguchi was never seen or heard from again. Some believe he met the same fate as the Kendalls, but the person they suspected—Mrs. Starbuck—stuck to her story. The Starbucks soon sold the ranch and their home in San Francisco and moved without notice.

And the Kendall family weren't the only victims of mass murder in Sonoma County. In 1949, another bloodbath involving an immigrant farm laborer made headlines. This time, however, there would be no question who committed the crime or why.

One night that November, Polcerpacio "Henry" Pio, a native of the Philippines, murdered four people with a shotgun. Pio was driven to anger when his former lover, Louise, arrived at his cabin with her brand-new husband and her sister to pick up some items she'd left there.

In a rambling, incoherent confession, the thirty-seven-year-old Pio said he warned Louise and the others to go away, but her husband tried to enter the cabin anyway.

"Give you warning not to push door. I am really shot you if you push the door," Pio said he yelled. "He push the door and so I shot him. Then I don't know what I do, and I maybe shoot some others."

Pio fired more than a dozen shotgun blasts at close range. Then he walked over to a neighboring ranch, where he emptied nine more shotgun shells into another Filipino hop picker. "That guy like to kill me before," Pio explained in his confession. An hour after the killings, he was apprehended "without resistance" while driving on the outskirts of Santa Rosa with the loaded shotgun on the seat beside him. He said he was going to turn himself in. Pio, whose smiling mug shot appeared on the front page the next day, pleaded guilty to the murders and was sentenced to life in prison. He served twenty-eight years before being discharged in 1977.

By then, Polcerpacio Pio had joined Henry Yamaguchi as part of Sonoma County's half-forgotten murderous past. By the time I started exploring what had happened to my own family, there were few residents left who still recalled the crimes of those earlier days, and their eerie foreshadowing of another immigrant dream that ended as a nightmare in the Valley of the Moon.

Two

The morning fog hangs low on the hills as the car rolls through the town of Sonoma, passing the plaza where the mission built by Padre Altimira still stands, restored and open to the public. Restaurants, bars, and boutiques surround the old plaza, catering to the tourists who come to town to sample the wares of more than two dozen wineries in the area.

Sonoma has long been among the top farming regions in the United States, with local towns having their own specialty. Sebastopol, near the coast, is famous for its apples, Cloverdale in the north boasts about its oranges, and Petaluma is the "egg basket of the world." Some of the towns—like Boyes Hot Springs and its neighbor Agua Caliente, or "Warm Water"—became resorts where wealthy tourists from San Francisco could be soaked and pampered at local spas. The Native Americans believed the warm, mineral-laden waters had healing powers. Santa Rosa, "the City of Roses," was a shipping hub and the county seat—the site of the local courthouse and jail—but the town of Sonoma has always been the true heart of the county.

The area's first vineyards were planted by monks at the Mission San Francisco Solano in 1823, and by 1870 California was the top wine-producing state in the nation. With its hot, dry summers, abundant sunlight, cool nights, wet winters, and fertile soil, it was the perfect growing environment for Cabernet Sauvignon, Pinot Noir, Zinfandel, Chardonnay, and Merlot grapes. In the next hundred years or more, Sonoma County attracted countless wineries, from major, established operations that had been in the family for generations to boutique wineries opened by wealthy newcomers. Wine tourism became a source of local lifeblood, and though the marketing-minded wineries of Napa Valley coined the term "Wine Country USA" for their advertising campaigns, the more laid-back Sonoma growers soon realized that there was money—and reputations—to be made in on-site tasting rooms and winery tours.

As the major employer in the county, the wine industry hired both locals and immigrant workers as field hands, to pick the crops or run the mechanical harvesters and to help on the production end. The field jobs didn't pay much— roughly eight dollars an hour by the 1980s—but that was enough to lure workers from Mexico. Many of them made their way to Sonoma and settled in Boyes Hot Springs and Agua Caliente, the last low-rent communities in the Valley of the Moon.

There is no physical boundary between Sonoma and Boyes Hot Springs, the first stop on Carmina's tour this morning. But one sees a decided difference between the two towns as the car swings onto the Sonoma Highway, Highway 12, and the resort town gives way to a collection of working-class neighborhoods. The businesses along the highway here cater to the local Hispanic population— taquerías, Mexican food marts, lunch-wagon trucks selling burritos and tacos. The Boyes Hot Springs Food Center on the corner of the highway and Mountain Road has signs plastered to its glass façade advertising beer and check cashing in Spanish and English. Men in straw cowboy hats

*and pointed cowboy boots gather in front of the stores;
many of them will return to the fields in the morning.*

*In the early 1980s, one of those working in the vineyards
and living in Boyes Hot Springs was Ramón Borjorquez
Salcido.*

What brought my father to Sonoma County was the same
thing that had lured millions of his fellow Mexicans to the
United States since the early part of the century: the opportunity to earn a better living than he could in Mexico.

Ramón was born March 6, 1961, and raised in Los
Mochis, a dusty, drought-plagued city in the Mexican state
of Sinaloa, halfway down the east coast of the Gulf of California. Los Mochis is only a hundred miles north of Mazatlán, a famous seaside resort, but it's no tourist town. There
are sugarcane and wheat farms there, but also fertilizer and
pesticide factories, and a gray-brown smog often hung over
the city from fires used to burn the debris from the cane
fields, and the residue of its industries. Still, compared with
its neighbors, Los Mochis wasn't the worst place to live; it
had lower unemployment, and a higher standard of living,
than some of the surrounding areas.

Ramón's father, Arnaldo—my paternal grandfather—was
a fisherman, but he died when my dad was seven. My paternal grandmother, Valentina Borjorquez, remarried. She and
her husband, Francisco Seja, lived in a simple, whitewashed
stucco house typical of a middle-class Mexican neighborhood. Ramón, his four brothers, and his two sisters helped
with the family finances by selling tamales their mother
made. But my dad didn't get along with his stepfather, and
he moved out of the house when he was just fourteen.

Ramón was a good-looking young man—only five feet
eight but athletic, with coal-black hair, a quick, charming
smile, and aspirations to improve his life. In 1980 he was
working at Tele Servicio Duarte, where he was considered a
good worker and "very honorable," according to his em-

ployers. He seems to have stayed out of trouble with the law, and that year he married a pretty young woman named María de Jesus Torres.

Unknown to my dad, though, María was already pregnant with another man's child. Jesus Ramón Salcido Torres was born September 21, 1980, and only then did Ramón discover María's secret. Ramón left María a short time later, but her betrayal affected him, planting a seed of jealousy in his mind that someday would bear bitter fruit.

The first sign of my father's potential for violence may have occurred shortly afterward. One night, when he was at his mother's house, he asked to use the phone, which she kept locked up. When Valentina refused, he became enraged and grabbed her. His older brother, Arnaldo, intervened, knocking him to the floor. Ramón left the house, and some say he threatened to return and kill his family.

Two weeks later he called to apologize to his mother. But he told her that she might not see him again for a while; he'd decided to head north and cross the border into the United States—where a man could start over, earn a decent living, and make something of himself. Carrying everything he owned, he slipped across the border at Jalisco.

Sometimes I wonder, if things had worked out differently, whether my dad might have lived out his life in Los Mochis—working, raising a family, enjoying a ripe old age in the sunny clime of his Mexican hometown. Or would the evil he was capable of have come out in some other way?

Ramón made his way to the Valley of the Moon. When he first arrived, he worked at a stable; then he got a job with one of the wineries lining Highway 12.

In Sonoma County, my father found himself in a land of haves and have-nots. There were wealthy neighborhoods of multimillion-dollar homes, including estates in the hills owned by international drug dealers who financed their lavish lifestyles with empires built on cocaine and marijuana. And there were places like Boyes Hot Springs, where the drug dealers were small-time nobodies who lived in the same dumps as honest, hardworking laborers.

Not every property in Boyes Hot Springs was trashed. Some residents fought to keep their homes and yards in good order and complained about the presence of criminals and run-down properties. But just as one bad apple can spoil the barrel, one yard full of weeds, trash, and broken-down cars, one house whose residents either don't care about or actually prey on their neighbors, can bring a neighborhood down to its level.

My dad was nothing out of the ordinary. His employers considered him an excellent worker, and he was well liked by others. He was seen often at the Boyes Hot Springs Food Center, picking up groceries, beer, and the occasional porn video. On evenings and weekends, he played soccer at Larson Park.

There's no doubt that my dad liked to drink and party, sometimes too much; in 1983 he was arrested for drunk driving. But instead of drinking at bars with other Mexican immigrants, he tended to hang out in working-class Anglo taverns like McNeilly's on Verano Avenue or the Valley of the Moon Saloon off Highway 12. He also liked to snort cocaine with his drinking buddies.

In the summer of 1983, he was at a party when a friend introduced him to Debra Ann Whitten. She was a divorcée, and he was an illegal immigrant who could help his residency status by marrying a U.S. citizen. They married on October 19, 1983, at the Heart of Reno Wedding Chapel in Nevada.

Within a few months, Debra Ann announced that she was expecting a baby in August. Before long, though, Ramón caught her cozying up to another guy. Flying into a rage, he accused her of being pregnant with the other man's child. He pinned his wife to the floor, punched her in her stomach, wrapped his hands around her throat, and threatened to kill her.

It was the second time Ramón Salcido failed to follow through on such a threat. Instead, he left Debra Ann and resumed the life of a carefree bachelor in Sonoma. Despite two unfaithful wives and two failed marriages, he had a high opinion of himself; his middle-class upbringing and education gave him an advantage over his coworkers, most of whom had left behind lives of abject poverty in Mexico, and his feelings of superiority gave him a glib, fast-talking way with women. He had a good job, a good relationship with his bosses, and he hoped to someday get a promotion and make more money. Maybe even afford something better than the 1979 Ford LTD sedan he was driving the day he met my mom, Angela Richards.

Three

The first stop in Boyes Hot Springs is an empty soccer field. "My mom wasn't allowed to date, or even hang out with guys," Carmina says. "But as she got older, seventeen or eighteen, she started to rebel and find ways around the rules. She used to slip out her window and come over here where the Hispanic men were playing soccer. The newspapers say that's where she met Ramón, but he has a different story about that."

Ramón Salcido says he was driving slowly down Gregor Street in Boyes Hot Springs when he noticed a teenage girl watering the garden in the front yard of a house. With her long, straight, dark-blond hair tied back from her face with ribbons, Angela looked like she'd stepped out of the 1950s. Even though she was working in the garden, she wore a formless skirt that fell below her knees and a high-collared blouse, both of which hid her figure. When she looked up, he saw a strikingly pretty young Anglo woman with large blue eyes and pale, delicate features.

"Ramón says Angela smiled at him when she saw him looking at her," Carmina says. "So when he got to the end of the block, he turned his car around and drove by my *grandparents' house again. He pulled up and whistled to get her attention. He says she turned off the water and hopped the little fence to come talk to him."*

Carmina's mouth twists, and she laughs ruefully. "Of course that's Ramón talking. So take it for what it is."

Whether my mom met my dad at the soccer fields or while she was watering the family garden, she kept their relationship a secret from her parents. Otherwise, it would have been nipped in the bud.

Mom's parents, Bob and Louise Richards, belonged to a conservative Catholic sect called Tradition, Family and Property, which didn't approve of dating or unchaperoned fraternizing between young men and women. As my grandparents saw it, they were providing their children with a safe haven in a sea of evil and immorality. Neither of them had felt that sort of protection from their parents growing up, and they wanted it for their kids.

When he was still a teenager, my grandpa Bob had watched his father walk out on his family. After that there wasn't a lot of money or a male role model. Although he'd been raised as a Catholic by his mother, my grandpa stopped attending church; he preferred drinking and carousing.

In 1962 he moved to northern California, where one of his sisters lived, and got a job working for Pacific Gas and Electric. One day he was visiting his sister when a young woman across the street was having trouble backing her car out of the driveway. He went over to help—and that's when he met Marian Louise Morehead.

My grandpa was a small, slender man, a full inch shorter than Louise, as she preferred to be called. They were both lonely and looking to settle down, and they hit it off right away. Grandpa was growing tired of his lifestyle, and Louise had a calming effect on him. She let him know that she wouldn't tolerate bad behavior, and he would have to change if he wanted to be with her. She, too, had had a rough, abusive childhood and not much in the way of reli-

gion or support; she wanted something different. She liked
that he was Catholic, and she insisted that he return to the
church, happily converting before their marriage.

My grandparents wanted a large family and started off
with a son, my uncle Robert. My mom came along next, on
June 15, 1965, when the family was living in Red Bluff, a
logging town in northern California. Then it was Uncle
Lewis, followed by Uncle Gerald. The family moved to
Davis for seven years, and then to San Jose in 1975. Twelve
years after my mom was born, they had another daughter,
my aunt Ruth Bernadette.

One day, on a visit to a San Jose flea market, Grandpa was
approached by some young men from the group known as
Tradition, Family and Property. Founded in 1960 in Brazil
by a Catholic professor named Plinio Corrêa de Oliveira,
TFP was probably the most conservative of the Catholic
groups that sprang up in reaction to the liberal Vatican II
reforms in the early 1960s. The young men told my grandfather that the group's name came from the three pillars of a
Christian society: tradition, family, and property. There
were some misguided sinners out there who dismissed them
as a cult, the men said, but they saw themselves as the last
great hope for Western civilization. They were opposed to
evil of all kinds, from liberal politics to the Vatican's misguided, weak-willed attempts to water down Catholicism
for the masses. They criticized the popes who had refused to
rescind the reforms, such as the heresy of conducting mass
in anything other than Latin.

Tradition, Family and Property wasn't a huge movement, but it had a presence in many countries. In the
United States it was called the American Society for the
Defense of Tradition, Family and Property. TFP was a
blend of politics, religion, and anachronism. The members
of TFP believed that humankind was better off under the
rule of God-appointed kings, queens, and other aristocrats.
They decorated their homes and offices with the trappings
of medieval courts, with heraldry banners and displays of

ancient armaments. Its members were staunchly anticommunist and longed for the dogmatic Roman Catholic
Church of their youth. In the United States the group en-
gaged in street politics—protesting outside of abortion
clinics and against any legislation advocating gay rights,
as well as organizing boycotts against films they considered blasphemous.

In the home, TFP called for all kinds of restrictions on
male and female relationships. Women were forbidden to
wear pants, makeup was discouraged, and from an early age
girls were taught that a woman's place was in the home
caring for her husband, who was expected to be the bread-
winner.

I'm not sure how much of this Grandpa knew when he
first learned of TFP, but he liked what the men at the flea
market had to say, and when he introduced Grandma to his
new friends, she felt the same way. After joining TFP, one
of the first steps they took was to pull their children from
the public schools, breaking them off from contact with
their friends and, to a large part, the world outside the Richards home. My mother and her siblings would be home-
schooled from then on.

In 1980, the same year that my dad arrived in Sonoma
County, the Richards family packed up again. This time
they landed in Boyes Hot Springs, in a small, two-bedroom
duplex in a neighborhood behind the Sonoma Mission Inn.
The boys here packed off to a TFP boys' school, St. Louis
de Montfort Academy in Herndon, Pennsylvania. Grandpa
got a job working as a UPS driver, while Grandma stayed
home on Gregor Street with the children, who were joined
in 1981 by another sister, my aunt Maria Ann. My Mom
shared the second bedroom with her two young sisters.

It was as if the Richards family was trying to turn back
the hands of time. Beyond their neatly kept lawn and gardens it may have been the 1980s, but inside it was the
1950s—with a dash of the Middle Ages thrown in. My
mother's childhood home was filled with shrines to the

Virgin Mary, votive candles, crucifixes, statues of saints, and images of Jesus. There were swords and shields with coats of arms on the walls and a full suit of armor in the foyer; a large statue of the Blessed Mother graced the front yard.

My grandparents tried to be as self-sufficient as possible, raising vegetables in the garden for immediate consumption and canning and keeping a beehive for honey. Grandma was an excellent seamstress, and she made all of the family's clothes. All the women in the family wore the same conservative elastic-waisted dresses hemmed below the knee and tied their long hair back with ribbons. Not only could women not wear pants, but on hot summer days the neighbors were surprised to see my mom and her sisters splashing in a blow-up wading pool in their dresses or terry-cloth jumpers because they weren't allowed to wear swimsuits.

Nor were they allowed to play much with kids in the neighborhood. They weren't supposed to go into other people's homes, and there were no sleepovers. What little contact they did have with other kids was always under the watchful guard of Grandma, who never let them out of her sight.

However strict my grandparents were with their children, there was no doubt that Mom and her sisters and brothers were loved. The family often went on outings together, and it was a common sight in the neighborhood to see my grandparents sitting in the front yard, happily watching their children play.

Grandma Louise was a kind and generous neighbor and friend, helping out when someone fell ill and delivering food and handmade gifts at Christmas. And her children were always polite and respectful of their elders.

It wasn't an easy neighborhood to raise children in, but Grandma was tough. She blew the whistle on a couple of drug dealers, and she kept an eye on a paroled child molester who lived down the block. Years later, I learned that she often drove to San Mateo at night to attend TFP meetings. Compared with San Mateo, Boyes Hot Springs was a Girl Scout camp. One day, a friend of hers asked if she was afraid when she went there.

Grandma, who always wore a large crucifix in plain sight around her neck, just shook her head. "I'm protected by Our Lady," she said, and winked. "And I carry a gun—just in case she needs some help."

For all the walls they erected and rules they enforced, my grandparents couldn't protect their daughters from the world forever. With her brothers off at school back east, and her sisters too young to be much companionship, my mother was left to make her way through her teens on her own.

Into her teenage years, she gave her parents no problems. Grandpa even called her "Angela the Angel." She was a good girl who spent her days going through her lessons with her mother, teaching her little sisters, working in the vegetable garden, and learning the arts of canning, cooking, and sewing from Grandma. She had an artistic side; she loved to sketch and paint animals, and she could sit and draw horses for hours, wondering what it was like to be free to run wherever she wanted. But she also had a tough, mischievous streak. Having been raised alongside three boys, she could hold her own in their rough-and-tumble world.

There was one thing that troubled her. Sometimes her mind—or something else—seemed to play tricks on her. She would be concentrating on a task when suddenly she'd catch sight of something out of the corner of her eye. It was dark, like a shadow, only it moved on its own volition. She'd turn her head to look, but it'd be gone, leaving behind only a chill that ran up her spine.

She told Grandpa about the apparitions, but he didn't think much of it—until one day they were standing in the backyard talking when, at the same time, they both saw something dark, unformed, move on the periphery of their vision. When they turned in unison to see what it was, he told me many years later, it disappeared into the shrubs, and their attempts to investigate turned up nothing more. Such things weren't discussed, of course, outside the family.

The family's next-door neighbor, Jana Morris, was delighted to have such a well-mannered girl as my mom to babysit her two young children. The first time she came over, Morris warned her, "No boys."

"You don't have to worry about that," Mom replied. "My parents wouldn't allow it."

But as her teenage years went on, Angela started bridling against her parents' restrictions. One day she confided to Mrs. Morris that she wished she could be like her brothers, who were away at school. "They're normal," she said.

The only time Mom felt real freedom was when she went out for a walk—and she walked everywhere. She'd walk to the library and into Sonoma, a six-mile round trip. When she was out walking, she noticed what other girls were wearing and their makeup. She saw them with boys and having fun. I think about that now, and I realize that she must have wanted so badly to have that sense of freedom. I went through the same thing myself. I know how it feels to just want to be normal, like everyone else. But sometimes things aren't that easy.

My mom was nineteen years old in the late spring of 1984 when she met Ramón Salcido. She was innocent and naïve. She'd never had alcohol or smoked a cigarette. She had no close girlfriends, no sleepovers with other teens, no chance to gossip or talk about boys. No dates. No proms. No treasured first kisses.

The young Mexican man in the old Ford didn't speak much English. She spoke even less Spanish. But he had a nice smile and a lot of confidence. When he invited her to watch him play soccer and maybe get together afterward, it must have been impossible for Angela to resist.

She couldn't ask her parents for permission. If Grandpa and Grandma were even willing to let her spend time with a boy—which they weren't—it certainly wouldn't have been with a Mexican farmworker. So she began slipping out her bedroom window at night to meet Ramón.

For my mom, it was a summer of many firsts: her first beer at the soccer fields where the signs prohibiting alcohol in English and Spanish were largely ignored. Her first young adult friends. Her first kiss. And, on those warm evenings, her first sexual experiences, in the backseat of a 1979 Ford LTD.

One day my mom decided it was time to tell her parents about their relationship. Grandpa was old-fashioned, so she told Ramón that she wanted him to ask his approval for them to see each other.

Ramón worked up the nerve and on a sunny afternoon walked up to the front door and knocked. When Grandpa answered, my dad tried his best in his broken English to explain that he wanted permission to date Angela.

Grandpa glared at him for a moment, his face turning red, and then yelled for his daughter. When she arrived, her father turned back to Ramón and demanded, "Angela, do you know this person?"

"Yes, Dad, please—" she began. But she hadn't even finished her sentence before Grandpa slammed the door in her boyfriend's face. Ramón stood there listening for a moment to the loud argument, but the door never reopened. Then he turned and walked back to his car.

That night Angela swiped a bottle of vodka from her father's liquor cabinet, drank as much as she could take, and then slipped out her window. She didn't return until the next morning—and when she did she was carrying a secret. Mother Nature had accomplished what Ramón's bravado could not: Angela was pregnant.

It didn't take long for the rumors to spread in the neighborhood. Angela Richards, the neighborhood good girl, was pregnant, and no one could believe it. But the truth was becoming as clear as her round belly.

When she finally told her parents, they were furious. But there was only one honorable thing she could do. She and Ramón had to get married.

The day of their wedding was fast approaching, but Ramón was keeping his own secrets. He'd never told Angela that he'd been married twice before, first to María de Jesus Torres and then to Debra Ann Whitten. Nor did he tell her when Debra Ann gave birth to a daughter, Maria Crystal, in August. When he and Angela drove to the Sonoma County courthouse in Santa Rosa to get their marriage license on November 28, 1984, they signed statements that it was the first marriage for each of them.

My parents were married ten days later, on December 8. Before the ceremony, Ramón, dressed in a borrowed suit, walked into the Boyes Hot Springs Food Center to buy a six-pack of beer for his wedding night.

"You look nice," store manager Bryan Mann said. As he later told the newspapers, he liked my dad, who had been a customer for years and always seemed to be smiling and friendly.

"*Gracias,*" Ramón replied and told Mann that he was getting married. He said he'd gotten a girl pregnant and "it's the right thing to do."

Two and a half months later, on February 24, 1985, Sofia Ann Salcido was born. She was a beautiful infant, with the dark skin and dark hair of her Mexican heritage, and she immediately became my dad's pride and joy.

Four

The Salcido family moved into a small, one-bedroom duplex house on Baines Avenue, just a few blocks from my grandparents. It was a low-slung box of a building, set farther back from the street than its neighbors; most of its large front yard was a dirt parking lot.

It wasn't much of a home, but then $350 a month was as cheap as it got in the Valley of the Moon, even in low-rent Boyes Hot Springs. The young couple didn't have much money, but they hoped for a better life someday. By 1986, my dad was working at St. Francis Winery near Santa Rosa on Highway 12. He was employed as a "vineyardist"—a fancy name for an experienced field hand—and as a bottler after the harvest. He was well liked by his bosses, but he was hoping eventually to find another vineyard where he might move into a higher-paying job.

The need for more income only grew when I was born on April 24, 1986. Unlike my sister, Sofia, who had remained dark-skinned and dark-haired, I inherited the pale skin, blond hair, and blue eyes of my mother's side of the family. I quickly became my mom's favorite; Sofia was Dad's girl.

When I came along, my parents decided that their daughters would sleep in the bedroom. They brought their king-sized bed into the living room, facing the television, which was in the dining room. The setup didn't lend itself to privacy or entertaining, nor did it give the family much room to spread out. But it was the best they could do in their tiny quarters.

Hoping to improve his financial situation, Ramón went to work at Grand Cru, a small but respected winery down a small gravel road behind the 130-year-old Dunbar Elementary School. In a region with plenty of better-known wineries, Grand Cru was off the beaten track—so much so that tourists who managed to locate its tasting room were given a pin reading I FOUND GRAND CRU WINERY. Dad was considered an exemplary employee, helpful with the other Mexican laborers and appreciated by his bosses, including winery foreman Ken Butti and assistant winemaker Tracey Toovey. But still he was making only eight dollars an hour; at that rate it was going to be tough to afford his dream of a new car, never mind a better home for his family. He kept his old LTD running with the help of his next-door neighbor, a local mechanic named Richard Clark.

To help out with the family finances, in 1987 Mom decided to go into business as a seamstress. Like Grandma, she made our family's clothes, and she was sure she could bring in a decent income with her sewing talents. She was so determined to make a go of it that she contacted the twice-weekly *Sonoma Index-Tribune* to ask if they'd be interested in her as a business story. The newspaper ran a small piece along with a photograph of Angela holding me. Even then it was easy to see the resemblance between us, with our big expressive eyes and smiles and the way we turned it on in front of the camera.

The picture in the paper revealed something else: Mom was wearing a maternity shirt. She and Dad were expecting again. With her hair swept back and her fresh-scrubbed look, she was the perfect picture of blissful young motherhood.

But pictures can be deceiving. By the time my little sister, Teresa Graciella, was born, on June 25, 1987, Mom was tired of living in their bad neighborhood—which became even more menacing a few months later when three people were murdered just blocks away.

On September 26, Sonoma County sheriff's deputies responded to a tip from a hysterical female caller reporting that there'd been several murders at a home in Boyes Hot Springs. The first time she called, the woman hung up before giving any details—not even a location. When she called back she gave them an address on Pine Street, but even then it took the deputies a while to locate the crime scene.

Entering the litter-strewn house just two blocks from the Sonoma Mission Inn, the deputies discovered three bodies in the back bedroom. Two men and a woman had been killed—bound and executed with multiple gunshots to the head—at least twelve hours earlier.

Finding this kind of violence at this particular address didn't exactly surprise the Sonoma County Sheriff's Department, which was responsible for policing unincorporated communities like Boyes Hot Springs that didn't have their own police departments. The house on Pine Street had been the scene of two successful narcotics raids in the previous eighteen months. At first the police declined to name any suspects in the triple homicide, but the next day the county's new sheriff, Dick Michaelsen, a former Santa Rosa police sergeant who'd been elected the previous year, gave all kinds of details on the case to local reporters—to the consternation of his detective unit, which liked to keep such information close to the vest.

If the police weren't surprised by the killings, neither were the neighbors, many of whom had been trying for years to reclaim the neighborhood from the criminals—

complaining about the all-hours coming and going at certain houses, trying to get the police to do something about the screeching tires and fights in the streets. They were tired of seeing beer bottles left on the curbs where their children played and drunks staggering out of certain disreputable bars night and day, including one where a Mexican laborer had been shot and killed over a drug deal the previous year.

Neighbors told the *Press Democrat* that the house where the murders occurred was filled with stolen property that had been brought over to trade for drugs, and that it had often been the scene of loud arguments and all-night parties. "We've called the police over and over," one local said. "It's gotten to the point where things seemed so lax that you'd think every dealer should be invited here to do their drug business." The neighbors were alarmed that no suspect had been nabbed in the Pine Street murders. The killer was out on the streets, and they worried that he would kill again.

The next day Michaelsen held another news conference to release the names of the victims, two men and a woman, after a local mother identified the young woman as her daughter. But the new sheriff ended up with egg on his face the following day, when the supposed homicide victim called the sheriff's office herself to report that she wasn't dead after all. "The mom didn't look close enough. Apparently, it was not a very close family," the sheriff snapped to the *Press Democrat*.

For my mom, the Pine Street killings were the last straw. Dad might have been pining for a new car, but Mom wanted to get the hell out of Boyes Hot Springs.

Twenty-two years old, the mother of three young children, Angela was no longer the naïve teenager who slipped out of her bedroom window at night looking to be free of her restrictive, religious parents. She had never quite rejected the teachings of TFP, and she was still a Catholic, though she wasn't exactly practicing. But she wasn't indoctrinating her daughters the way she had been; there was no religious imagery around our house, no strict rules to follow. Angela had started wearing clothes that showed off her slim size-six figure—including pants, miniskirts, and bathing suits, which scandalized her dad. She also had "worldly" girlfriends to confide in, like Barb Bradley, who lived next door with her boyfriend, Dan. Barb saw my mom as an innocent who didn't understand the ways of the world—especially when it came to men.

Barb didn't dislike Ramón, at least not completely. He obviously loved my mother, and that counted for something. Sometimes he seemed a little possessive, but Barb just attributed it to Latin machismo—protective, but not in a bad way.

In the early days of their marriage, Mom seemed content to let Dad do his thing while she stayed home with the children. She was always with us, occasionally bringing us over to Barb's to play in her bathtub, a luxury our family didn't have. Sometimes Mom told Barb that she wished Ramón wouldn't go out quite so much, especially without her. And she didn't want to stay in Boyes Hot Springs. But otherwise she seemed happy enough.

But Barb sensed that there was trouble under the surface, at least on my dad's side. She knew he liked to party, that he often stayed out all night, and that he used cocaine. In Barb's eyes, his excuses for his absences were pretty lame, but Angela believed him.

Sometimes, when he was in the right mood, Ramón did take Angela along to his favorite bars. There some of the other men looked at the young couple with envy. Many of them thought Ramón was the crazy jealous type, afraid to let her out of his sight. But John McNeilly, the owner of McNeilly's, one of Ramón's favorite pubs, later told the newspapers that my dad seemed like a proud, attentive husband who enjoyed showing off his good-looking wife. Mom was attractive, and friendly and articulate to boot—if much quieter than her happy-go-lucky husband.

True, McNeilly remembered, Ramón always had his

hands on Angela, as if to demonstrate to everyone else that she belonged to him. But so what if the guy wouldn't leave her alone for two seconds, except for a quick dash to use the restroom?

There was the one time when Dad, staggeringly drunk, made a bet with another patron that Mom would do a strip-tease on the bar. Mom didn't want to, but Ramón demanded that she comply. "Do it! We need the money!"

So she did.

Five

The car rolls slowly down Baines Avenue as Carmina points out the duplex with green trim where she was living in April 1989. The neighborhood isn't much different now—an assortment of neatly kept properties, even a few newer homes, sprinkled in with the tattered remnants of better times that line the narrow streets.

Yet a few things have changed about the house since her childhood. Steel bars have been installed over the windows and front door, making it look a little like a third-world jail. A tall fence now surrounds the property, with a metal gate that bars the entrance to the driveway. There are no tricycles or bikes with training wheels in the yard, just a broken-down car and some other junk. A young man in dark sunglasses sits at the entrance of the yard in a restored vintage Ford Mustang, watching as Carmina cruises by. A rap beat throbs from the canary-yellow car for a few minutes; then the driver peels out, heading in the other direction.

This is the way Carmina found her old home when she first returned to Sonoma after more than fifteen years. "When I arrived in Sonoma with Grandpa it was April *twenty-sixth, just a couple of days after I turned nineteen. I hadn't been back since my dad . . . since Ramón took me . . . when I was almost three. Grandpa didn't tell me where we were going, but I knew. I told him how to get here. 'Turn left, then turn right.' He hit the brakes. He was just dumbfounded. 'How could you know that?' he asked. But I remembered . . . just like I remember everything that happened that day."*

Baby Teresa's cries woke me and Sofia. It was late at night and we were alone—not just in the bedroom we shared but in the house. Our parents were gone, off to the bars or their friends' houses again.

It wasn't the first time we'd been left on our own, nor would it be the last. By 1988, Mom was insisting more and more on joining Dad's social life. Having gone from a repressed youth to a young, impoverished motherhood, she wanted to live a little.

On these nights it was Sofia, the oldest of us kids, who filled the role of parent. If Teresa woke up needing her diaper changed, Sofia got up and changed her and soothed her back to sleep before she returned to bed. Sometimes I cried out in my sleep and Sofia would wake up and comfort me, often letting me crawl into bed with her until I fell back to sleep. She truly had the temperament of a little mother.

With Dad's dark coloring, Sofia couldn't have looked more different from me and Teresa—Teresa, like me, had our mom's dark blond hair and blue eyes. Emotionally, too, Sofia was different, especially from me. Perhaps because she had so much responsibility heaped on her shoulders so early, she acted older than her years. Quiet and reserved, she seemed to observe the world with her deep brown eyes as if she'd seen it all before and was no longer surprised by it. Some people said she had an "old soul." Teresa and I couldn't have had a better big sister.

On the other hand, I was a little hellion. My grandpa remembers that I was physically strong for my size. Once, around the time I turned two, I wanted to see what was on top of the dining room table—so I reached up, grabbed the edge, and pulled myself up by my arms like a mountain climber. He says I was also strong-willed. Some nights I insisted on sleeping in my parents' bed; Dad wasn't happy about it, but if he tried to bring me back to my own bed, I'd put up such a fuss that my mom would laugh and say, "Let her stay." My nickname was Mina, but the more stubborn I got, the more often my mom seemed to be saying it "Meana," as in "*Mean*-a, quit being mean to your sisters."

I was my mother's pet, and I was determined to fend off any competition from my sisters. Sofia was shy, and Teresa too young to be much competition, but I loved being the center of attention—especially if there was a camera nearby. All I had to see was a lens pointed in my direction and my face would light up and I'd pose. Polaroid cameras were my favorite, because I got to see the results almost as soon as the flash popped.

I could be a handful—the kind of kid who was hard to keep track of, who was always finding new ways to give my mom a panic attack. I loved exploring on my own, and I wasn't afraid to try new things, including the gasoline I found in the garage one day when my parents weren't looking. When mom found me with it she called the hospital, but fortunately the gas tasted awful, so I hadn't sipped enough to endanger my life.

As I grew older, more and more people commented on how much I looked like Mom. Years later, Grandpa showed me a photograph of Mom when she was about three; at that age, we were almost the spitting image of each other.

My relationship with Dad, on the other hand, was a mixed bag. Sofia may have inherited his looks, but I got his personality and temperament. I was the daughter he was most likely to have an adventure with—like riding between his arms on his motorcycle.

As I got older, it seemed like my parents were around less and less, especially at night. When Sofia awoke and discovered that they were gone, she handled whatever needed to be done. But one night she got up, told us to wait, and left the house. She walked to the home of Connie Breazeale, a neighbor who sometimes babysat for us. "I woke up and my mommy and daddy aren't home," Sofia explained when Connie answered the door.

Connie didn't know quite what to do. Like some of the other neighbors, she knew my parents often left us to fend for ourselves. She wondered if she should contact child protective services. But she knew that would cause problems for my mom, so she didn't call.

"Go home, honey," she told Sofia. "Lock the door and get back into bed. I'm sure your mommy and daddy will be home soon."

We girls spent a lot of time at our grandparents' house, and we loved it there. Grandma doted on us. We were actually closer in age to our aunts Ruth and Maria than our mother was, and they liked playing with us. They weren't allowed much contact with the neighborhood kids, so Sofia, Teresa, and I were living dolls for them to dress up and direct, like the porcelain dolls in their collection. We were their playthings, but we didn't mind it in the least.

The other reason we loved going to my grandparents' house was that we knew we'd get a decent meal there. Mom was an indifferent cook, especially now that she always seemed to be busy with other things. Once, when I demanded dinner, Mom tossed me a package of ramen noodles—which I proceeded to eat uncooked. Grandma, on the other hand, always had something tasty and nutritious to eat.

Birthdays were a big deal at our grandparents' house. Grandpa saw to it that our parties were something to remember, with pony rides, big cakes, and lots of presents.

Like any little headstrong girl, I thought all the parties should be for me. I loved my second birthday party, in April 1988, but I wasn't so thrilled when it was time to celebrate

Teresa's first birthday in June. When I realized that the party—and the presents!—were for her, I threw a fit. I even tried to steal one of my sister's gifts, and raised a howl when I got caught. "You already had your birthday," Grandpa told me. "Now it's Teresa's turn." To a two-year-old, that wasn't much of an argument.

Unfortunately for us, by that time our grandparents had moved to Cotati, about a thirty-minute drive from Boyes Hot Springs. They were no longer just a few blocks away, and it wasn't as easy for Mom to drop us off for Grandma to babysit. So we didn't see them as often.

For Grandpa, the only good thing about that was that he didn't have to deal with his son-in-law. He didn't like Ramón much—he thought he was full of himself, a smart aleck—and he especially didn't like the way Ramón treated Angela. When my father left my mother alone all night, Grandpa suspected it was because he was seeing other women. And though Ramón liked to brag about his pretty wife, he often treated her with contempt. One rainy morning, when Mom was pregnant with Teresa and my grandparents were still living a few blocks away, Dad's car wouldn't start. Mom called Grandpa to ask if he could borrow a car to get to work. Sure, Grandpa replied, expecting to see his son-in-law in a few minutes. But a few minutes later it was Mom who appeared on his doorstep, soaking wet and chilled. My dad had sent her to pick up the car.

Then there was the day Mom gave birth to Teresa. When her labor pains started, Dad couldn't be found; nor did he show up at the hospital. When she got out of the hospital, she had to track Ramón down at a bar to give him a piece of her mind.

But that wasn't the worst of it. One night, after my grandparents had moved to Cotati, my parents got into a fight and Dad pulled a knife on Mom. She grabbed us kids and fled to her parents' house, afraid and unsure what to do about her marriage.

As a Catholic, Grandpa told her that divorce wasn't an option except in extreme cases. Still, maybe there was some other option, he said. But it was late, and Grandpa had to get up early for work the next morning. "Let's sleep on it," he said. "We'll talk more tomorrow when I get home." But when he got home the next day, Mom had already packed up us girls and returned to Boyes Hot Springs.

Six

The car swings around and back past the house on Baines, stopping in front now that its guardian in the Mustang has gone.

"I didn't know what to expect the first time I came back here," Carmina says. "I knew I was in the presence of something that had to do with my past. It was emotional, knowing where I was and what happened here, but it's hard to describe that emotion."

As the car heads back toward the highway, Carmina tries to recall life before what she calls simply "the tragedy." She shrugs. "I have some memories, but they're sort of mixed together, and some of them aren't very clear." Some of them are like fuzzy snapshots that have drifted in and out of her consciousness since childhood; others were nudged into recollection by conversations with others, or by things she's read since returning to Sonoma. The image of sitting in front of Ramón on his motorcycle is one such memory. "My sisters were scared of the noise and would run off when he started it up," she remembers. "But I liked the motorcycle. I thought it was exciting."

In recent years, though, she's heard more about her father's driving games—how he would drive his car down their street with her standing on his lap, steering, then duck down when another car pulled up next to them so it looked like his daughter was driving all by herself. That story she heard from Ramón himself.

But most of her early memories are her own. They roll through her mind like old home movies—missing scenes and transitions, a little out of focus and discolored with time, but still reasonably clear. There was a family outing to Bodega Bay on the Pacific coast, when her father made a small tent of towels and beach chairs to keep them out of the sun. She remembers the ocean—how she wasn't afraid of the waves like Sofia was and dashed right into them, only to be knocked down and carried away in the surf. She doesn't remember being afraid as she tumbled around. Just her mother frightened on the beach and her father diving through the waves to reach her.

But she also recalls her father coming home drunk and yelling at Angela. "I'm hungry—where's dinner?!" She remembers her parents screaming at each other, and Ramón pulling Angela's hair. "It was terrifying," she says. "We'd just try to stay the hell out of the way, go to our room and play with our toys and pretend we couldn't hear."

Then there was Christmas Eve 1988. Their parents had gone out for midnight Mass at the local Catholic church after putting the girls to bed. But Teresa's cries awakened her sisters, and they all ended up in the living room looking at the Christmas tree.

"Santa had come. There were all these presents under the tree. We sat down and ripped everything open. We were still sitting in the middle of all this paper, playing with our new toys, when my parents came home. Ramón was furious. He exploded, saying terrible things in English and Spanish. We ran to our mom, who told him to calm down. "Look at how cute they are. We can't be mad at them." After he finally calmed down, we took photographs, then *wrapped all the presents back up again. That's one of my last good memories."*

The highlight of that Christmas was a party we all attended at the home of Grand Cru assistant winemaker Tracey Toovey and his wife, Catherine.

According to those who knew him, Toovey was a nice guy, well liked by everyone. The story was that one day, when he was a teenager, he and his best friend, Ken Krohn, were drinking wine and Toovey blurted out, "One of us needs to learn how to make this." Right there and then he'd decided on his career.

Known for his ever-changing crazy haircuts and bushy mustache, Toovey was a family man, dedicated to his wife and best friend, Catherine, and their two children, four-year-old Kerissa and infant son Kiernan. Otherwise, he didn't seem to need much to make him happy. Heck, he'd been driving the same old Volkswagen Karmann Ghia for twenty years.

After Christmas, Mom found herself in the doldrums again. She needed something to give her a spark. She found it one day when she was strolling around the Santa Rosa Mall and a young woman approached and handed her a flier advertising the Covers Modeling School. "You'd be perfect," the young woman said.

Angela took the flier home. A friend of hers had told her that her daughter was looking into modeling school, and she said she thought Mom should think about it, too. Growing up, Mom had been taught that vanity was a sin, and she'd never considered herself pretty, at least not until she started going for her walks and getting attention from men. Yet she was beautiful—so much so that my jealous, obsessive father wouldn't leave her for a minute in a room full of men.

Maybe she could model, Mom thought now. Models made a lot of money, didn't they? But the flier said the ten-week course cost $510; how could she afford that? When she got home that day, there was an application for a Visa credit card in the mail. She decided to take that as an omen, she later told her friend Barb Bradley. "I filled it out and I told Ramón that if we get it, I'm going to use it to go to modeling school."

Mom said that Ramón had agreed to the idea, but to Barb that seemed doubtful. She knew Ramón didn't want Angela working, and he certainly didn't like the idea of other men looking at her. Then again, Mom was getting more assertive at home. She'd started letting Dad know when she thought he was going out too much. Of course, that led to loud arguments and threats, but she wouldn't back down.

Angela confided to Barb that she'd let herself get pregnant in order to escape her parents' home. At the time, marriage had seemed like a good way out. But now she was feeling trapped; something had to change, even if that something cost money.

As soon as Visa approved her application and sent her a card, Mom headed over to the Covers Modeling School, where she met owner Patricia Rile. A short, energetic woman who also represented some of her modeling-school graduates for advertising work in the Bay Area, Rile thought my mom had potential. She was pretty, fresh-looking, and wholesome. A bit too short for runway work, but with a little help she might land some work with retailers looking for that "young mom" look. Still, she didn't like to lead anyone on. Making a career in modeling, even a modest one, was tough, and at twenty-four my mom was getting a late start. She was also a little too demure and soft-spoken, but that could be addressed. And Mom did have a very cute laugh—not loud, but genuine and unrehearsed. If she wanted to work at it, there were real possibilities.

In any event, Angela would never have taken no for an answer. Paying for the class with her new Visa card—which had just enough credit for the classes—she told Rile that she wanted more than anything else to learn to model.

Mom took her three-hour-long classes more seriously than

most of the other students, paying rapt attention and catching on quickly as Rile and the other instructors taught her how to carry herself, apply makeup, walk, pose for the camera, and dress for success. Before long, she was undergoing a transformation. She cut her hair in a bob, wore more makeup, and started upgrading to a more fashionable wardrobe. If the patrons at McNeilly's and the Valley of the Moon Saloon thought she was pretty before, they were really noticing now. Ramón wasn't sure just how to handle the change; he went out of his way to show off his beautiful "model" wife, but he would glower jealously at anyone who looked a little too long.

Where Angela really stood out was in front of a camera. It takes more than a pretty face to make it as a print-media model. It also takes attitude and the ability to project that in a photograph. And when Mom stepped in front of a camera, the metamorphosis was startling. She went from an almost painfully shy young woman to a vivacious, captivating model whose eyes could blaze or soften sweetly on command.

Though she was still soft-spoken, she was becoming more self-assured. Rile thought her chances of making it as a print model were getting better every day.

Mom didn't say much about her private life, and Rile didn't ask. Most of the time she drove herself to the modeling school. But Dad came along twice, sitting politely and smiling as he watched the class. Rile thought that he was a nice, attractive young man. He didn't say much, and what he did say was heavily accented. But it was clear to Rile that he worshipped his wife.

Still, there were things about the relationship that Rile thought odd. When Angela locked her keys in the car outside the modeling school one day, for instance, she called her parents to come get her, not Ramón.

And twice, after Mom made an appointment with Michael Beehler, a local photographer, she canceled at the last minute. The second time, she said she couldn't afford the session because her husband wanted to use the money for a trip to Mexico.

Mom put her modeling career on hold when Dad decided to take our family to visit his hometown of Los Mochis in February 1989. It was the first time he'd been back home with his wife and children, and he was anxious to show us off. He spent much of the visit raving about his good life back in Sonoma. I don't remember much about the trip, but I know we were fussed over and pampered by a multitude of aunts, uncles, cousins, and grandparents.

As far as Sofia was concerned, though, the biggest excitement was that Dad had promised to take us to Disneyland on the way back to celebrate her fourth birthday. She could hardly wait to leave Mexico. But things didn't work out. Sofia later told our babysitter that we didn't go to Disneyland because "my daddy couldn't find it."

When Grandpa heard the story, he thought even worse of his son-in-law. He was growing increasingly worried about my dad's behavior. On New Year's Eve, after picking up his own son at the airport, he'd caught Ramón trying to break into his house. He got home just in time to see my dad hanging out of a bedroom window.

"What are you doing?" Grandpa asked him, scowling, glad his son was there with him.

Ramón, who was obviously drunk, just shrugged. "I need to borrow your shotgun."

"My shotgun? What for?"

"To celebrate the new year," Dad replied, mimicking firing a gun into the air.

"Well, I'm not going to give you my shotgun!"

Ramón's face contorted into a mask of rage. He stalked over to his car. Reaching in through an open window, he pulled out a large knife and stood there for a moment as if making up his mind what to do next. Then, after shouting a threat, he got into his car and drove away.

Grandpa knew that Dad had already tried to attack Mom with a knife, and now he was afraid that Ramón would really lose his temper someday and someone would get hurt. For the moment, though, he put his concerns aside and threw a big birthday party for Sofia to help her get past the disappointment of missing out on the Magic Kingdom. It was a great success, and everybody got along—everybody but me, that is. Once again, I couldn't understand why every birthday wasn't *my* birthday.

"Now, Carmina," Grandpa told me, "today is Sofia's day. Yours is coming up in April."

After the trip, Mom returned to her modeling classes, more determined than ever to make a career of it. She told Rile and her friends that she really needed the money.

Barb Bradley suspected that Mom's desperation had to do with more than just making ends meet or even moving out of Boyes Hot Springs. Barb worked for a nonprofit company that helped place disabled people in new jobs, and she was connected to the social services network. She told Angela that there were shelters for women trying to get out of abusive relationships. But she warned her that if she was planning to leave Ramón, she'd have to figure out how to support herself. "Welfare is just a big trap."

Rile also noticed that Mom kept saying she was going to pursue her modeling career with or without her husband. At one of her last classes, when Dad showed up to drive her home, Mom made a point of turning to Rile and announcing in a loud voice, "I'm going to do whatever it takes to be a model."

If Dad understood what she was saying, and its implications, he didn't react. He just stood there smiling until his wife was ready to go.

The modeling classes were capped off by a student fashion show that Pat Rile sponsored through a designer dress shop she owned. It was a chance for the women to get a little runway experience in front of an audience, while showing off Rile's dresses to the women of Santa Rosa. It was a big affair, held at the Flamingo Hotel, and Rile was expecting a large turnout. In a video taken that day, Mom looked pretty and self-confident as she walked the runway in a white polka-dot midriff top, white pants, and a white jacket. At one point, her voice is heard in the background, laughing in her free and easy way.

Seven

One person who worried about our family that year was our neighbor Richard Clark. He liked Ramón and Angela, but it sounded like things were getting pretty bad between them, and he was concerned about us kids. My parents were leaving us home alone a lot, and Clark thought about calling social services, thinking that maybe someone could come over and calm things down. But he was worried that the agency would overreact and take us away, so he never did.

Life in our house was really deteriorating. Even at not quite three years of age, I knew things weren't right. Mom and Dad were fighting all the time—mostly verbally, but it was getting physical, too.

Richard later told the police that Ramón, in particular, seemed like he was under a lot of stress and might be cracking. One night, when they were working on their cars together, Ramón broke down and started crying, telling Richard that he suspected Angela was having affairs with other men.

Clark told him that he hadn't seen any evidence of it. Angela was almost always home during the day taking care of us, and he'd never seen other men dropping by. In fact, the only man he'd seen around our home during the day was my dad, who drove by in a Grand Cru truck as much as three times a day.

Ramón conceded that he'd been checking on Angela. He said he'd even been reprimanded at work for letting his marital problems affect his job performance.

According to Clark, Ramón was doing more and more cocaine, and he'd been bragging about carrying a gun. He told Clark he wasn't afraid to use it, either, and claimed to have shot at people one night over some disagreement. Clark didn't know how much of this was posturing and how much was true. But he did know that Ramón was in a financial pinch. Angela wanted money for her modeling career, and Ramón confided that an ex-wife was after him for child support.

One night my sisters and I were back in our bedroom when Dad came stumbling home drunk and angry. He and my mom started fighting, and soon they were screaming at each other.

"I'm going to blow your head off!" my dad shouted.

"Living with you is like living in jail!" Mom yelled back.

Sofia and I crept out of our room to see what was happening. We stood in the entrance to the hall and watched as Dad grabbed Mom by the hair and slapped her across the face.

It was too much for me. Always the fearless one, I rushed between my parents and tried to push them apart. Then I turned and started hitting my dad—until he struck me back, hard enough to send me stumbling away.

Mom lunged at Dad, but he hit her and knocked her to the ground. "Get out!" she screamed at him. And, to everyone's relief, he left.

My father was telling Clark the truth about his financial problems. On March 11 a Fresno County judge handed down an order demanding that he repay the state welfare system the roughly $5,800 it had paid to support Debra Ann Whitten and their daughter, Maria Crystal. The judge also ordered him to start paying Debra Ann $511 a month in child support. If that wasn't bad enough, Dad was also in default on a $6,500 loan and needed to catch up and start making his $112 monthly payments.

Up to this point, he'd managed to keep his other marriage a secret from my mother. Now that the law was after him, though, it was bound to blow up in his face.

And that's what happened on April 11, when sheriff's deputies showed up at the door to serve Ramón with a court order for child support. My father admitted to my mother that he had been married—there was no getting around it—but he swore the child wasn't his. He told Angela to call Debra Ann Whitten and ask her to call the court and tell them Maria Crystal wasn't his. My mother made the call, pleading with Debra as if it had been her idea. But Debra later told reporters she could hear Ramón in the background telling my mom what to say.

Debra Ann assured Angela that she wasn't trying to cause trouble. It was the district attorney who was after Ramón for the money. But she could hear Ramón get furious when he heard her response.

A short time later my mother called Nevada to get a copy of Ramón's other marriage certificate, as well as the divorce decree. That's when she learned that Ramón was still legally married to Debra Ann; they'd never bothered to get a divorce. My mom was living with a bigamist.

After the initial shock wore off, Angela began to see Ramón's predicament as another sign that it was time to take a new direction in her life. As her dad had always said, the church didn't recognize divorce—but neither did it recognize the marriage between a woman and a man who was already married. "Maybe now I can get an annulment," she confided to Connie Breazeale.

Around this time, my father later claimed, Mom told him Sofia wasn't his daughter, but she didn't know who the father was. On that long-ago night when she drank a bottle of vodka and slipped out of her bedroom window after fighting with her father, she claimed, she was accosted and raped by another Mexican man.

Yes, she'd told him, two people could have secrets. He'd been married and fathered a child and never told her. She'd been raped and let him think the child was his.

Was it true? I'll never know. But the seeds of secrecy were blossoming into a disaster.

The argument Richard Clark overheard late on the afternoon of April 13 ended with my dad storming out of the house.

Mom let him go. She had more important things on her mind. The next day she was finally going to do her photo shoot with Michael Beehler. Pat Rile had suggested that she bring one of her daughters along, to take some shots with that clean, wholesome young-mother look Rile thought might interest agencies in San Francisco. So Mom decided to bring me—the child who looked the most like her.

When Angela called to confirm the appointment, Beehler was skeptical. She'd already canceled twice. "What about Ramón?" Beehler asked. The last thing he wanted was to be dodging bullets from a jealous husband.

"Don't worry about him," she replied. "I can handle him."

After the argument, Ramón headed for the Valley of the Moon Saloon, where he started drinking beer and brooding. He was angry about what Angela had told him about Sofia, about the idea that he had a third "unfaithful" wife. The more he drank and stewed in his soup of jealousy, the more sure he became that Grandma must have known her daughter was pregnant with another man's child. He'd been duped.

The bar owner noticed him scowling, as though in some internal argument. "You're awfully quiet," she said.

"Just tired," he replied. In search of a little pick-me-up, he told his friends he wanted to score a little cocaine but would settle for methamphetamine if necessary. He left the pub at about seven-thirty, telling the owner to put the beers on his tab. He'd pay later.

Ramón made his way to McNeilly's, where he sat next to another regular, Mark Ondrasek. In need of money to buy coke, he told Ondrasek he had some expensive Grand Cru sparkling wine in his trunk, and he'd sell it to him cheap, five dollars a bottle. Ondrasek bought four, giving Ramón a check for twenty dollars; later on he gave Ramón a forty-dollar check and took another eight bottles. But that still didn't get Ramón the cash he needed, and he wanted a drink, too. The bartender wouldn't take his checks, but because Dad was a regular, he lent him five dollars.

Somehow, Ramón finally came up with more cash and ordered several Separators—brandy, Kahlúa, and cream, saying he wanted "something sweet." He also found cocaine. He offered some to a woman drinking at McNeilly's, but she turned him down. His friend Michael John Coratti was happy to go out to Ramón's car to snort a line with him, though. Ramón told him that he was throwing a party later at the Sonoma Mission Inn "with some ladies" and invited him along.

Later that night, after the cocaine ran out, Mario Mata, who had known my father for five years, was sleeping in his own bedroom when he woke up to find Dad sitting next to his bed, wielding a knife. He said he'd crawled in through an open kitchen window. "You should be more careful," Ramón warned him. "I could have killed you."

My dad wanted to know if he had any money he could use to buy cocaine. Mata said he was broke, but he agreed to go with Ramón as he went looking for money and drugs.

A few minutes before 3 A.M., the two men met up with Coratti at the Sonoma Mission Inn. Dad told the others to wait in the parking lot while he went in to check on his "reservations." He walked up to the registration desk and asked clerk Lela Brooks if she had a reservation for employees of the Grand Cru winery under the name of Salido.

Brooks said she had nothing under that name. Ramón told her he wanted a room.

When the clerk looked over, she saw a security guard, William Buker, trying to catch her eye. He'd seen Ramón standing with two other men in the parking lot, and he knew the inn's upscale clientele wouldn't appreciate the drunken bash these characters were trying to bring into the hotel.

Brooks suggested to Ramón that perhaps his reservation was at the Sonoma Valley Inn in downtown Sonoma. She called the motel for him, but they didn't have a reservation either. Defeated, Dad went back to the parking lot and told his friends the party was off. The three split up and went their separate ways.

What my dad did for the next couple of hours would remain a mystery. But he showed up at our home on Baines Avenue at about five-thirty that morning.

According to the official version of the events that followed, when my dad got home we were asleep in the back bedroom but Mom was gone. Dressed in a sweatshirt and baseball cap, she'd left the house early, walking through the chill morning air to an ATM at the Wells Fargo bank on West Napa Street in Sonoma. A woman who saw her there in the near-dark mistook her at first for a man because of her clothing. The woman later told the police that she thought my mom looked like hell, that she was acting strange and took ten minutes to finish her transaction, and then stood around watching her.

Bank records show that a little after 5:30 A.M., on April 14, 1989, Mom withdrew two hundred dollars from the family account. It was the last of the cash my parents had in the bank. Whether she took it to pay the photographer later that day or as part of some escape plan would become a matter of speculation in the years ahead. I choose to believe she withdrew it because she wanted to take us and get away from my father, but no one knows for sure.

At some point that morning, Angela also mailed a letter to a records clerk in Washoe County, Nevada, with a check for three dollars and a simple request for a copy of a marriage certificate of Ramón Salcido and Debra Ann Whitten. That was all the proof she would have needed to have her marriage annulled.

Even as she mailed that letter, though, her husband was sitting in his house fuming. He later told the authorities he was so angry that Angela had left him alone with the kids that he wanted to kill someone. But that's not exactly how I remember it.

What I remember is that, after their fight the night before, Mom took us back to our room and tucked us in. Despite our fear, we were soon fast asleep.

The next thing I recall is waking up and hearing my dad walking across the room. It was still mostly dark in the house, but I could see him pick up Teresa from her crib and walk out. Then he came back and picked me up from my bed.

"Where are we going, Papa?" I asked him. But he just laid my head on his shoulder.

It was dark in the house, but when we walked past their bed, I know I saw my mom sleeping there. I can still picture her face. I called out to her, and that's when my dad put his hand over my mouth.

Teresa was awake and crying in the backseat when dad put me in the car. Then he went back and got Sofia. He put her in the back with us, then got behind the wheel and pulled away from our house.

"Where are we going, Papa?" I asked him again. But he didn't answer. He didn't seem furious. It was more like he was somewhere else.

Eight

Early that same morning, Detective Sergeant Mike Brown picked up his copy of the *Press Democrat*. He always read the paper before heading in to work at the Sonoma County Sheriff's Department, where he was in charge of the Violent Crimes Investigations Unit.

One item that caught his eye had to do with the so-called Trailside Killer, a fifty-three-year-old sexual predator and serial killer named David Carpenter who'd been arrested in May 1981 and eventually charged with nine execution-style murders, most of which had occurred near trails in San Francisco's Golden Gate Park. Carpenter had been found guilty of two of the murders and sentenced to die in the gas chamber; he'd since been convicted and sentenced to death for other murders as well. But so far he'd managed to escape the executioner. In fact, there'd been no executions of California death row inmates since 1967, even after the U.S. Supreme Court lifted a moratorium on the death penalty in 1976. And it didn't look like there would be any executions any time soon.

As a young man, Mike hadn't been a fan of the death penalty. But after becoming a deputy and seeing the carnage some killers were capable of causing, he came to the conclusion that some people deserved the ultimate punishment.

Mike also supervised the Crime Scene Investigations Unit, and assigned and directed his detectives on cases ranging from assault with a deadly weapon to rape to homicide. His father had always taught him that it didn't matter how much money he made at his job, or how many people he had working for him. What mattered, he told me later, was that he "get a job that makes a difference." As someone who'd grown up with a well-defined sense of right and wrong—something else he got from his father, as well as his uncle, Morris Lucy, a Los Angeles County sheriff's deputy—he'd found it in law enforcement.

After finishing the paper that morning, Mike kissed his wife, Arlyn, left his home in a quiet, well-kept Santa Rosa neighborhood, and headed to work.

Mike had never heard of the 1910 Kendall murders or Polcerpacio Pio's massacre in 1949. But the county had seen other sensational crimes since then, from an execution-style murder committed by a notorious mob hit man known as Joe "the Animal" Barboza in the 1960s to a shotgun murder by a well-known local character named Ernest "Kentucky" Pendergrass that dominated the newspapers for weeks. Most violent crimes didn't get that sort of notoriety, but there were plenty of rapes, assaults, shootings, and homicides in Sonoma County to keep his Violent Crimes Investigation Unit busy. The county averaged twelve to fifteen murders a year, most of them over in the Russian River area, which was riddled with drug use and criminal activity.

The 1987 triple murder in Boyes Hot Springs that frightened my mother so much had been another one of those homicides where the suspect was unknown. In fact, by April 1989 the case still hadn't been solved. But it was clear to most people that it was drug-related and that the killer knew his victims, therefore the neighbors weren't in much danger.

The case had caused Mike Brown some consternation

after Sheriff Michaelsen called him at midnight the day the murders were discovered, asking if Mike had a positive identification on the dead woman.

"We're not sure yet," Brown replied. "We'll be able to nail it down tomorrow."

That wasn't good enough, Michaelsen said. He needed to get something to the press as soon as possible. That didn't make sense to Mike. The next day's newspapers were already at the printer, and there wouldn't be any television news until the next morning anyway.

But Michaelsen, who'd been elected the previous year, was turning out to be something of a media hound. During his campaign, he'd received the backing of the Santa Rosa Police Department, where he'd been a patrol sergeant, but he'd never been a detective and didn't really know how they operated. Nor did he have a detective's reluctance to talk about an ongoing investigation, especially to the press.

The sheriff had heard that the dead woman was the daughter of one of the victims, and he told Mike to contact her surviving parent, her mother, and take her to the morgue to see if she could identify the body.

Mike balked. There was no need to put the poor woman through that ordeal, especially in the middle of the night.

"I'm giving you a direct order," Michaelsen snarled. "Take that woman down there, and I don't want to hear any more about it."

Mike had no choice. Reluctantly, he contacted Melissa's mother and brought her to the morgue. The coroner hadn't even had time to clean and prepare the victim, whose face was covered with blood and distorted from a gunshot wound. But the woman took one look at the body lying on the steel morgue table and started screaming that it was her daughter. Mike told the sheriff, and Michaelsen told the press that the dead woman had been positively identified by her mother.

The next morning, however, Mike was sitting at his desk when he got a call from the reception desk. "There's a woman here claiming that she's not dead."

* * *

The hardest homicides for Mike to deal with were those committed against children. What bothered him was the fact that the victims hadn't even had a chance to live, but also that they were never in any way responsible for the situations that led to their deaths. It wasn't their fault that they were raised in a bad environment, that their parents were drug dealers, or that some sick adult had chosen to prey upon them. As a parent himself, Mike took their deaths especially hard.

One such case had an enormous impact on him. In June 1980, when he was new to the Violent Crimes Investigation Unit, he was assigned to a case in which a fifteen-year-old girl had set fire to her parents' home, killing her stepmother and ten-year-old brother. He was watching the coroner examine the woman when he glanced over at the boy, who was lying on an autopsy table, still in his pajamas. His mind suddenly superimposed the face of his own son, Tim, on the dead boy's.

The vision shook him to the core, and he had to step out of the room. *You're not here to cry for these people,* he told himself. *You're thinking with your heart, not your head, and it's your head they need to bring them justice.* Calmer, he imagined a mask dropping into place over his face so that he could operate as a disinterested third party. He couldn't let emotions get involved, or he wouldn't be able to see clearly.

Over the years, Mike later told me, he'd worn the mask many times, bottling his emotions within himself as he went about his job bringing justice to those who had no one else to speak for them.

There were a few clouds in the sky that April morning as Mike Brown drove to work. But the sun was up and temperatures were expected to reach the mid-sixties.

Arriving at the sheriff's office, he gathered the reports written the night before to review and assign to his detectives. It was usually a quiet part of the day, before things started rolling. It wasn't long, however, before all hell broke loose.

It started simply enough at 8 A.M., when Dispatch called him to report a possible homicide at the Grand Cru winery off Dunbar Road. A patrol car had been dispatched.

Mike usually had five detectives working for him at VCI, but that morning only three were available. One had retired and had not yet been replaced; the other, one of his best and most experienced men, Detective Randy Biehler, was home with the flu. Usually his detectives worked several cases at a time, but when one was assigned a homicide, that was all he did. That morning, Detective Dave Edmonds, the newest and least experienced member of the unit, was on call.

Mike told Edmonds to head over to the Grand Cru and sent Detective Larry Doherty, who'd been with the unit for a couple of years, with him. A short time later, as Mike was getting ready to catch up with Edmonds at Grand Cru, Dispatch called again to say that there'd been a shooting at the Kunde Estate winery. "A man's been wounded."

Mike paused. Kunde was in Kenwood just a little way up Highway 12 from Grand Cru. That meant that there was a good chance the two crimes were related. Mike decided to check out the Kunde shooting himself before heading to Grand Cru. He and Dave Sederholm, an experienced detective, headed out together.

He had no idea where this day was about to lead him, or how many years later it would still bring tears to his eyes.

Nine

Immediately to the north of the Kunde Family Estate winery rise a series of round hills, draped with concentric rings of grapevines. A stone arch at the base of the closest hill leads to the vineyard's famous caves, dug into the red volcanic earth, where 5,500 barrels of wine are stored. The caves are a favorite stop for tourists who visit the tasting room in the large building thirty yards from the house.

The vineyards had been in the Kunde family for four generations, beginning with Louis Kunde, a German immigrant who settled in the Sonoma Valley in 1904. The estate had grown to two thousand acres, stretching along two miles of the highway and rising to as high as one thousand feet. Along with their grapes, the Kunde family raised cattle, and the estate also served as the headquarters for Grand Cru.

Earlier that morning, the Grand Cru's foreman, Ken Butti, had been sitting on the porch of the small house at the Kunde Estate winery where he lived with his wife. Butti wasn't particularly surprised to see my father, who was one of his Grand Cru employees, drive up in an old Ford LTD and park a few yards from the porch.

Nor was he particularly pleased to see him. Ramón had once been a model employee, but his work had been deteriorating, especially in the last month, since he'd been hit with child-support payments for the child of his ex-wife. He was calling in sick a lot, and when he did come to work—usually late—he looked like he'd been partying all night, with dark circles under his bloodshot eyes.

All Butti knew was that my parents' marriage was going downhill. Ramón told him he suspected that Angela was cheating on him. Butti told him he was going to have to shape up or lose his job, but the ultimatum didn't seem to have much effect, and he'd recently told the Grand Cru management that he didn't want Ramón working for him anymore. But my dad didn't know this yet, so Butti had no clue why he'd shown up this morning.

"Hi, how you doing?" Ramón asked, as if they'd accidentally met somewhere.

Butti nodded at him. Something wasn't right. "What's going on, Ramón?"

Dad turned away and looked over at the passenger seat. He mumbled something that Butti didn't understand and then reached down. When he sat back up, he extended a hand out the window.

The first thing Butti noticed was that Ramón's forearms were covered with blood. Then he noticed that a gun was pointed at him. The gun fired. One. Two. Three shots, one of which struck him in the right shoulder. Stunned, Butti fell onto his side with his back to Ramón and waited for more shots. But instead he heard the car drive off.

Standing at the kitchen window inside the house, Butti's wife, Teri, had seen my dad drive up. She heard several *pop*s, but thought it was just the two men fooling around. As Ramón's car left, it rolled slowly by her open window. When she looked up, she saw a gun pointed at her. As she stared into Dad's eyes, which were wide open and focused, she heard a click. But there was no *pop*, no bullet. The gun had jammed.

* * *

A little after eight-thirty, Detective Sederholm turned in to the driveway at Kunde and raced up the long, gently climbing road to the ranch house. He and Mike Brown arrived just as Butti was being loaded into an ambulance.

"Do you know who shot you?" Mike asked.

"Ramón Salcido."

Did he have any idea why Ramón Salcido would want to shoot him?

Not really. He told Mike about Ramón's failing marriage and his financial problems, both of which were affecting his work performance. But he couldn't think of any reason Ramón would want to shoot him.

As the ambulance drove off, Mike went to his car and radioed the dispatcher in Santa Rosa. "Check with the records section and see if we have anything on Ramón Salcido."

A few minutes later she called back. A Mexican male named Ramón Salcido, age twenty-eight, five feet eight, 180 pounds, had been arrested for drunk driving in 1983. His booking papers listed an address of 201 Baines Avenue in Boyes Hot Springs.

Mike wondered what was going on. He had a dead man at one winery and a shooting victim at another. The second victim said Ramón Salcido was having money problems and marital problems.

Suddenly, as he later told me, Mike Brown knew where he needed to be—Boyes Hot Springs. "Do we have any patrol units available in the valley?" he asked the dispatcher.

"There are only two on duty, and they're both already at the crime scenes," the dispatcher replied.

"Start calling in off-duty patrol and tell them to respond to the valley," Brown said.

He thought for a moment. It was going to take some time for the off-duty units to get moving, and something told him he didn't have that kind of time. He needed to get to Baines Avenue.

Mike would have liked to take Sederholm with him. He

was a good police officer, and they'd been in a number of tight situations together. But Sederholm was needed at the Kunde winery to help the CSI detectives process the scene. "When you get done here," Mike told him, "meet me at 201 Baines Avenue." Then he jumped into his car and took off.

When he got to the highway, he saw his lieutenant, Erne Ballinger, parked at the bottom of the drive. He pulled up to him and explained what they had so far. "I've called in off-duty patrol, but there's no time to wait for them. Let's go get this guy."

A moment later, Mike Brown and his lieutenant were roaring down Highway 12, headed for Boyes Hot Springs and my family's home on Baines Avenue.

Ten

They must have driven this same way, Ramón and his three little girls, south out of Sonoma along the serpentine highway leading toward the Petaluma dump. The hills on either side of the road rise and fall as they reach toward the horizon, and on that morning they would have been cloaked in gray slumber before the dawn.

As her father drove, Carmina was aware of the occasional passing car. And every few minutes she'd ask him where they were going. "He finally told me to shut up and sit down," she remembers. "Now we were terrified. Something was very wrong.

"It seemed like we drove for a long time. Then I was aware that we had turned onto a dirt road and then we stopped. . . . Something had changed. The air seemed thick for some reason, and everything was silent. There were no sounds at all. . . . "We were just lambs being led to the slaughter."

Outside the car it was just about dawn, so the light was dull and gray. Inside, the shadows were darker; everything was black and white, including her father's face as he turned toward them.

"I remember looking over at Sofia. She was holding baby Teresa, who was asleep. Then he called to me. 'Carmina, get up here.' He didn't sound like Papa anymore. I don't know how to explain it, but it wasn't his voice. I was afraid, but I didn't know what else to do. I started to go up. But Sofia said no. She pushed me down on the floor behind his seat and motioned for me to stay there."

Ramón demanded that Sofia hand him Teresa. "But she wouldn't. Maybe she saw the knife. She held on tight, but he leaned over the seat and took the baby. She wasn't strong enough to hold on."

Carmina grows quiet, sniffling every few seconds as the car turns onto the gravel road into the dump where the nightmare began.

Detectives Brown and Ballinger arrived at our house on Baines Avenue and parked around the corner. They knew the street was only a block long, and they didn't want to take the chance that my father would spot them if he was there.

Getting out of their cars, they popped the trunks, pulled out bulletproof vests, and put them on, all without saying a word. Then they slipped back into their suit coats, pinned their badges to their lapels, checked to see that their guns were charged, and started to walk toward our house.

Mike Brown was sure they were going to catch Ramón Salcido. He just hoped it wasn't too late for whoever else might have been in the home.

They had no idea what they were getting into. They couldn't even discuss a plan until they got close enough to see the house. They did know that the suspect was armed; that he had committed a murder and an attempted murder with cold-blooded efficiency; and that he'd already proved willing to look a man in the eyes and shoot him without warning or provocation. There was no telling what he would do faced with two armed detectives.

Slipping quickly through a neighbor's yard, they peeked around a corner. It didn't look good. There wasn't much cover between the street and the front of the house. Just a big, open front yard. Near our front door Detective Brown saw two small bicycles with training wheels—one of them tipped over onto its side—and a tiny tricycle. *Kids in the house,* he thought. *That complicates things.*

Normally, with only two officers, one of them would have gone to the front of the house and the other to the back to cut off the possible escape routes and come at the suspect from two directions. But a thicket of thorny blackberry bushes blocked their way to the back. They were going to have to take the house head-on, which was dicey because of the open expanse they would have to cross.

Just as they were about to move, a woman came out of a neighboring house and asked what they were doing. "Sheriff's department! Get back in your house," Brown demanded. When the woman retreated, the two detectives rushed forward, their .45-caliber semiautomatic handguns held shoulder high, aimed at the house. They stayed about ten feet apart so that if a gunman appeared, he'd have to choose one or the other.

As he advanced, Brown saw a bright red smear across the white front door. *Blood.*

Reaching the house, Ballinger positioned himself to the side of the door. Brown crouched beneath the large picture window. He popped up to look in the window, then dropped out of sight. In that split second he saw blood splatters inside the house, on the wall opposite the window.

Ballinger pushed the door open slowly and took a quick look inside. Then, as Mike Brown covered him at the picture window, he went in the doorway and found himself in the living room with my parents' bed in it. A second later, Brown followed him inside, clearing the television room as Ballinger covered him from anyone suddenly appearing in the hall.

Furniture was overturned. The television was on, and the screen was splattered with blood, as was the wall behind it. There were more blood splatters and smears on the walls in the hallway. And there, lying in a pool of thickening blood, was the body of a young woman.

It was my mother, Angela Salcido.

The two detectives quickly cleared the rest of the house, covering each other as they moved. They came to our bedroom, with its two small beds and a crib. But the killer was nowhere to be found, and neither were us children.

My sisters and I were gone.

The detectives returned to my mom in the hallway and tried to piece together what had happened. Judging from the state of the room, Angela had put up a hell of a fight. Her face was bruised as though she'd been beaten, and she'd been shot more than once, until one final bullet to the back of the head killed her.

Looking around the kitchen, Brown saw an address book lying open on an ironing board. On one of the pages, the killer had left behind a fingerprint in blood. The fingerprint was next to a phone number for my grandmother, Valentina Borjorquez Seja Armendariz, in Los Mochis, Mexico. There were more handprints on the phone itself. Apparently, my dad had paused long enough to call home.

Brown and Ballinger moved on to the attached garage. When it was clear, they went outside, where they were soon joined by Dave Sederholm and two uniformed deputies in marked cars. Mike put Sederholm in charge of this crime scene and headed out front, where he met Randi Rossmann, the *Press Democrat*'s police reporter.

Rossmann knew better than to expect Mike Brown to make any inappropriate statements about the crime scene or the condition of the bodies. But he told her what he could. They had two murders and one attempted murder. No suspect in custody, no cause of death. Next of kin hadn't been notified, so he couldn't comment on that either.

Then Brown went back to work. The case was too hot to stand around talking. He needed to find Ramón Salcido and the three little girls, according to the neighbors, who lived in the house.

* * *

Rossmann understood. Twenty-six years old, she had been the police reporter for the *Press Democrat* for almost a year. As the paper's first female in that job, she'd had to earn respect the hard way. She never burned a source or played favorites. She asked tough questions and wouldn't be put off until she had answers. But she also understood the difficult roles that police officers had—that their job was dangerous but also psychologically treacherous, especially for those who dealt with violent crimes.

Rossmann had taken off from work that morning to spend some time with her fiancé looking at tile samples for their new home. When a sudden burst of activity cropped up on her police scanner, she knew something big was going down. "I have to go," she told her fiancé, and headed off for 201 Baines Avenue in Boyes Hot Springs. She arrived right after Brown and Ballinger went in the front door.

Aware of the magnitude of the story, Rossmann stayed at the scene for more than an hour, interviewing neighbors and trying to learn what she could from the police. Before too long other reporters started arriving—along with television crews from San Francisco—and suddenly the pressure was on to stay ahead of the competition.

At about ten-thirty, Rossmann noticed a new flurry of activity among the police on the scene. After huddling with his detectives, Mike Brown headed for his car. Something told her that things had gone from bad to worse. She got into her car and followed the detective sergeant.

Eleven

Just before seven o'clock that morning, thirteen-year-old Vern Inman was jolted out of his sleep by a woman's screams. Lying still for a moment, he could tell the cries were coming from my grandparents' house across Lakewood Avenue in Cotati.

"No! No!" the woman shrieked. Inman jumped up to look out his window, but the screaming had stopped. *Must have been a family fight,* he thought.

The teenager dressed and left for school. So he wasn't home a few hours later to see two Cotati Police Department cruisers pull up at the house across the street.

A few minutes earlier, the officers had received a call from the Sonoma County Sheriff's dispatcher about the homicides that morning in Kenwood and Boyes Hot Springs and the nonfatal shooting in Kenwood. The sheriff's office had asked that the three officers, two men and a woman, respond to the Lakewood Avenue address to make what's called a "welfare check." They were supposed to make sure that everyone was okay and warn them that Ramón was on the loose and dangerous.

One of the officers knocked. There was no answer, but the

door was unlocked and ajar. As one of the male officers stayed on the doorstep to watch the yard, the other two stepped inside cautiously, guns drawn.

The living room they entered was decorated with paintings of saints, religious statues, crucifixes, and images of Christ. But the rest of the house was a scene from hell.

As they reached each victim, it was clear that there was no need to check for vital signs, so after making sure that the killer wasn't hiding in the house, the Cotati officers quickly retreated. They called the Sonoma sheriffs department and asked for help. The house was in their jurisdiction, but their small department had no crime-scene investigators, and lacked the experience to handle something that horrible. Ramón Salcido's killing spree had started in unincorporated Sonoma, on the sheriff's department's turf. I think the Cotati officers were relieved to let someone else handle it.

Mike Brown arrived at the Cotati residence about half an hour later, after first stopping at the Grand Cru to clear the crime scene with detectives Edmonds and Doherty.

Just inside the open gate at Grand Cru, Brown had seen the body of a young man dressed in a cherry-red Grand Cru winery sweatshirt sprawled in an old Karmann Ghia. His feet and legs were still inside the car, but his upper body had fallen out onto the gravel. Edmonds told him that some Grand Cru employees had identified the victim as Tracey Toovey, a well-liked assistant winemaker. None of them could think of a reason why my dad would have shot him. Toovey wasn't even Ramón's boss.

Brown filled in the other two detectives on the situations at Kunde and Boyes Hot Springs, as well as the report he'd just received from Cotati. Then he got back into his car and raced out to my grandparents' house, lights flashing and siren screaming.

When he arrived at the Lakewood Avenue house, it had already been cordoned off with crime-scene tape. A small crowd of neighbors had gathered and were being interviewed by the police officers. When he heard that there were three victims in the house, Brown wondered if they were me and my sisters.

As Mike entered the house, he slipped on the emotional "mask" that usually protected him in such situations. But nothing the Cotati police officers had said prepared him for what he found. The body of a middle-aged woman, my grandmother Louise, was lying in a large pool of blood against a wall near a hallway. Her throat had been slashed open, and she appeared to have been beaten. Furniture was overturned and the religious paintings on the walls were knocked askew. Given the blood smears on the floor and the walls, and the defensive wounds on her hands and arms, it was clear my grandmother had put up a fight, but she'd been overwhelmed by her attacker.

Brown soon saw the reason she'd fought so valiantly. At the very end of the hall, the body of my eight-year-old aunt, Maria, lay in the doorway of the master bedroom. Her throat had been cut so violently that she'd nearly been decapitated, but even that hadn't been enough for the killer.

Judging by blood trails on the floor of the hallway, Mike saw that Maria had been dragged to where she now lay, and then had her legs spread apart with her feet flat on the floor and her bent knees up in the air. Her nightgown had been pulled up and her panties yanked down around one ankle, exposing her genitals.

The positioning of the body, with her feet facing her parents' bed, struck Mike Brown as such a statement of hatred that it was hard to fathom what could have caused it. Given the amount of blood beneath her, it was clear that she'd still been alive while the killer was doing this. Maria's heart had beat on until she was drained.

As horrific and degrading as Maria's death had been, it was the sight of my aunt Ruth that would haunt Mike Brown for years. He found her in the kitchen, lying facedown in her own blood. Her throat, too, had been sliced open to the bone. Her nightgown had been pulled up above her waist.

Her panties, soaked in blood, lay wadded at her feet. The killer had then moved her legs back and forth, making a pattern in the thickening blood like some sort of obscene snow angel, leaving them spread apart. And the murderer had left a pair of bloody red handprints on her buttocks as he pulled them apart.

Years later, I asked Detective Brown how he got through such a horrible scene. "By focusing on my job," he said. But it was clear the images still haunted him.

There were now four crime scenes, five dead people, and another victim with a bullet wound in his shoulder.

The sheriff's department was prepared to take on the case, but Brown was running out of detectives. He hated to do it, but he called Randy Biehler, suffering at home with the flu, and asked if he could get himself to Cotati. The poor guy sounded half-dead, but he told Mike he was on his way. Then Mike asked Dispatch to call the California Department of Justice to see if they could spare some of their CSI specialists. They quickly agreed.

Now all Mike Brown could do was wait. And wonder where my dad was. And what he'd done with my sisters and me.

As the crowd gathered outside the police cordon, they felt the first waves of a panic that would eventually envelop Sonoma County. Rumors were already beginning to spread: Ramón Salcido had gone crazy. My entire family had been murdered. Ramón was still out there, ready to kill some more.

This was no drug deal gone bad. No foiled burglary turned violent. It was a case of uncontrolled, unconscionable, inexplicable violence. And the likely suspect was nowhere to be found.

My grandparents' next-door neighbor Colette Thomas stood at the crime-scene tape aghast. She and her two girls, Calah and Mary, had met the Richards family one day soon after they moved in, when Grandma was walking past their yard with Ruth and Maria. My young aunts, never shy, introduced themselves.

Thomas noticed right away that the family was "a little different." Grandma told her that she sewed all of her girls' clothing, which was well made but looked like fashions from the 1950s. Whatever the case, the Richards family seemed happy. The girls laughed a lot; they obviously loved their dad and were devoted to their mother, with whom they spent most of their days.

My grandparents weren't shy when it came to talking about their very devout Catholic lifestyle, and Colette knew they belonged to some sort of underground Catholic group. Grandma was protective of her girls; they weren't allowed to go farther than a few houses away. Nor were they supposed to go into other homes—even for birthday parties— though the Thomas girls were welcome to visit Ruth and Maria at theirs. Once they'd gone along with Colette and her girls to a horse show at the Sonoma County Fairgrounds. Grandma talked about how much her daughter Angela loved horses and riding—even though she'd only been allowed to ride in a skirt—and about my mom's talent for drawing the beautiful animals.

Mom always brought us along when she went to visit Grandma. But Colette noticed that Ramón didn't come as often. The few times she'd met him, he seemed quiet and reserved. My aunts told her daughter Mary that her parents didn't like my dad very much.

Now Colette and the other neighbors wondered in fear. Where was Ramón now? And where was my grandfather?

Grandpa was out making deliveries for UPS around noon when he got a call from his supervisor telling him to bring the truck in. There was an emergency—he was needed at home.

Grandpa couldn't imagine what could be wrong. Things were good at home. After work that day, he was scheduled to fly back east to see his sons. The night before, as he was packing for the trip, he had felt a sudden wave of peace and contentment. "A good feeling just came over me," he told my grandmother, taking her hand.

"Me too," she replied gently.

There was no sleeping in at my grandparents' house, and the girls were up when he left for work that morning a little before seven. Ruth had a cold, so he didn't get his customary kiss good-bye from her, but Maria gave him one. "Bye, Daddy," she said, smiling.

Five hours later, Grandpa arrived back at the UPS station. The others there fell silent when they saw him; some averted their eyes as if afraid to look at him.

"What's the matter?" he asked his supervisor, fear rising in him like bile.

The man shook his head. "You just need to go home."

When Grandpa reached Lakewood Avenue, the street was filled with police cars and TV-news trucks. It looked like a parking lot for some big event. A crowd of people hovered near the wide yellow tape that cordoned off the area in front of his house.

As he drove up, a young police officer motioned for him to stop and roll down his window. "What happened?" Grandpa asked.

"Who are you?" the officer demanded.

"Bob Richards."

The cop's demeanor changed. He asked Grandpa to get out of his car and have a seat in the back of his police cruiser.

Grandpa did as he was told, sitting with the door open and his feet on the ground as he waited for the officer to tell him what happened. But the young man seemed unsure of what to say. All Grandpa could gather was that someone had done something bad.

Then he understood. "All of them?" he asked, his voice cracking.

The officer nodded. "All of them."

The young officer was relieved when a Sonoma County

detective walked up and introduced himself. He asked Grandpa to come with him to the police department head-quarters in Cotati. He'd be safe there, and they could talk about his son-in-law, Ramón.

After speaking to the detective at the station, Grandpa called his sons and told them what had happened. As if trying to shake off some horrible dream, he drank cup after cup of coffee, but that just left him awake and numb. That morning, when he left for work, he'd had three beautiful daughters and a wife. Now they were all gone. And his granddaughters—Sofia, Teresa, and I—were missing.

Twelve

It was midnight before Mike Brown had finished his initial reports and was ready to go home. The other detectives had just left to try to grab a few hours' sleep before starting up again.

It had been one long, horrible day. He'd spent most of the afternoon and evening driving between the various crime scenes, keeping his detectives updated and getting briefed on what they were learning. None of them had ever handled a case this complex or wide-ranging. Mike was serving as the clearinghouse for information, and the task was overwhelming.

All he could think about was that the killer was still free. They needed to catch him and assemble the makings of an airtight case against him. More urgent still, they needed to find me and my sisters.

The media had been showing up at the crime scenes all day—first the locals, then the Bay Area TV, radio, and print reporters, followed by the national media. There'd even been calls from international news agencies. As the news spread, the sheriff's office started getting tips: Someone somewhere had spotted a Mexican male who fit my dad's description. Then someone reported seeing him somewhere else many miles away. He was seen in a station wagon, in a beat-up older-model sports car, or heading down the highway on foot.

In the meantime, the sheriff's department had to think about its own community, which was worried about its safety. Many of the people who called wanted to know if they were in danger. But the one person who should have been assuring them that they were safe was doing just the opposite.

Sheriff Michaelsen had shown up at Cotati that morning. He set himself up in the Cotati PD's "command post," a van equipped with communication gear, outside my grandparents' house. And there Michaelsen proceeded to have "strategy" discussions with the Cotati police chief as nearby TV crews listened in through the open door.

Mike Brown later told me he and his men didn't think the community had much to worry about from my father. He'd obviously gone after specific people—his family and two employers—and wasn't just running around killing whoever he saw. The people who might still have to fear him—remaining family members and winery employees—were in hiding; a deputy had even been placed at Dunbar Elementary School on the road to Grand Cru, where frightened parents had come to pick up their children early. But most people would be safe unless they happened upon Ramón accidentally or tried to apprehend him—and by this point, hours after the killings, there were indications that he'd already left the county.

For some reason, though, Sheriff Michaelsen held several press conferences during the day, proclaiming that everyone in the area was in danger. As the VCI Unit looked on in anger, he released details about the murders—especially Cotati, which he called "the worst in county history." Experienced investigators know to keep as many details private as possible, to help them spot errors in false tips and suspect statements.

The detectives were particularly appalled when Michaelsen announced that my aunts Ruth and Maria had been sexually assaulted. It was true that sexual abuse could be construed from Ramón's manipulation of the bodies, but the crime-scene teams had not established whether they'd actually been raped. It was an unnecessary invasion of my aunts' privacy, especially because no one knew if my dad would eventually be charged with that crime.

There wasn't much Mike Brown and his detectives could do about the sheriff. But that didn't mean they had to feed his appetite for the limelight. For the moment, Brown told his men not to tell Michaelsen or the other brass any more details about the case. "If you see them coming," he told his men, "head the other way. Find something you suddenly have to do. Our goal is to catch Salcido and put him on death row. And I'm not going to allow anything to happen that might compromise that."

"If they find out you said that, you'll be in trouble," one of the detectives warned.

"I'll worry about that later," he replied.

As they tried to piece together the events of the day, the detectives began to realize that they'd arrived at the crime scenes in reverse order. It was clear that my father had struck first at Cotati.

They knew that Grandpa had left his home a little before 7 A.M. and that Vern Inman had heard screams coming from the house a few minutes later. So Ramón had arrived at the front door right after Grandpa left—had, perhaps, even been hiding in his car waiting for Grandpa to leave. Then he'd wasted no time attacking his victims. He also spent several minutes ransacking my grandparents' home—his bloody fingerprints were found all over it.

The detectives also knew that a call had been placed from

the Cotati house at 7:14 A.M. to our house in Boyes Hot Springs, and that Ramón's bloody handprints had been found on the telephone. So he'd already committed the Cotati murders and taken the time to arrange my aunts' bodies, then decided to call our house. Why did he call home from Cotati? It seemed unlikely that he'd told Angela what he'd done, since my mother didn't flee or call the police. Perhaps it was to make sure she would be home when he arrived.

The investigators weren't quite sure what my father did next. There were two ways to reach Boyes Hot Springs from Cotati. One was to head north on Highway 101 to Santa Rosa and then east on Highway 12, past Kenwood, to our house on Baines Avenue. The other way was to head east from Cotati, past Petaluma on Lakeville Highway to Stage Coach Road, and loop around through Sonoma and then to Boyes Hot Springs. Either way, the trip would have taken about thirty minutes.

Our Boyes Hot Springs neighbor Richard Clark told Dave Sederholm that he'd heard a woman screaming around eight o'clock that morning, followed by a series of gunshots. Another neighbor, a Hispanic woman who didn't speak English, said through an interpreter that she'd also heard screams around that time, then several gunshots, more screams, and finally silence.

Assuming that Ramón left Cotati immediately after his 7:14 phone call, he could have made it home to Boyes Hot Springs by around 7:45, where it seemed as though he'd attacked Mom immediately, judging by the reports of the neighbors.

My mother had put up a fight. She had tried to get away, but my father struck her in the face and head with a blunt instrument and fired at her several times before he finally killed her with a shot to the back of the head.

It couldn't have taken long, Mike Brown later told me. It would all have been over for my mom in a few terrifying minutes.

* * *

When the sheriff's department dialed the number my
father had looked up in that bloody address book in Cotati,
the woman who answered was his mother, Valentina Borjorquez Seja Armendariz. My grandmother confirmed that
her son had called her that morning. He was crying, she
said. "Mama, this is the last time you will hear my voice,"
he told her. He confessed to her that he'd killed my mother
but claimed that he'd left his children with a friend.

If this was true, then it seemed as though my father must
have driven out to Grand Cru and waited for Tracey Toovey
to arrive at work a little before eight o'clock. As Toovey
stepped out of his car, Dad shot him several times in the
face, then jumped into his LTD and sped off for the Kunde
estate. But this theory only worked if he had made it back to
our home with enough time to kill Mom and get to Grand
Cru—a ten-minute trip—before eight, which is when the
sheriff's dispatcher received that first call about the shooting at the winery. That would conflict with the accounts
given by the Baines Avenue neighbors. But Mike knew that
witnesses are often unreliable in estimating times, so their
account wasn't necessarily conclusive.

The second call to the sheriff's department had come in at
8:18, which would have left plenty of time for my father to
have killed Toovey and driven to Kunde to shoot Butti. This
chronology jibed with a report from a school bus driver who
claimed to have seen Dad at about eight-thirty that morning,
speeding past him on Highway 12 in an older Ford sedan.

That one eyewitness report wasn't enough to settle the
matter, though. It was entirely possible that after leaving
Cotati, Dad had gone first to Grand Cru, then backtracked a
quarter mile to Kunde. Which would have meant that, even
as Mike and the Violent Crimes Investigation Unit were re-
sponding to the first two calls, my father was driving to
Boyes Hot Springs to kill my mother. Or he might have
killed Angela, then driven to the wineries and attacked
Toovey and shot Butti—and then *returned* to our house in

Boyes Hot Springs to clean himself up and call his mother in Mexico. If that was the case, Brown and Ballinger would just have missed him when they got to the house.

That was the problem with such a complex case: There was a good amount of evidence, but much of it was contradictory, or inconclusive, or subject to multiple interpretations. For instance, Butti said that he'd seen blood on my father's forearms. Was that blood from the Cotati murders? Or was it my mother's blood? It was impossible to know.

All of that would be important at the trial. But right now what Mike was thinking about was finding me and my sisters before anything happened to us, and catching the mass murderer who had killed my mother.

The detectives did have an idea of where Dad had gone after he left Sonoma County. At 9:34 A.M., someone had tried to withdraw $140 from our family account at a Wells Fargo ATM in San Rafael, forty minutes south on Highway 101. The request had been denied for insufficient funds; the account had been cleaned out earlier that morning. At this point, the detectives didn't yet know what to make of that earlier transaction, the $200 withdrawal from a Wells Fargo ATM in Sonoma at 5:39 A.M. Who was it that had made that withdrawal—Ramón or Angela?

This gave Harvey Head, a financial-crimes detective, an idea. He contacted Wells Fargo and asked them to keep my father's card active and allow him to make withdrawals, despite the fact that his account was empty. That would allow the sheriff's department to track his movements. The idea paid off almost immediately. That same day, Dad used his card to buy tan slacks and a light-colored sports shirt at a Ross department store. A little later, he cashed two checks—one for forty dollars and another for twenty—at a Wells Fargo branch in San Francisco. They were the checks from Mark Ondrasek that he'd been holding since the previous night.

* * *

One thing that was troubling both the detectives and the general population was the question of my father's motive. And there, too, a number of theories existed.

Some of the neighbors, as well as a few of Ramón's drinking buddies who'd called the department when they heard the news, pointed out that Dad was the jealous, possessive type. He didn't like other men looking at his woman. Both our neighbor Richard Clark as well as Ken Butti said that Ramón suspected Mom of cheating on him.

Clark told Sederholm that he'd heard my mother and father arguing the night before. He heard Mom shouting that Dad never let her go out, and he even said that Dad had threatened to "blow your head off." That might have explained his attacking my mother. But why would my father want to shoot Toovey? The assistant winemaker was a dedicated family man who was rarely without his wife and kids except when he was at work. My father had been having trouble at work, but Toovey had nothing to do with that. And it certainly didn't explain his attacking my grandparents or their other children.

Mike and his detectives learned pretty early on that my father had been drinking and snorting cocaine the night before the murders. And a clerk from the Sonoma Mission Inn told the media that he'd been turned down for a room because he'd been drinking. But getting high didn't explain Ramón Salcido's murder spree. This wasn't some spur-of-the-moment, drug-crazed frenzy or a lethal flash of uncontrollable anger. Even if my father had been under the influence—or provoked into some insane fit of rage—when he attacked Grandma and my aunts in Cotati, he'd had plenty of time to sober up and cool down before he reached his other victims. He'd wasted no time committing the murders, but he wasn't so rushed or crazy that he didn't rummage through my grandparents' house and make two phone calls.

The detectives' interview with Ken Butti suggested another motive—that Dad had suddenly snapped due to financial pressures. The court records revealed the mess my father had gotten himself into with his overdue child support and bank-loan obligations. Still, it was hard to imagine a $5,800 debt and some child-support payments sending Ramón on a killing spree—and none of his victims had had anything to do with that.

But this theory gained ground after the San Rafael police got a tip that our Ford LTD had been spotted in a San Rafael shopping-mall parking lot. Once the local police officers confirmed that it was my father's car, the Sonoma County investigators joined them to stake out the car in case Dad returned to claim it. When he failed to show after several hours, the car was towed back to Santa Rosa to be processed by the Crime Scene Investigations Unit.

Inside the car, the investigators discovered a fully loaded .22-caliber handgun and a large, bloody fishing knife under the passenger seat. They also found my father's Social Security card on the front seat and a handwritten note in Spanish on the dashboard. "Forgive me, God, but this law made me do it," the note read. "We could live a better life, me and my children, but they won't let me." The note seemed to point to the child-support law as my father's motive—or at least his excuse—for the killings.

The front seat of the car was soaked with blood—more, it seemed, than my father was likely to have brought into the car from his known victims. In the car was a pair of blood-soaked pants with three photographs in a rear pocket.

The first photograph was of Mom. "To my Ramón. I love you. Angela," she had written on the back.

The second and third photos had been inscribed on the back by my father, apparently on the night of the murders. One was of him with my mother. For some reason, he'd written on the back: "I hope they arrest Arturo and Richard because they sell cocaine."

The last photo was of us, his three daughters. On the back

of it he'd written that he loved us very much, and "We will be together in God's other world."

When he saw that final photograph, Mike Brown's heart sank. Richard Clark had told Dave Sederholm that he'd heard a car trunk slamming several times over in our drive-way that night. "I was worried that he hurt his little girls and put them in the trunk," Clark said. Now Mike wondered if the man was right.

Yet none of the detectives, or the dozens of other law-enforcement personnel who were now working the investi-gation, were ready to give up on finding us. After all, my father had told his mother that he'd dropped us off with a friend. Maybe it was true.

Or maybe we were still with him. The bus driver who'd reported seeing my father claimed to have seen us in the backseat of the car. Neither Ken Butti nor his wife, Teri, re-membered seeing any kids in the car, but we could have been lying down, out of view.

The detectives told themselves there was still a chance that the blood on the seat was Ramón's. Grandma had obvi-ously fought back; perhaps she'd injured him. But now they knew that Dad had taken a bus from San Rafael to San Francisco. With all the publicity about the case, it seemed unlikely that a single Hispanic man could board a bus with three children without being noticed.

Just as Mike Brown was about to leave the office that night, Sheriff Michaelsen walked in. The detectives might have been exhausted, but the sheriff was beaming. He asked if Mike had seen him on television. "I'm even going to be on in Japan," he announced.

Mike said nothing. The VCI detectives had watched the sheriff performing all day and were disgusted. They knew that being sheriff had more to do with politics than law en-forcement. But even Michaelsen should have known better than to tell the press everything he had about the crime scenes. Instead of calming the community, he'd been stirring the pot of fear—and exploiting my family's tragedy to get attention. Mike got up and walked out of the office. *Those kids didn't die to give you a photo op,* he thought.

As he drove home, Mike Brown later told me, he said a prayer asking God to protect me and my sisters. He was a deeply spiritual man, and he believed in a compassionate God and the power of prayer. "Please God, keep them safe," he pleaded again as he crawled into bed.

Thirteen

*T*he view at the Petaluma dump hasn't changed much over the years. In April 1989 the leaves on the grapevines along the highway would have been the freshly minted color of lima beans. The wild grasses at the dump, now brown and brittle, were green and already as tall as a three-year-old girl.

And it was an early, dull gray morning—not sunny midday—when Carmina's father opened his door with Teresa in one hand and a large butcher knife in the other.

"I could see everything," Carmina says, wiping her eyes as she looks over to where her father must have parked. "I was down on the floor, looking out between the seat and the car. He stuck a leg out and pinned Teresa down on it. I watched him cut her throat."

She pauses a moment. "She didn't even struggle."

Her father stood up and walked a couple of feet from the car. "He threw her down the embankment and then came back," she recalls. "Sofia was trying to open her door, but there were child-safety locks or something; she couldn't get it open."

Carmina's shoulders slump. "Sofia . . . the little mother. When we were left at home alone, she was the one who changed Teresa's diapers, who would get up and get me my bottle. She was trying to protect me to the end."

That morning, Ramón stood outside the car and called Carmina's name again. He didn't sound angry, just different, cold. She started to get up, but once more Sofia stopped her, leaning over the front seat so that their father could reach in and take her instead.

"There were no sounds, no sounds" as he placed Carmina's older sister across his knee and sliced hard across her throat. The blood flowed down onto his pants and the front seat, pooling on the floorboard and the ground. No sounds, no sounds, except the crunch of his boots across the gravel as he carried Sofia over to the embankment and tossed her down next to Teresa.

Ramón walked back to the car and called Carmina's name for the last time.

The next morning's *Press Democrat* devoted almost its entire front page to the case. Its headline told the story as it was known at that moment:

FIVE SLAIN IN SONOMA COUNTY RAMPAGE; WINERY WORKER SOUGHT

Beneath the headline was one of my mother's modeling head shots, and a mug shot of Dad from his 1983 drunk-driving arrest. The paper's front page also carried a photo of the covered body of my mother—misidentifying her as "Angelia" Salcido—as she was being removed from our house. It would be several days before the papers corrected the spelling. "Believed to be in the custody of the suspect," a chart inside noted, "are his daughters, Sophia [*sic*], 4; Carmina, 3; and Teresa, 2."

The main story, by Randi Rossmann, Bony Saludes, and

James Reid, led with the biggest unanswered question—
what had happened to us, Ramón's three daughters:

> Fears mounted Friday for the safety of three little
> Boyes Springs girls whose deranged father took them
> along Friday on a vicious killing rampage, the worst
> in Sonoma County history.
>
> After killing five people—including his wife and
> her mother and two sisters—Ramón Bjorges [*sic*] Sal-
> cido, a winery worker, apparently fled Sonoma Valley
> with his three children, according to Sonoma County
> Sheriff Dick Michaelsen.

The story was full of details, from Dad's problems with
child support, his marriage, and his job to the discovery of
his car in San Rafael. But much of the story was colored by
Sheriff Michaelsen's hysterical pronouncements at his press
conferences. The sheriff revealed that the victims had been
beaten and stabbed so viciously that "it's difficult to determine the exact nature of the weapons used." My aunts were
"severely attacked," he said, using a sharp "unknown instrument." They'd also been "sexually assaulted and sodo-
mized . . . and one of the children was nearly decapitated."

As his own detectives cringed, Michaelsen went on
sowing the seeds of fear. "He is bent on killing a lot of
people today," he'd warned the assembled reporters. "His
path of violence has been a really gruesome one." After reviewing the evidence and talking with a local psychologist,
he announced that my father was a "totally deranged, insane
individual," and that "based upon the type of traumatic injuries that he inflicted upon these young children . . . his own
children are in great, great danger. He has literally no at-
tachment to those children at this point in time."

Bony Saludes, a longtime *Press Democrat* reporter, contributed another front-page story that day. Under the head-

line SUSPECT KNOWN FOR JEALOUSY OF HIS WIFE, he recounted his interview with Richard Clark, who called his friend Ramón "extremely jealous of his pretty wife." My father carried a gun, Clark said, "and threatened to kill any man he caught paying attention to her.

"He's crazy," Clark told Saludes. "He's convinced that his wife is having affairs. He went around with a gun and he threatened to blow her head off. He said if anyone messed with his old lady, he'd kill them."

Ramón's former employers at the St. Francis Winery, who were also quoted in the story, painted a somewhat different picture. They'd thought a lot of him and wanted to hire him back after he left. He did seem to have something of an ego, they noted, and liked to lord it over some of the other workers that he was from a wealthy family in Mexico.

One of the St. Francis managers said she'd even helped Dad apply for his naturalization papers. "But I don't know if he ever became a citizen."

Roy Curtis, one of my grandparents' neighbors in Cotati, told the reporter that he'd often seen my family visiting. My father was always neatly dressed and seemed nice enough, he said, but he told Saludes that he'd "detected some racial tension between him and his father-in-law."

In another story inside, under the headline BRUTAL SLAY-INGS STUN QUIET COTATI NEIGHBORHOOD, Michaelsen told Saludes that "the blood goes throughout the whole house." He said his detectives believed the attack on my grandmother had begun the moment she opened the door.

Grandma's neighbor Colette Thomas was interviewed with her eleven-year-old daughter, Calah. She called my young aunts "two little angels with halos on top of their heads," and Calah said that "it was like their mother didn't want them out in the real world." Her twelve-year-old friend Jennifer Shultz agreed: "Their mother was pretty over-protective and wouldn't let them go very far."

Many of the neighbors said that things would never be the same on Lakewood Avenue. "They've shot our neighborhood all to hell," said Leonard Mathys, a fifteen-year resident. "It's real scary to realize it's your own street. This is an extremely quiet, peaceful neighborhood. It proves anything can happen anywhere."

The paper also carried a background story about my mother, the " 'gorgeous' slaying victim who sought a career in modeling." It quoted Barb Bradley as dismissing the rumors that Ramón was insanely jealous, saying that he attended Mom's modeling classes and shows and that he was proud of his wife's ambitions.

"They were a very happy couple," Barb said. "He loved his wife. He loved his kids, and she loved him and the kids, too. I never saw any violence or anything like that." She acknowledged that my father had been doing a lot of cocaine lately but said that the day before the murders Mom had told her that he hadn't done any for a week, "at least not to her knowledge." My mom, she said, was not a drug user.

An unnamed patron at the Valley of the Moon Saloon said he couldn't understand why Angela stayed with her husband. "She was absolutely gorgeous," he said. "She must have loved the hell out of him, because she could have had any man in this valley."

With Michaelsen sounding the alarm, the news reports spread fear throughout the county. As she told me herself many years later, Pat Rile was in her dress shop when she heard the news. It didn't take the media long to find her, and suddenly she was fielding calls from reporters asking about Mom's "modeling career," and whether she'd seen the jealous side of my dad. They didn't seem to listen when Pat said that Angela didn't really have a career, that she'd just taken some classes. The more calls she got, the more Rile began to worry that Ramón might perceive her as the enemy, as the person who'd filled his wife's head with dreams of a modeling career. She closed the shop and went into hiding.

She wasn't the only one who feared that Ramón might strike again. Deputies were assigned to guard the Toovey and Butti families. Schools in the Cotati district as well as the Dunbar school were closed. At Dunbar the children had been traumatized by a police helicopter that passed back and forth over the school on the day of the murder; the kids and some of the teachers were convinced the helicopter must be tracking the killer nearby.

The Grand Cru winery closed. The employees went into hiding, and some of them kept guns nearby; their neighborhood began to resemble an armed camp.

And everywhere, people wondered what had happened to me and my sisters.

On the morning of April 15, after a sleepless night, Mike Brown got up before the sun and headed out to San Francisco. Ramón had gone to the Bay Area, too, but that wasn't why Mike was driving there.

Sonoma County had no central morgue. They usually used funeral homes for autopsies, but none of them were prepared to handle five autopsies in one day. So Sonoma County's chief deputy coroner called Dr. Boyd Stephens, San Francisco's well-known medical examiner, and Stephens agreed to conduct the autopsies.

One at a time, Stephens examined each victim, recording his findings as he went along. My mother had been severely beaten, suffering head trauma from repeated strikes with what appeared to be the butt end of a handgun. She'd been upright and moving, he said, during the beating. She'd also been shot once in the shoulder and twice in the head.

Tracey Toovey had been shot three times in the head and once in the shoulder. My grandma, Louise Richards, had suffered a powerful blow to the back of her head with a blunt instrument, hard enough to fracture her skull. Then her throat had been slashed ten times.

My aunts Ruth and Maria had defensive wounds to their hands, apparently acquired in attempting to ward off their attacker. The wounds to their necks had been so deep that all the major structures—the muscles, windpipes, the major veins and arteries—had been cut through, right down to the spine.

If the positioning of the bodies, and my father's bloody handprints on Ruth's buttocks, weren't evidence enough of the killer's sexual deviancy, Stephens's examination found one piece of evidence that confirmed it. One of Ruth's long, dark hairs had been inserted partway up her rectum. There was only one way it could have reached that spot, and that was that the attacker—accidentally or intentionally—put it there.

Despite the severity of the throat wounds, Stephens noted, my aunts would not have died instantly. They would have lost consciousness fairly quickly but lived on for several minutes before death took them.

As the medical examiner did his work, it was hard for Mike Brown to keep his mask of objectivity in place. The sheer number of victims—four of them related females, a mother and her three daughters—was terrible. But so was the horrific overkill. My mother and Tracey Toovey had been shot several times in the head; the others were slashed and abused while still alive. It was pure, conscienceless viciousness.

About seven hours after the autopsies started, Mike was crossing the Golden Gate Bridge into Marin County to return home when suddenly the police radio picked up a flurry of communications coming out of Sonoma. The reception was bad, and he could only catch every other word, but it was enough to go Code Three. There was another crime scene—this time at the Petaluma dump.

Fourteen

A gentle breeze rattles the dry brown grasses at the top of an embankment at the Petaluma site, a lonely spot and somber despite the bright blue sky.

It was here that Ramón returned to the car to collect Carmina. She made no attempt to answer his call. Having watched from no more than a few feet away as he murdered her sisters, she knew what was coming next.

"He reached in and unlocked my door, then opened it and dragged me out. He sat down on his seat and put me on his lap and grabbed the knife."

Carmina gazes up into the heavens, then sighs heavily. "I begged him, 'Please, Papa, stop!' I was putting up a fight and I think that surprised him a little. He grabbed my hair and pulled my head back so that my neck was exposed. But I put my hands out to push away the blade."

She holds up her right ring finger; a white scar bisects it. "It was nearly cut off. He had to let go of my hair and grab my arms and pull them down. I remember looking at his face; it was all twisted and angry, like he was mad at me for giving him a hard time. I said, 'Please, Papa, don't cut me. I'll do whatever you want.'"

Ramón paused—not out of some last vestige of humanity, she believes, but out of some other, darker impulse. "But then the fury returned, and he cut my neck."

Carmina's hand goes up to the pale scar that encircles her throat. "I remember a sharp sensation, but it didn't really hurt. I think I may have blacked out, because the next thing I can remember was being thrown down the embankment, and then rolling over on my stomach, crying. I tried to climb the embankment, but Ramón turned around and kicked me in the head. Then everything went black."

When she regained consciousness, the day was warm and sunny, like it is now. She was surrounded by a sea of tall green grasses and all alone.

"I just lay there in a daze, but when I gained some strength, I sat up and called for Sofia—he'd thrown me very close to her—but she didn't answer. I shook her, but she wouldn't wake up. I looked over and saw baby Teresa. She'd been slaughtered. It was my most terrifying moment."

Carmina was not quite three years old. She could hardly grasp what had happened. "But I knew something was terribly wrong. I had to move away from them, so I crawled about three or four feet. Then I curled up on my side and went to sleep again."

As the memory surfaces, Carmina mimics the movements of a child curling up on the ground. Her eyes close, then fly open, as if she's once more watching what happened eighteen years ago. "I woke up with the hot sun beating down on me. I was so thirsty. . . . I remember standing up and looking out over the grass. We had driven that way many times to go to Grandma's house, and I think I must have recognized the hills over toward Cotati because I said, 'Grandma, I'm thirsty.'"

A perplexed look crosses Carmina's face. "I've wondered about that. Why did I call for my grandma and not my mom? Maybe because I knew I was facing her house. Or . . . or maybe because Grandma Louise was there with me. She *was already dead, and she had always taken care of me when my mom wasn't around."*

The little girl kept sleeping, fitfully, through the rest of that afternoon of April 14. Her waking moments remain in her mind like snippets of a silent movie that fades to black between scenes. She remembers seeing a shed on the hill above her and hearing the sound of men working up there. But there was nothing she could do about it, except sit in a field of grass waiting to be rescued.

At one point, barely able to see over the tips of the grasses, Carmina got to her feet and tried walking toward the hills of Cotati. *"But I got dizzy and fell down. I remember staring down at my pajamas—my nightie—I think there were bear shapes on it. It had been white, but now it was bloody. I looked over at my sisters and saw that their faces and necks were covered with flies. I just knew I had to stay away from them."*

Carmina believes that she slept through the night. *"Or at least I can't recall anything. I just remember waking up to the sound of footsteps on the road above me. I froze. I thought it was my dad coming back to hurt me again. If I was like my sisters, I thought, he would leave me alone. So I closed my eyes."*

The footsteps stopped directly above the spot where she was lying at the bottom of the embankment. Then they started away again. *"I moved so that I could look. He must have turned and looked back, because he saw my leg move. Then I heard a yell . . ."*

"Oh my God!"

That afternoon, a young man had been poking around the Petaluma dump as he waited for a friend to get off work at the quarry. When he wandered over by an embankment and looked down, the man saw three large dolls lying at the bottom. At least he thought they were dolls—a bit worse for wear, unwanted, discarded with the rest of the trash. He started to walk away, but something about the dolls made him look back.

That's when I moved my leg.

"Oh my God!" I heard him yell, and he took off running up the road to the quarry.

The young man, Mike Mikesell, found the quarry superintendent, Tim Smith, and told him what he'd seen. Tim ran to the road above the embankment and looked down, where he saw three little girls lying in the grass below him. Two of us were dead; he saw that at a glance. But I was sitting up in the grass.

Tim told Mike to run back and call 911 to report two dead children and another who needed an ambulance.

Tim scrambled down the embankment to get to me. When he saw the wound—a straight line of crusted blood from just below my right ear to just below my left—he gasped. I squeezed my eyes shut. When I heard the footsteps returning, I'd kept them closed as tight as I could. I was terrified. Then Tim picked me up and carried me up the embankment.

As we reached the top, I looked back. It was the last time I ever saw my sisters.

Tim Smith set me down on a piece of cardboard. Then he sat down next to me and put his arm around me. "Where's your mommy?" he asked. I tried to answer but it came out as a gurgle. "That's okay," he said. "Shhhhh." He didn't want my wound to start bleeding again. So we just sat quietly and waited for help to come.

I remember Tim trying to comfort me. And I remember when the helicopter arrived. The light and the noise terrified me. When they put me on the stretcher to load me onto the helicopter, I started screaming and kicking, flailing my arms so wildly that they had to send the copter away and wait for a regular ambulance.

Strapped to the stretcher, surrounded by strangers poking me with needles, I started to cry. I didn't want to be hurt anymore.

On the way to the hospital, the paramedics asked me what happened. "Daddy cut me," I said. "Please don't hurt me."

Like almost everyone in the community, Dr. Linda Beatie had been horrified by the murders and worried about my sisters and me.

There was a lot of fear out there in Sonoma County, and Michaelsen's press conferences hadn't helped. But not everyone thought they were in direct danger. Linda Beatie felt safe in Petaluma, a nice small town. She wasn't worried that Ramón Salcido might be walking the streets of her neighborhood. In her nearly twenty years as an anesthesiologist at Petaluma Valley Hospital, Dr. Beatie had been fortunate; since it wasn't a trauma hospital, they didn't get the really bad traffic accidents, and there was little violent crime to speak of in the area; she'd never even seen a gunshot wound.

Dr. Beatie was about to start preparing a patient for surgery when the nursing supervisor called and told her to put that case on hold. One of the Salcido children had been found alive nearby and was on her way to the hospital with a throat wound. The anesthesiologist rushed to the ER, arriving just as I was being wheeled in.

Two images from that moment would stick in the doctor's mind for years to come. One was of a blond female paramedic who was helping with the gurney; it was the first time Linda Beatie had ever seen a female paramedic, and this woman, she thought, looked like an angel.

The second image was of me, sitting up on the gurney as they carried me in. At first, she thought, I didn't seem too badly traumatized. I was alert, not terribly bloody—just a little girl sitting calmly as everyone rushed around her.

When Dr. Beatie learned of my condition, however, she started to tremble with fear. When my throat was slashed, the cut had missed the major blood vessels. But my trachea, or windpipe, had been completely severed. By all rights, I should have suffocated. The only reason I was alive, the doctors later realized, was that my head had fallen forward and kept my airway intact long enough for the blood to congeal and seal it off. Otherwise, I wouldn't have been able to breathe and would have died with my sisters.

But that didn't mean I was going to survive now. In fact, as she confronted my situation, Dr. Beatie was increasingly afraid that she might kill me herself.

She would normally have prepared me for surgery by sedating me and then passing a tube down through my mouth and throat, working it past the vocal cords and into the trachea. But my trachea was in two pieces. Not only would it be difficult to pass a tube from one end of it to the other, but manipulating my head to accomplish this might cause the severed ends to part. If that happened, I would die very quickly.

In that moment, Dr. Beatie was overwhelmed by the challenge before her and the possible consequences if she failed. Petaluma had only three anesthesiologists, and they worked rotating shifts. There was no one on standby, no one to consult with or even to offer support as she performed the procedure.

She left the ER and went into a small adjoining room. Leaning over and resting her head on the bed of an X-ray machine, she prayed for the strength to go back and help me. And she cried and cried—until two veteran nurses who'd followed her out of the ER helped her pull herself together.

"I can't do this," Beatie cried. "I'll kill her."

"No, no, you'll be fine," one nurse assured her.

"We can do it," said the other.

The doctor looked at their faces, said another quick prayer, and walked back into the ER.

Beatie saw that the surgeon, Dr. Dennis MacLeod, was getting ready to take me into the operating room. As he prepared, one of the nurses stepped forward with a Polaroid to document the wound for evidence purposes.

When I saw the camera pointed at me, I did what I had always done: I smiled for the picture. When the photo popped out of the camera, I reached for it.

At first the nurse began to hand me the picture, but she stopped when a collective gasp went up in the room. Realizing then what she'd almost done—shown a young child a photo of her own severed throat—the nurse mumbled something and turned away.

As I was wheeled into the operating room, Dr. Beatie went in search of every size tube she could find. Dr. MacLeod had already determined that my other injuries weren't life-threatening; my survival depended entirely on Dr. Beatie maintaining the integrity of my airway. After that, it would be a matter of sewing the wounds together.

As it turned out, Beatie's fears were unfounded—in large part because of the sharpness of the blade with which I'd been cut. As MacLeod gently tilted my head back to view the wound, they could see both ends of my trachea. Beatie wouldn't have to try to get the tube down through my mouth, past the vocal cords, and into the airway. Tilting my head would give them just enough room to insert one end of the tube into my trachea leading into my head and the other end into the part of my trachea leading into my body.

With that one swift action, I was saved. At least for the moment.

By the time she drove away from the hospital after the operation, the world looked different to Linda Beatie. Now she *was* afraid. When she got home, she wanted to talk about the horror of what she'd seen, but her family was already on their way out the door to a high school ball game. "That sounds awful, Mom," they said, and then left her alone with her fears.

Beatie walked through her house and turned on every light. What if Ramón Salcido *was* lurking in her backyard? Evil had become real for Dr. Beatie, as real as a Polaroid photo of a child's severed neck.

Though I didn't know it at the time, I had one other visitor that night.

When Detective Mike Brown walked into the emergency

room at Petaluma Valley, he learned from a local police sergeant that I'd been conscious and talking when I was brought in. I had calmly said, "Daddy cut me," and made a slicing motion across my throat.

Brown went into the operating room and watched as Dr. MacLeod explored the gaping wound. As he turned away, he later told me, he grew more determined than ever to catch my father. But that wasn't going to happen at Petaluma Valley Hospital.

As Brown returned to his car, the sight of the doctor's fingers probing my throat wound was etched in his mind. It was the only memory of me he would have for the next sixteen years.

The next day my sisters and I looked out at readers from a photo in the top left corner of the *Press Democrat*'s front page. We were wearing our Easter dresses, and Sofia and Teresa were smiling, but I looked petulant—an accident of the photo editor's hasty choice.

In the days that followed, I'm told, the community reacted to my story like a lifeline in a time of crisis. It was as though, by following the tale of the one little girl who had survived the horror, they might save their own spirits as well. A trust fund was set up for me (and another for the Toovey family), and toys, flowers, gifts, and letters of support started arriving at the Petaluma Valley Hospital.

The letters came from near and far. "May God bless you, little Carmina," Deborah Devine wrote from Saudi Arabia, where she was living with her husband and young son. "Please get well and when you grow up try not to remember any of the bad things that happened. The world prays for you."

Some sent thousands of dollars; others gave what little they had. "I usually send flowers to be put on my son, Dave's, grave on Mother's Day, but I feel this year he would like for this money to be put to good use for Carmina." Even the inmates at the Sonoma County jail started a trust fund for my welfare.

Many of the letters called for retribution. "I hope the monster who calls himself her father is quickly caught, sentenced and given the death penalty," one said. Another, from a thirteen-year-old girl, declared that "the father needs to be put in jail and executed for what he did to these children."

Other letters reflected the fear that had rippled into the community and beyond. "Are we safe anymore?" asked one woman. "I have a daughter and the fact that a father could kill his own children is beyond my comprehension," wrote another.

Nor was the fear limited to the adults. A young preschooler sent a heartfelt, if misspelled, letter with her donation of "moey for the litte gril." At the end of her brief note, she added, "I am getting worried He will take my Brother and sister."

Many included their hopes that I would heal physically and psychologically. "I hope this darling little girl will end up in a very happy home with people who love her," a woman wrote from Long Beach. "I hope she will get the very best of counseling in the years ahead so that she will be able to lead a normal, happy life."

At the same time, the community—especially people who had known my dad—grappled with what could have caused him to snap. Most of his onetime friends and drinking buddies described him as "happy-go-lucky," but they argued over whether it was his obsession with Angela that pushed him over the edge.

"What I saw was not jealousy," bar owner John McNeilly told Bony Saludes. "I'd say he was overly possessive. He always had his hands on her and he'd never leave her by herself."

Richard Clark now said he had sensed that a tragedy was coming. "I was in his garage and we started talking about his gun," he told Saludes. "He always carried this handgun.

He mentioned the child support payments and his ex-wife. He told me that whenever anyone owed him money, he took a gun to them.

"I tried to tell him he shouldn't do that, that he shouldn't be using a gun, and then he changed the subject."

Clark repeated what he'd told the police about my parents' argument the night before the murders. "I think if she had a place to go a long way away, she would have left him," he speculated, adding that he'd once considered turning the parents in for leaving the kids at home alone.

At the Valley of the Moon Saloon, the owner still couldn't believe the killer was "our Ramón—the Ramón that we knew." But the McNeilly's bartender who'd lent Dad five dollars that night said he'd been hoping my father would "blow his own brains out."

At the sheriff's department, Mike Brown was swamped with requests from the media. Every time he came back to the office, there was a new stack of pink message notes on his desk. All the major national news outlets—CNN, ABC, NBC, CBS, the *Los Angeles Times, The New York Times*, the San Francisco papers, and the national magazines—wanted his time, as did the international press corps. On the night of April 16 the sheriff was featured in an interview with Connie Chung on the *CBS Evening News*.

Mike watched as the media, especially the big national outlets and the international press, played up the most sensational aspects of the case. The Mexican press, in particular, was all over the story. They'd obtained a copy of Ramón's drunk-driving mug shot, interpreting his expression as "smirking" and nicknaming him "the Jackal." The media speculated wildly about Dad's motives: the jealous husband with the gorgeous "model" wife, the money problems, the drug abuse. The reporters Mike talked to all wanted him to guess the killer's mindset, but he was careful to say no more than "We're still working on that."

Brown tried his best to ignore the media circus and concentrate on finding the killer. He was the point man for dozens of law-enforcement officers—including all the detectives with the department, uniformed deputies, the coroner's office, local police departments, and the California Department of Justice CSI unit that had been assigned to help the investigation. Most of them would never see their names in the newspapers or hear them on television, but they were all professionals doing important work.

Detective Brown knew he was going to need more help to find my father. Although there was a chance that Ramón was holed up in the Bay Area, Mike was convinced he was heading south to Mexico. And that would spell trouble.

The United States and Mexico had an extradition treaty— at least on paper. But while American suspects wanted for crimes in the United States had been caught across the border and returned by Mexican officials, the same had never been done with a Mexican national. As I learned later from Mike Brown, the Mexican penal code mandates that Mexican nationals arrested in Mexico for crimes committed elsewhere must be tried and sentenced in their own country. Mexico does not have the death penalty, and its leaders had stated more than once that they would never send one of their own back to a country that did.

If my father reached his native country, Brown and his team would be in uncharted waters. Fortunately, the detective knew where to turn. A month earlier, during a training program given by the California Homicide Investigators Association, he overheard a conversation about prosecuting Mexican nationals who committed crimes in the United States. He'd introduced himself to one of the men, Enrique Mercado, a California Department of Justice agent with expertise in pursuing such cases.

Now Mike Brown tracked down Mercado's number and called him for help. "He may be on the way to Los Mochis," he told the agent, pointing to Ramón's call to his mother during his killing spree. "I need to find an honest cop in Mexico." He knew that sounded politically incorrect, but

Mexican police were notoriously corrupt, as Mercado well knew.

Mercado said he'd see what he could do. There were some tricky politics involved, the agent said. The people of Mexico often accused their leaders of allowing themselves to be bullied by authorities in the United States. Marching down there and demanding that they hand over a Mexican national accused of a crime in the United States might not sit well with the Mexican people or their politicians. Mike Brown and his team would have to walk a fine line.

Sixteen

A s the community struggled to make sense of the murders, fear turned to anger. Most of it was directed at Ramón Salcido, but in his absence there was concern that some of it might be redirected toward innocent people.

At Tracey Toovey's emotional memorial service, Rev. Rich Gantenbein, the pastor of Saint Andrew Presbyterian Church, urged the congregation not to blame all Hispanics for what my father had done. "It was the act of one very sick person. Tracey would not call for vengeance. Trust the law enforcement people; trust the judicial system; or we will sink to the level of Ramón. . . . God alone can deal with Ramón."

So far, there had been no reported incidents directed at Mexicans in the area. But local Hispanic residents feared a backlash. If you're a Mexican man, some joked bleakly, you'd better watch your back; someone's bound to mistake you for Ramón and call the cops.

It was no joke at the sheriff's office, which continued to field dozens of calls from concerned citizens who'd "seen" my father—only now the sightings were coming in from all over the country. It seemed "like every Mexican male in a car has been reported," a sheriff's office representative told the *Press Democrat*.

Beyond the immediate danger of some vigilante shooting an innocent person, the Hispanic community worried that Americans would treat the case of Ramón Salcido as confirmation of their image of Mexican men as hard-drinking, drug-using, undependable, wife-abusing, hot-tempered criminals. That stereotype could affect their ability to get jobs and housing, they said, as well as their standing in the community. "Americans are going to start thinking, 'Why should we allow these people into our country if they're going to do bad things,'" a young Mexican woman living in Boyes Hot Springs told the *Press Democrat*.

Hispanic activists complained that the media was misusing the word *machismo* in describing Ramón. In the proper context, machismo was a good thing, reflecting "manly" virtues of integrity, courage, and pride in one's accomplishments; it described the good, hardworking man who took care of his family and honored the woman he was with. Only in America had the word been bastardized to describe hotheaded Hispanic males who were boastful, physically abusive, violent, and at odds with the law.

Gaye LeBaron, a longtime columnist for the *Press Democrat* and a respected local historian, wrote that every Mexican male in Sonoma and surrounding counties could expect to see flashing police lights in their rearview mirrors. "This is a terrible, terrible time for the whole community, but for the Hispanic community it must be worse. Pray we get through this without accident to add to the tragedies."

Most Hispanics expressed anger and disgust with my father, holding him wholly responsible for his actions. But a few in that community, including one local priest, voiced the opinion that Ramón Salcido had arrived in the United States as a good man who would not have committed such atrocities—only to be corrupted by the loose morals and drug culture of America.

With the killer still on the loose, one thing that united

Mexicans and Americans was fear. Neighbors in Boyes Hot Springs and in Cotati kept their doors locked and their children inside. The Grand Cru winery's employees and their families were in hiding, the vineyard closed until further notice, owner Walter Dreyer told *Press Democrat* reporter Bonnie Cohen. "We cannot place the lives of our staff or the general public at risk since we have no idea where Ramón Salcido is or what he may do next."

In the Tooveys' Glen Ellen neighborhood, the residents slept with their lights on. "And they keep their shotguns handy," Cohen wrote.

At the Boyes Hot Springs elementary school, counselors visited classrooms to check on any children who might have known the Salcido girls. Many parents kept their children at home. "This is not just something kids are fantasizing about," said Sonoma Valley school superintendent William Levinson. "They know that people were murdered. Their fears are real."

Pat Rile kept her dress shop and modeling school closed. With the media intimating that Ramón had resented Angela's modeling "career," she lived in constant fear that my father might hold her responsible.

And Sheriff Michaelsen wasn't making it any better. In yet another press conference, he warned that Ramón could kill again. "It doesn't have to be a relative or a co-worker. Every one of us should be in fear of this man."

On April 18 the *Press Democrat* ran a number of letters to the editor complaining about its "sensational" coverage of the killings. But the murders still dominated the front page, and the paper continued to update readers on the investigation and our family's background.

By now the media had discovered my mother's "cloistered upbringing" in a home filled with Catholic crucifixes and imagery. They reported that her family was deeply devoted to Our Lady of Fatima, the statue of the Virgin Mary that was said to have wept real tears. Reporters interviewed former neighbors who talked at length about how my mother and her siblings had been "kept apart from the world beyond their doorstep." Many of these comments seemed to imply that my grandparents' conservative outlook was somehow responsible for the death of my mom, her mother, her sisters, and two of her daughters.

The world around me was filled with harsh suspicion, but I knew nothing of it. In the wake of my surgery I remained at the hospital—"resting comfortably and playing with her new teddy bears," as their press representative reported. So many new toys and stuffed animals had been delivered to the hospital that an entire room had been dedicated to storing them. And the hospital switchboard had been deluged with calls from people who wanted to adopt me.

Seventeen

Carmina stands quietly on the gentle slope of the Calvary Catholic Cemetery outside Petaluma, looking down at the graves of her grandmother and two young aunts. The horror that threatened to overwhelm her at the dump has given way to a deep sorrow.

"They say Ramón waited outside to make sure Grandpa was gone." Her eyes harden. "I don't know why—Grandpa was a lot smaller than he was—except that Ramón's a coward. He only attacked women and children."

She shakes her head as if trying to understand the depths of her father's depravity. "After Grandpa left, he went up to the house and said he needed to borrow a car jack. So Grandma took him to the garage. When she turned, he hit her over the head with the tire iron—so hard it knocked her out and sent her glasses flying all the way across the garage. Then he went into the house with a knife and found Ruth."

Carmina shudders. She's read the reports at the district attorney's office on what happened next, including the parts that didn't make it into the trial. "He molested Ruth and Maria, before, during, and after he killed them."

She moves over a few steps to the grave markers for

Angela, Sofia, and Teresa. There's a marble horse-head bookend—half of a set that had belonged to her mother and had been given to Carmina by a cousin after her return to Sonoma. She left one and kept one—a small thing she could share with her mother, along with their love for horses.

Mike Brown has told Carmina that he believes her mother went to the bank that morning to get what money she could so that she could leave Ramón. "I like to think she was going to get out of there with the three of us," Carmina says.

But she'll never know for sure. Too many answers to the questions she'd like to ask are buried here, six feet down and lost forever.

Carmina lifts her head and looks around. It's a plain, simple cemetery, with few trees or statues or even head-stones. Just a series of plaques set into a low hill of mown grass—a few flowers, the occasional small American flag, and little remembrances like the bookend. "When I first came here with Grandpa, I felt such peace. I wanted to stay. He had to take me by the hand and say, 'Let's go.'"

A simple mausoleum stands at the top of the hill. Her eyes retrace the steps Bob Richards and his sons took six times on the day of the funerals. She is quiet for a long time, trying to hold back the tears. "I want to be buried here," she says at last. "It feels like home . . . like another home where we can be together again."

Grandpa didn't start crying until the sixth trip. One at a time, he and my uncles carried the caskets from the Calvary Cemetery mausoleum down the gently sloping hill to the grave site.

First had been his wife, my grandmother. Then Angela, Ruth, and Maria. Four silver-gray coffins, from eldest to youngest. Then the white coffin of quiet Sofia, the little mother. And still he did not cry.

Throughout those first five trips down the hill and back up, Grandpa just remained numb. He had been ever since the young police officer let him surmise that they were all gone. Every female member of his family—except me. He hadn't come to the hospital to see me yet; he didn't have the strength. He'd been told I was continuing to improve and was even sitting up and watching cartoons. *As soon as this is over,* he promised himself.

In the days that followed the murders, my grandfather was in shock. He would wake up in the middle of the night, wondering where he was. Then he'd remember and go numb again. It wasn't his dreams that were troubling him; it was the nightmare that began when he opened his eyes.

If any emotion got through the veil he pulled around his mind for protection, it was fear. He didn't know why Ramón hadn't tried to kill him, too, but he believed that his son-in-law might return to finish what he'd started. The fact that twenty uniformed sheriff's deputies stood guard during the funeral seemed to confirm that his fears weren't groundless. He was grateful they were there. Even if my dad didn't show his face, the deputies kept the press at a distance; emotionally, he couldn't talk to anybody and didn't want to try.

After helping to bear six caskets down the hill to the grave site, Grandpa made his way past the fifty or so attendees and back up the hill to the mausoleum. He and his sons took their places around the last small coffin and lifted. It was so light that he wondered for a moment if there'd been a mistake, if the coffin was empty. But then he remembered that this was Teresa's casket. She was hardly more than a baby. He wept for the rest of the service. It would be two years before he could stop crying for more than a few hours.

After the services were over, Grandpa was approached by assistant sheriff Gene Fahy. It wasn't confirmed yet, Fahy cautioned, but he wanted to let him know that someone matching my dad's description had been apprehended in Mexico.

Eighteen

<hr/>

*C*armina turns from *the graves and walks purposefully back to the car. It's time to go see Mike Brown. The thought invigorates her. Her laugh returns and she is able to resume her story at the point where she was still in the hospital.*

The road heads past Petaluma and then Cotati before reaching Highway 101 and then Santa Rosa. It's been a long day by the time the car pulls up in front of a neat ranch-style house in a quiet, tree-lined neighborhood. The crêpe myrtle trees in the yard are blossoming; Carmina pauses a moment to admire them before opening her car door.

Telling her story has meant confronting the memories left to her by an evil man who was also her father. But now she looks forward to seeing a different sort of man—the one who fought for her when it all started, who never forgot her when she was lost to the Valley of the Moon, who was there for her when she returned and needed a friend.

Carmina rings the doorbell. The door opens and Mike Brown stands there smiling. He welcomes her into his home and guides her into his library/family room. It's a comfort-

able room, a good place to sit back and read one of the books that line his walls—Jack London, Mark Twain, John Steinbeck.

Mike Brown has since retired from the Sonoma County Sheriff's Department—with the rank of captain—and few souvenirs of his career are on display in the room. Just two small shadowboxes on the wall, each holding a medal from the sheriff's department. One for solving a two-year-old missing-person case that turned out to be a homicide. The other for his work on the Salcido case.

He did have a hand in creating one of the books on the shelf: The History of the Sonoma County Sheriff's Department (1850–2005). Along with some of the other sections, he wrote the "In Memoriam" section paying tribute to the deputies who had lost their lives in the line of duty.

One more name had been added to that list since the Salcido murders. On March 29, 1995, Deputy Frank Trejo, a former narcotics detective who had helped with the Salcido case, was working graveyard patrol when he pulled into a parking lot next to a bar in Sebastopol to investigate a pickup truck that was sitting in the dark.

The truck was driven by Brenda Moore, whose passenger, Robert Walter Scully, was on parole from the Pelican Bay State Prison, where California housed its roughest customers who weren't on death row. Scully was a member of the Aryan Brotherhood, a white supremacist gang, and had an extensive criminal record. That night he'd instructed Moore to pull into the parking lot so that he could rob the bar next door.

Trejo got out of his patrol car and was walking up to the truck when Scully got out of the passenger side with a sawed-off twelve-gauge shotgun. Scully ordered the deputy to put his hands in the air and get down on his knees, then shot him point-blank in the face, killing him.

Scully was now on death row with Salcido. But so were more than six hundred other condemned men while the State of California dragged its feet on executions, granting

*the killers years and years of useless appeals while ignoring
the innocent lives they'd taken.*

*Mike puts the book back on the shelf, settles into an easy
chair, and begins to unravel the events that began at 8 A.M.,
April 14, 1989.*

It's not something he enjoys talking about.

The Sunday after the murders, the Sonoma County Sheriff's Department took a call from Los Mochis, Mexico. The
man on the other end spoke Spanish, but the operator who
took the call understood only two words: *Ramón Salcido.*

"Uno momento," the operator said, then passed the call to
Frank Trejo, a narcotics detective and Spanish speaker. The
caller identified himself as the husband of one of my father's
sisters and told Trejo that my father was hiding out at his
mother's house. The sister thought Ramón was endangering
the family and wanted him out. The man also asked about
the reward.

As soon as he got off the call, Trejo told Mike Brown and
the VCI Unit detectives what he'd learned. Brown immediately asked that Trejo be reassigned to VCI until further
notice. He then had Trejo call Enrique Mercado at the California Department of Justice and say it was time to contact
that "honest cop" they'd talked about in Mexico. Mercado
had been assured by his Mexican contact that he'd have no
problem arresting "the Jackal" if the opportunity arose.
Nobody liked a child killer.

Ever since the murder, preparations had been under way
at the county and state levels for what to do when my father
was caught. District attorney Tunney had already filed the
necessary paperwork to make it a death-penalty case, and
the California Attorney General's Office was prepared to
initiate extradition proceedings from Mexico if needed.

Not every request for help was granted, however. Brown
tried contacting the FBI, but the Bureau contended that it
had only one agent in all of Mexico and he was unavailable.

Brown suspected that the reluctance had more to do with international politics than manpower issues, but there was no time to argue.

If the FBI had no one who could help in Mexico, he knew the U.S. Drug Enforcement Agency had agents in that country, which was the main portal for drugs entering the United States. He contacted the DEA, which was much more cooperative. Officials there offered to help in any way they could, as long as they could keep a low profile. The Mexican government knew they were operating in that country, but it wouldn't do to advertise the fact to the population at large.

The best offer came without Brown having to ask. Soon after the murders, he got a call from Gilbert Moya and Arturo Zorrilla, detectives with the Los Angeles Police Department's Fugitive Unit. They'd been reading about the Salcido case and thought they might be of assistance if the suspect made it to Mexico.

Moya and Zorrilla were experts in bringing back fugitives from south of the border. They were well acquainted with the Mexican authorities and dealt with them on a regular basis. "We know the people to talk to, and it could save you time." And they knew plenty of ways to get fugitives "kicked across the border," where American law officers would be waiting for them.

If Mexican officials tried to prosecute my father in Mexico for his crimes, the LAPD officers warned, the cards would be stacked against them. First of all, they said, after a suspect is arrested in Mexico he must be brought before a judge with a complaint filed against him by a Mexican prosecutor within forty-eight hours or the suspect would be released. That wasn't much time—especially when a Mexican prosecutor would have to review unfamiliar evidence from U.S. officials in order to determine the appropriate charges for a complaint. Mike and his team would have to translate enough of their reports and case summaries and get them to a prosecutor in Mexico, along with relevant photographs, at once. The clock would start ticking as soon as Salcido was arrested.

Mike called the LAPD officers and told them an arrest appeared imminent. They immediately offered to help his team start preparing the paperwork.

"We can do this one of two ways," the LAPD detectives said. "You can come down here. Or we can come up there."

"Can you guys come up here?" Mike asked.

No problem, they replied, and were soon on a jet headed north.

As Mike and his team would later learn, after his rampage my father had caught a bus from San Francisco to Calexico on the Mexican border, where he arrived at around 2 A.M. on Saturday, April 15. He then made his way to Los Mochis, where he stayed with his mother and with various other relatives.

On Monday morning, April 17, a Mexican *commandante,* six Mexican marines, and DEA agents from Mazatlán converged on Los Mochis to locate and arrest my father. But the press had beaten them to town, and when Ramón learned that they were snooping around he left town to stay with his grandmother in the nearby village of Guasave.

The move foiled the Mexican government's first attempt to nab him. But my father's sister didn't want him staying with their grandmother either, and soon the family decided that he needed to leave and take the train to Guadalajara. A large city in western Mexico, between Puerto Vallarta and Mexico City, Guadalajara had a large, mobile population and harbored a lot of criminal activity, including drug cartels. It would have been an easy place for a lone fugitive to get himself lost.

Before he could leave, though, Ramón's sister turned him in. The Mexican Marines and DEA agents swooped down upon the Guasave neighborhood, but they got the wrong address and rousted a terrified family of eight across the street from Ramón's grandmother's shanty. In the confusion my father slipped out and stole away in the light of a full moon. He left so quickly that he forgot his prized lizard-skin cowboy boots. By the time the agents returned ten minutes later with the correct address, their quarry was gone; they hauled away his grandmother and her son-in-law instead.

Now, one last time, Ramón's sister called the authorities to tell them that my father was taking a train from the local station. If they hurried, they could still catch him.

Around one-thirty on Wednesday morning, the agents converged on the train station, where they found Ramón waiting for his ride. He gave up without resistance.

Later that morning Mexican authorities trotted my father in front of the media in Mazatlán, where he was waiting to be flown to Mexico City. Smiling for the cameras, my father told the reporters, "I'm guilty. I did the killings in the United States, and I expect to be judged there."

For domestic political reasons, the Mexican authorities told the press that Ramón Salcido had been riding a bus that was stopped at a "routine" antidrug roadblock. When he was unable to present identification, they said, he was removed from the bus, whereupon he confessed.

Mexico's attorney general, Enrique Álvarez del Castillo, announced that my father had given authorities an extensive statement about the killings. In it, Ramón presented what he said was the motive for his murder spree: My mother, he claimed, had been having an affair with Tracey Toovey.

As my father told the story, when he arrived home from work on Thursday afternoon, April 13, Angela was gone, leaving me and my sisters unattended. He then went out for a beer, returning at about 7 P.M. to find that Mom was still not home. An hour later, he said, he watched as Toovey's car pulled up to my house and my mother stepped out.

When she came inside, he said, the two of them argued. After that he headed out to the bars. It was then, he said, that he decided to kill my mother, using a "nine-millimeter handgun" he said he kept in his car with two clips of ammunition. Sometime before seven o'clock the next morning, he said, he put me and my sisters in the car so that we wouldn't see him kill our mother. Then he returned to the house and shot Angela three times, killing her in the hallway. After that, he went to look for Toovey and shot him "twice in the chest."

Next, Ramón said, he went to Cotati. He wanted to kill Louise, he said, because he thought she approved of Angela's affair with Toovey. He told the Mexican officials that he went into my grandparents' house and shot my grandmother and my aunts Ruth and Maria. Finally, he claimed, he drove to San Rafael, where he told me, Sofia, and Teresa to get out of the car. He said he intended to kill us and then himself.

According to Castillo, "he admitted to assassinating with a nine-millimeter pistol his wife, Angela Richards, and to have cut off the heads or slit the throats of her daughters, Sofia, Carmina and Teresa, 4, 3, and 1 respectively. With the same pistol he killed his mother-in-law Louise Richards, 47, and his sisters-in-law, Ruth, 12, and Maria, 8, and finally his friend and work companion, Tracey Toovey, all because of jealousy."

A few hours after this "press conference," my father was flown to Mexico City, where another media mob awaited him. Ramón smiled again for the cameras, but now he seemed weary. "I came to Mexico to see my parents for the last time," he said in response to a shouted question. "I think I'm going to be tried on the other side. I don't have anything else to say at the moment."

Before he was whisked away, though, he did give the press one final response. Later it would be debated which question he was addressing. Some believe he was answering someone who asked if he had anything else to say. But most of the press thought that he was answering a different question asked at the same time: "Do you have any remorse for the killings?"

"Not really," he answered.

* * *

About the same time that Ramón was talking to the media in Mexico, Sheriff Michaelsen was holding another press conference in Sonoma. The killer was under arrest, he announced, and he would be handed over to Detective Sergeant Mike Brown on the U.S. side of the border. Brown and his team were already flying south to bring him back, he said.

The word spread quickly throughout Sonoma County, and it was greeted with a collective sigh of relief. People who hadn't been outside of their homes for days, or at least hadn't let their children out, finally unlocked their doors.

When asked about their reaction to the arrest, however, some members of the Mexican community in Sonoma said they questioned whether the authorities had the right man. They knew how things worked in their country, and this seemed too fast and easy. Other citizens told reporters that they weren't looking forward to a long and expensive trial. Justice would be too slow for Ramón, and some wanted to bypass the system and "string him up."

The Reverend Rich Gantenbein, who had been acting as the spokesman for the Toovey family, told Chris Smith of the *Press Democrat* that the family was glad they would finally be able to go home. Toovey's widow, he said, "was glad that the reign of terror was over."

The minister paused a moment and then added, "Thank God, we can unload our guns."

Nineteen

On April 19, 1989, as most of the country was absorbed by the trial of Colonel Oliver North, the *Press Democrat* ran a five-column front-page headline: I'M GUILTY.

The subhead, "Quiet end to brutal slayings," led into an article on the funerals in Petaluma, with a photograph of Grandpa and my uncles standing at the grave sites. But the lead story was my father's arrest.

The busloads of journalists who'd beaten the Mexican police to Los Mochis had sent back a raft of raw information, some of it accurate and some of it not. Most of them ran with the Mexican version of the arrest—the supposedly "accidental" discovery of my dad during a routine roadblock—and reported some variation on the response my grandmother, Valentina Borjorquez Seja, had given to the accusations against her son.

In tears—captured by a photograph that ran in the *Press Democrat*—she recounted the call she'd received from her son in Sonoma. When he hung up, she said, she thought she'd never hear his voice again. He had made a chilling comment—either "I'm going to kill myself" or "They're going to kill me," she wasn't certain which.

When my father arrived in Los Mochis, my grandmother said, she tried to talk him into giving himself up. "If he's not guilty, he should have nothing to fear. He believed in his family. He loved them and was very proud of them. I don't believe that Ramón could have done this."

The journalists spread out through the city, looking for every angle they could. Just as the residents of Sonoma County couldn't fathom what would cause an otherwise ordinary winery employee to slaughter his family and a coworker, the citizens of Los Mochis were puzzled by the inexplicable crime. As if anxious to establish that there had been no warning signs in my father's former life, the local police held a press conference to say that he'd never been into any trouble with the law there. They even produced documentation from his former employers noting what an exemplary worker he had been.

His former friends and schoolmates remembered him as a quiet man and a decent athlete. Some ventured that drugs must have led to his downfall. My grandmother's husband, Bitasio Seja, recalled the trip my family had taken to Los Mochis the previous February. "He was a good boy," he told Saludes. "Never had any trouble. I can't understand what happened. His mother is very, very worried."

Before Ramón's arrest, most people in town assumed he would not live to be captured. When the Mexican state police went to apprehend a suspected murderer or child rapist, one neighbor observed, they tended to shoot first and handcuff suspects later.

Back in Sonoma County, Ramón's attempt to blame his anger on my mother's supposed affair with Tracey Toovey was met with new fury from Toovey's family and friends. There had never been a more dedicated or faithful family man than Tracey, they said. He and his wife, Catherine, were more than married; they were best friends. And he spent his free time with his children, not cheating on his wife.

This accusation by my father added cruel insult to injury. Not only had he murdered Toovey, now he was trying to explain his crime away by pulling the winemaker's name through the mud—and my mom's along with it. To Rev. Gantenbein, it seemed that my father had created his own private hell, and now he was trying to "drag other people into it. To try and respond to these bizarre allegations is to further allow him to control us. We just have to draw the line and say, 'That's it.'"

Some fifteen hundred miles to the south, in Mexico City, Mike Brown and his team were waiting in the U.S. embassy to see whether their work tracking Ramón was going to pay off. It seemed like the first time they'd slowed down in a week, but they weren't happy about the delay.

When the LAPD officers Moya and Zorrilla arrived in Sonoma, the sheriff's department put them up in a nice hotel in Santa Rosa, but they were hardly able to enjoy it. They spent the next twenty-four hours preparing documents for the Mexican authorities, as well as getting hundreds of photos developed. They worked straight through Tuesday night and well into Wednesday morning to finish preparing the materials. Then they had to get it all to Mexico City.

The materials were too important to trust to a fax machine or even an express service; they would have to be hand-delivered. But the detectives couldn't just send someone on a commercial jet—their tight timeline couldn't be subject to an airline schedule. They also didn't know where the trip would take them—Ramón had been arrested in the state of Sinaloa, but he'd been transported to Mexico City. There was no telling where he might be moved next, and the American detectives would need mobility. They also hoped to bring my father back with them—a major security challenge, since by now the media attention had made him a reviled figure throughout the world—and Mike Brown was hoping that his team could interview him on the way. Providing security and conducting an interview would have been impossible on a commercial jet.

So he called Walt Smith, a childhood friend who happened to be the manager of the Sonoma County Airport tower, and asked if he knew anyone who might lend them a private jet. "I need one that can hold six people," Mike said.

Smith called back a little while later with a piece of surprising news: The cartoonist Charles Schulz, the creator of *Peanuts,* lived in the county and immediately offered the use of his private jet. Schulz's son Craig, a licensed pilot, had also volunteered to fly them along with a copilot friend.

Even with all the help, the VCI team found themselves rushing to the airport early that Wednesday afternoon for the flight to Mexico City. When Mike Brown stopped home to pack a toothbrush and a change of clothes, Arlyn wasn't there, so he scribbled her a note on a legal pad and left it on the counter: "Gone to Mexico don't know when I'll be back."

At the airport, Mike met the team of detectives who'd be flying with him: Dave Edmonds, the "case agent" and detective at the Grand Cru crime scene; Larry Doherty, who was also familiar with the Toovey murder; Dave Sederholm, who'd handled both the Butti shooting and the Baines Avenue crime scenes; Frank Trejo, who spoke Spanish; and the LAPD's Arturo Zorrilla, who would help them negotiate the Mexican legal system. When they left Sonoma County a little after 1 P.M., the funerals in Petaluma were still in progress.

During the flight, Mike and his team discussed their strategy. They needed to remember that they had no official standing in Mexico; they would essentially be arriving as guests, with hats in hand. If they succeeded in bringing my father back with them, they decided, Dave Edmonds would be the detective who questioned Ramón. Edmonds was the least experienced at conducting interviews, but as case agent he would be responsible for assisting the prosecutors at trial; he had to know the case backward and forward. And it was important that only one detective interview my father so that no defense attorney would later be able to claim that they'd ganged up on the suspect. But Edmonds knew his fellow detectives would be there the whole time to assist him. "If you have questions you want asked, write them down and give them to Dave," Mike said.

The team arrived in Mexico City at about 9 P.M. local time and crammed into a taxi for the trip to the U.S. embassy. Even the cab ride was an adventure; on every corner there were police officers—or army personnel, they couldn't tell which—with automatic weapons, looking on with only mild interest as fistfights broke out in the streets around them.

The detectives had been told that someone would meet them at the embassy, but after standing outside for more than a half hour, they decided to check in to their hotel, which was fortunately located next door. They were exhausted; none of them had slept for more than a few hours at a time since April 14. And they were starving. They'd had no time for breakfast, lunch, or dinner; the only thing to eat on Charles Schulz's jet had been—you guessed it—a can of peanuts. After checking in, the detectives regrouped at the hotel restaurant and ordered steaks; they arrived looking gray and unappetizing, but the detectives wolfed them down before retiring for the night.

The next morning they returned to the embassy, where they cooled their heels and caught up on the local coverage of the Jackal, who was pictured on the front pages posing with Mexican authorities.

The detectives were surprised that my father had confessed so easily to the Mexican authorities. But they were really taken aback when Trejo and Zorrilla began translating his "confession." They didn't know if the rumored affair between Toovey and Angela was true—so far, they'd seen no evidence of it. But much of the rest of what he said didn't jibe with the facts.

For instance, they knew that Ramón had used a .22-caliber handgun, not a nine-millimeter. And he'd shot Tracey Toovey in the face, not the chest—a pretty hard detail to forget when the victim was only a few feet away. He also claimed that he'd shot Grandma and my aunts, when the detectives knew that he'd bludgeoned and butchered them, probably with a knife. And that he'd killed my sisters (and almost killed me) at the Petaluma dump, not forty minutes farther south in San Rafael.

Who knew why he lied? Was he was trying to make his cowardly acts somehow more "manly?" Did a nine-millimeter sound more like a man's gun to him than a little .22? If he was going to confess to murdering women and children, did he think it sounded better to say that he'd shot them, instead of admitting that he'd chased them around a house and slashed open their throats with a knife? Did he think the murders would make more sense if he claimed they were "crimes of passion" triggered by his wife's unfaithfulness? Did he actually believe he could play the victim? He was obviously willing to lie, even in a confession. To the Sonoma and LAPD detectives, though, the details of his flawed Mexican confession weren't so important. They intended to get the story straight from Ramón.

Finally, after a couple of hours, the detectives were told to report to the Mexican attorney general's office, where they presented their translated investigation reports and summaries, as well as the photographs. After the materials were accepted, they were summarily dismissed and sent back to the U.S. embassy, without so much as a question from the Mexican authorities.

After waiting several hours more, they got word that they were to return to the airport and prepare to leave the country. There was no mention of any further involvement with the case or of what would become of my father. It was a huge disappointment—they would have to return to the United States empty-handed, without the fugitive they came to collect—but the detectives did as they were told and headed for the airport, where they were directed into a private building to wait for their plane.

At one point, Mike Brown and Dave Edmonds wandered away from the group to get something to drink at a nearby snack bar, where an American man walked up to them and started chatting. Obviously unaware of who they were, he introduced himself as an FBI agent and started boasting about his role in apprehending the Jackal. The Sonoma detectives knew that what he was claiming wasn't true; he was taking credit for work that had been done by the VCI Unit and those who had actually helped them—from the LAPD detectives to the California Department of Justice to the DEA. They excused themselves and left him standing there, still talking about his feats.

After they returned to the waiting area, the group was joined by a young, well-dressed Mexican woman. They had no idea who she was, and she didn't bother to introduce herself. "You'll be leaving in ten minutes," she informed them. "All incoming and outgoing air traffic has been put on hold until you have left."

The detectives nodded, disappointment on their faces. They'd done everything they could to bring my father back, but it looked like it was all in vain. Until she said, "Ramón Salcido will be going with you."

While Mike Brown and his team were busy putting together the case against my father, it turned out, an international behind-the-scenes campaign had been waged to bring him back to the United States.

Ever since my father's arrest, the Mexican government had been under pressure to return him to U.S. custody. Extradition papers had been submitted to the U.S. Department of State, which had passed them along to the Mexicans. But the State Department wasn't the only governmental body involved. The House Foreign Affairs Committee, which had a lot of political and financial clout abroad, cast a vote asking the Mexican government to cooperate and conduct any extradition proceedings with dispatch. President George H. W. Bush even called Mexican president Carlos Salinas to intervene.

In truth, the Mexican government was happy to cooperate. Everyone recognized that my father's actions were heinous. But the Mexican authorities needed a pretext to release him—some extenuating circumstance they could point to as evidence that they weren't capitulating to U.S. demands or easily agreeing to hand over a Mexican citizen to a country with the death penalty.

In the end, my father himself gave Mexico the excuse it needed. When he was arrested, he made a point of declaring that he was a U.S. citizen. All the president had to do was declare him an illegal immigrant and order him deported. In fact, he wasn't a U.S. citizen, but the Mexican government didn't know that.

A short time later, my father made his final appearance on Mexican soil, before a mob of more than eighty reporters and camerapeople. Wearing what appeared to be a new dark blue sweatsuit, he smiled as reporters shouted questions at him. At first he tried to respond, but he gave up when no one seemed interested in hearing his answers.

A few minutes later, my father was walked out to the tarmac by Mexican authorities—including the airport manager, who had him by the elbow as if the prisoner was in his personal custody. Walking with the Mexicans was the FBI agent who'd been bragging about the operation to the Sonoma detectives at the snack bar; his eyes grew big when he spotted Brown and Edmonds. Trying to recover, he pointed to the badges on their belts.

"You might want to hide those," he suggested, apparently because of the politics of the moment.

Mike Brown shrugged. "You might be ashamed of who you work for, but we're not. The badges stay."

My father was handed over to the Sonoma County team, who lost no time escorting him onto the jet. The Americans knew they had no authority to arrest him in Mexico, and they didn't want to give defense attorneys grounds to claim they'd dragged him back across the border improperly, so they deliberately chose not to handcuff or restrain him until they'd returned to the United States; if he had decided he wanted to fight the extradition, he could actually have turned around at any time during the transfer and stayed in his native country. It wasn't as if they were worried that he might overpower them. *He's just a little worm,* Mike thought. *A punk and a coward.*

On Mike's instructions, however, the detectives treated Ramón politely. The detective sergeant had told his men that they would have to put aside their personal feelings toward their prisoner. "He knows he's the most hated man in the world, and we're the only friends he'll have on that plane," he said. "It's the only way he's going to talk. If we mistreat him, or he gets the feeling we're looking down on him, he'll clam up."

The jet had six passenger seats, three in a row on each side of the aisle. But my father made seven, so they put him in the "best seat on the jet," seated across from Edmonds at the rear; four of the other detectives took the remaining seats, while one had to sit in a luggage closet at the rear of the plane. From the time they boarded the plane, no one said a thing to the prisoner—and they wouldn't until they reached American airspace.

When they stopped in the Mexican city of Hermasillo to refuel and check in with U.S. Customs before crossing the border, Mike called his lieutenant, Erne Ballinger, to let him know when they were expected to land. Ballinger told Mike that one of the major American TV networks had chartered a jet to follow their plane as it headed north. Sure enough, Mike looked down the tarmac and saw the camera crew filming outside their jet. It wasn't a happy sight; Mike was still concerned that some vigilante might be out there looking for a chance to kill his prisoner, and if so, the TV crew was giving the would-be assassin a good sense of where they'd be and when.

A U.S. Customs agent standing nearby must have noticed the look on Mike's face; he asked if there was a problem. When Mike explained, the agent smiled and suggested that there might be a problem with the other jet's paperwork. "How long do you need?"

Brown smiled in return. "How about twenty-four hours?"

"Consider it done," the man replied and walked off.

Back in the air, the detectives and their prisoner were soon on their way to California. The pilot had originally intended to fly directly from Mexico City to Sonoma County by crossing over New Mexico and Arizona and then into California. But flying over other states without reporting to their magistrates might have given defense lawyers an excuse to quibble about whether my father had been denied his rights to fight extradition from those states to California, so Mike Brown asked that they swing around and fly directly to California, where they could land in San Diego and clear U.S. Customs. "Let me know when you're fifty miles inside California airspace," he said to the pilot. "Then I'm going to want you to throttle back and take your time getting to San Diego."

As they waited to cross the border, my father sat looking out the window. At one point, Mike decided to take a picture of his prisoner "enjoying" the view, as proof that he hadn't been restrained or made uncomfortable during the flight. Dad agreed happily, even asking what speed film Brown was using.

"Four hundred," the detective replied.

"Plenty of light." My father nodded and then smiled for the camera.

Soon Mike got the word that they were fifty miles inside California airspace. He gave Dave Edmonds the signal to begin, which he did by informing Ramón that he was under arrest for murder and attempted murder. "Do you understand?"

"No problem," my father replied. "Yes, I understood." He said he also understood his Miranda rights and waived them.

"First thing I want to get clear with you is, as long as you've been with us, have we battered you or hit you or mistreated you in any way?" Edmonds asked.

"Not at all. No problem."

"Do you feel like we've done anything to coerce you, to make you do something you don't want to do?"

"Not at all. Everything is fine."

Edmonds began by following up on a statement my father had made to him earlier—that he'd intended to surrender to authorities. "Why were you going to turn yourself in?"

"Because I already know that I would do the crime in your country, and part of it was my family . . . and I would feel guilty about it."

Edmonds then asked my father a key question: why he'd killed my mother. According to Mexican authorities, he had blamed it on his anger at hearing that she'd had an affair with Tracey Toovey. Now, however, he changed his story. In flat, broken English, he told Detective Edmonds that he'd killed her because he'd learned that Sofia was not his child.

"She didn't tell me about what's my own daughter," he said. "She married me when she was pregnant, and then later on when we was married, she told me about the little kid that was not my own."

But that wasn't the last excuse my father would give. A few questions later, he changed his story again. Now he said that he'd killed Angela because after he got home from a night of drinking and snorting cocaine, she left him alone with the kids. "She say, 'I'm gonna go outside, you know, looking for, you know, for somebody or what, I don't know.' Then I say all these things to myself, you know, okay, so, my wife left three childs with me there at home, then I say what I have to do."

My father quickly confessed that he'd "cut the throat" of me and my sisters at the Petaluma dump and then proceeded to Cotati, where he murdered his mother-in-law and two young sisters-in-law. After that, he said, he'd returned to his home in Boyes Hot Springs, intending to kill Angela and himself. After he killed my mom, he decided to kill Toovey—because the assistant winemaker had threatened to fire him—as well as "another man," whose name, Ken Butti, he couldn't recall until Edmonds reminded him.

This first interview was intended to be quick, and Detective Edmonds finished it in half an hour. All Mike Brown wanted now was a straightforward confession to all seven murders, as well as the attempted murders of Ken Butti, his wife, and me. They knew that a defense attorney might be waiting for my father in San Diego, ready to shield him from any further questions. These few minutes before reaching San Diego might be their only chance to get a useable confession.

Even without one, there was plenty of evidence tying my father to the murders. Two of his victims had lived, and I had told that police officer that "Daddy cut me." My father's blood was found in the Cotati home and on the bodies of my grandma and aunts—although the detectives now saw that Grandma hadn't managed to inflict more than a small cut on my father's finger. And my father's bloody prints had been found at the Cotati and the Baines Avenue houses, including on the buttocks of my aunt Ruth.

As they'd hoped, my father now confessed quickly to all the murders, as well as the assault on me and Ken Butti. The confession came just in the nick of time: San Diego air-traffic control had allowed them to hold up other aircraft in order to accommodate the jet with the killer aboard, but now they were insisting that it land immediately.

Looking out the window as the jet taxied, Mike Brown saw that their arrival was no secret. The San Diego Police Department SWAT team, as well as agents with the U.S. Bureau of Alcohol, Tobacco and Firearms, were there to keep a whole new contingent of reporters and cameras—and any would-be assassins—at bay. Mike ordered the plane's window shades drawn; he didn't want this to be any more of a spectacle than necessary.

As the jet rolled to a stop, the control tower relayed a message from Ballinger asking Mike Brown to call the sheriff's office when they landed. With the crowd milling outside, however, Mike replied that there was no way he could get to a telephone immediately.

They'd been on the tarmac less than five minutes when there was a knock on the cabin door. Mike Brown knew this might be the defense attorney they'd feared. Instead, when they opened the door, it was another U.S. Customs agent.

"You have anything to declare?" he asked, poking his head in.

"Nope," Mike replied.

The agent nodded. "Didn't think so. You're clear to proceed." He closed the door, and five minutes later, the jet took off.

Once they were back in the air, Brown asked the pilot to take his time getting back to Santa Rosa. They had my father's confession. Now they wanted the details.

Twenty

"Can we start from when you were first considering these killings?"

As soon as they were airborne, Edmonds had once again read my father his rights. Once again he waived them and confirmed that he had not been physically harmed or coerced. Now it was back to the questioning.

My father had no problem with any of it. In fact, he seemed to enjoy all the attention, answering the questions politely and unemotionally, as if he were a candidate for the school board. "I don't remember exactly when . . . the police come to my work for to let me know that I have a child support suit from Fresno County," he said. "And then my wife and I have some arguments at home about it because I been married before with a Debbie Ann. And I have one child with her."

"So that started making you feel like you want to kill?"

"Yes, I feel," Ramón started to answer, then changed his mind. "I don't feel like I wanted to kill nobody. I wanna have some beers, you know, and forget everything else. But my wife made me feel that way when she left me at home with my kids and take off . . . That's when I start to feel like I wanted to kill."

My dad said he took me and my sisters out to the car, and then he drove us around Sonoma looking for my mom as he swigged from a bottle of champagne and snorted cocaine. He kept this up for about an hour, he said, without any luck.

"You were mad because you could not find your wife?"

"Yes."

"So you decided to kill your three children?"

"And kill myself, yeah."

Edmonds asked why he picked the Petaluma dump.

"Because nobody can, you know, I don't want nobody to see me."

My father described how he'd taken Sofia and Teresa out of the car one at a time and slit their throats, then thrown their bodies into the ravine. "I walking back and pull out my third child, Carmina, and then do the same thing. I just take the knife, cut her and then dump her there."

He claimed that he and my mom had previously discussed killing themselves. "She told me a couple times, you know, 'Why don't we kill ourself and don't live in this world? Everybody take our money and we don't have very much money. . . .' She asked me a couple times, and we were mad and fight about it."

"But you didn't kill yourself."

"I didn't because, uh, I wanted to," he answered confusingly. He said he decided that my mother had probably gone to her mother's house, so he went there to kill her, as well as Grandma, Ruth, and Maria.

"Were you gonna kill your father-in-law, too?"

"No, sir."

"Why not?"

Because he wasn't upset with my grandfather, he explained. He was upset only with his mother-in-law and sisters-in-law, who had known about Sofia's real father and kept it a secret from him. Grandpa didn't know about that, he said. "They're scared about him," he said. "My mother-in-law scared about telling him because she thought he was gonna be mad . . . knowing that my one daughter was not mine."

Then, as if realizing it was ludicrous to blame my young aunts for keeping such a secret, he corrected himself. When he left the dump for Cotati, he said now, he was intending to kill Grandma but not my aunts.

By the time he reached my grandparents' house in Cotati, he went on, it was getting light outside. He parked about a block away, watched as Grandpa left, and then pulled up in front of the house. Getting out of the car, he retrieved a tire iron from his trunk and walked up to the house. "I knock the door and I . . . I was still, you know, scared and nervous." When Grandma answered the door, my father told her he needed to borrow a screwdriver to fix his car.

"Then she say, 'I have one in my garage.' So when she walked in front of me into the garage, that's when I hit her on the head."

"Did you think you killed her?" Edmonds asked.

"I thought it was . . ." Ramón started to explain, then started over. "I said to myself I'm gonna go get a knife, you know, to make sure she was dead."

Dad was walking into the kitchen when Ruth appeared. "She saw me and then I thought she hear something . . . so I say, 'I need a knife.'"

At first my twelve-year-old aunt didn't answer him. She asked where her mother had gone. "I thought she gonna see her mother dead or something, so before she see that I say, 'Come in here, show me where a knife is.'"

Ruth did as she was told, but my dad had already found a large butcher knife. When she entered the kitchen and turned her back to show him where the knives were kept, he grabbed her by the hair, pulled her head back, "and just cut the throat with the knife."

"Did she have a chance to scream?"

"No. Not at all."

"What did she do?"

"She just fell down on the floor."

Ramón said that when my aunt fell, he could see her buttocks and that she wasn't wearing any panties. The detectives knew better, but for the moment Edmonds let it slide.

As he walked out of the kitchen, Dad said, he saw Maria standing in the dark hallway. "I walk in front of her. I don't say nothing. I just turn her around and cut the throat."

"Did she say anything to you?"

"No, sir."

"Did you touch her body after she fell down?"

"No, sir. I . . . I . . . I just move her out of my way."

Maria wasn't wearing underwear, he said. "You saw her without panties?" Edmonds asked.

"Without panties, yes," he agreed.

Again, Edmonds let it slide. They wanted to nail down the murders before pressing him about any sexual assaults.

As he was getting ready to leave, Dad said, Grandma staggered back into the house. "I thought she was in the garage dead." They struggled and he knocked her to the floor onto her stomach. Then he reached down, pulled her head up by the hair, and cut her throat as well.

With all the occupants of the house dead or dying, Ramón went looking for the guns he knew his father-in-law kept there. "I opened the closet and was all kind of guns there." He took a .22-caliber semiautomatic and several boxes of bullets.

"Why did you get the gun?" Edmonds asked.

"I get the gun with the intention to kill my wife and kill myself." Then he drove off.

When he got back to our house, my father said, "I walk in my home. I wanted to tell my wife that I already killed my daughters and, uh, my mother-in-law and her sisters, and then we can kill ourself." But when Mom saw him, she ran for the telephone. "She was trying to call the police when I shoot her right in the head."

At first Dad denied hitting my mother with the gun. But

My mother, Angela Richards, with my grandfather Robert and grandmother Louise, and my uncles Lewis, Robert Jr., and Gerald.

My mother as a young woman, at a TFP conference.

My father, Ramón Salcido, with the motorcycle we used to ride with him.

My mother with her younger sisters, Maria *(left)* and Ruth.

My father with friends in Sonoma.

Ramón and Angela Salcido.

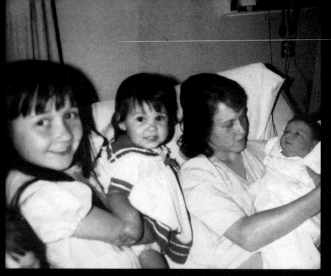

At the hospital the day I was born: Ruth, Sofia, my mom, and me.

With my sisters Teresa and Sophia.

With my mom and
Sophia at Christmas.

All dressed up with Sophia.

Reward! $25,000 Reward!

For Information Leading to the Arrest
of Murder Suspect

RAMON SALCIDO

NOTE: An additional reward of $10,000 is being offered by the Governor's Office for the arrest and conviction of Ramon Salcido.

DESCRIPTION:

Mexican Male Adult

Age: 28

D.O.B.: 3-6-61

Height: 5'9"

Weight: 175 lbs.

Hair: Dark Brown

Eyes: Light Brown

Mustache

ALSO KNOWN AS:

Bojorquez, Ramon Salcedo

Lopes, Ramon

Lopez, Ramon

Ramon-Salcido, Rodriquez

Salcido, Ramon Bojorquez

Ramon Salcido is believed to be responsible for the brutal murders, on April 14, 1989, of 3 adults and 4 children in Sonoma County. Some of the victims were members of his own family. Weapons used: knife and gun. Salcido may be enroute to Mexico, and should be considered armed and extremely dangerous.

If you have information regarding Salcido's whereabouts
PLEASE CALL

SONOMA COUNTY SHERIFF'S DEPARTMENT
(707) 527-2650

At my mother's grave.

My father's wanted poster. He was free for only
days before being apprehended in Mexico.

One of the few photographs in which my scar can be seen.

discovered music at an early age.

With my grandfather and my uncles, Gerald *(far right)* and Robert.

At my first holy communion,
New York City, at the age of seven.

With my grandfather, 1997.

At fourteen, with the Swindells' kitten and their mastiff

later in the interview he admitted that the gun jammed after he shot her the first time, so he began hitting her with it instead. Then he replaced the bullet clip, which allowed him to fire at her again. He shot her one final time after she'd fallen to the ground.

Fortifying himself with more champagne and cocaine, my father said, he then decided to kill Toovey and Butti. He knew Toovey would get to work first, he said, so he waited until the winemaker drove up to the Grand Cru winery gate and flashed his lights to get him to stop. Then he stepped out of his car. "I said, 'I'm gonna kill you.' He said, 'What'd I do to you?' And I said, 'Because you was trying to fire me a couple times on the job.' I said, 'I'm gonna kill you,' and I shoot him."

"Do you remember how many times you shot Tracey Toovey?"

"Absolutely? No. I just shoot . . . I remember three or four times."

Ramón said he then hurried to get away and drove to the Kunde Estate to shoot Ken Butti. "He say, 'Oh, what are you doing so early,' and I say, 'I'm gonna kill you,' and so I shoot him one time. I was scared, and I have another shot of champagne and I take off."

After shooting Butti, my father went home to Baines Avenue. "I was gonna shoot myself there in front of my wife." But first he called his mother. "I said, 'Mother, I'm gonna say good-bye. I'm gonna kill myself. I already killed my wife and her sisters and my mother-in-law, and a couple people.'"

He told his mother that he had a gun and was ready to shoot himself. But then she started to cry, begging him to come to Mexico to see her and his sister. Then, she said, he could turn himself in—or kill himself if that's what he wanted.

After leaving his house, he told Detective Edmonds, my father headed to San Rafael. From there he went to San

Francisco, and from there to Calexico. "I walked across the border," he told them. "Nobody asked me anything. Border Patrol seen me walkin' but they don't ask me nothing."

With my father's detailed confessions to the murders in hand, Edmonds returned to the attacks on my aunts. "We found fingerprints that we think are yours on Ruth and Maria, bloody fingerprints."

"Yes," my father replied.

"Are those yours?"

"Uh, I think, I think."

"Why were your bloody fingerprints on the little girls' legs?"

"I think I was pulling back in there or something."

"Okay. Her legs were opened up wide. Did you open her legs up wide?"

"No, sir."

"How did her legs get opened up wide?"

"I lifted up. I pull her up is all what I do. I don't do anything else than that."

Edmonds didn't relent. "It looks like, to me, that you tried to molest those girls, and I know this is hard but it's important to tell the truth."

But my father wouldn't give in. "I already told exactly everything that true and that I don't try to molest her at all."

"Did you take off either one of the girls' panties?"

My dad hesitated and mumbled something. Then he said he thought he remembered using one of the girls' panties to stop the bleeding from his finger.

"Which girl? Both?"

"Uh, I think both, but I don't remember. There was blood on my finger, and I don't find nothing I can clean . . ." His voice trailed off.

"You saw they had clean panties on?"

"Yes," he answered. Earlier, of course, he had said the girls weren't wearing underwear; he was losing track of his story. It was obvious that my father was getting nervous, and the detective knew he might clam up at any moment, but he pressed on.

"Okay, Ramón, I know this is hard, but we found bloody handprints on Ruth's butt."

"Yeah."

"Why are there bloody handprints on her butt?"

"I don't . . . I don't remember, sir. I don't do nothing to her. I would like to help you but I . . . I don't remembered I do. I don't know any prints or something I can said that it was me."

Now my father had had enough. "I don't want more question about this. I wanted to kill her and I . . . I . . . I don't do any rapes to them. I just only killed her and I . . . I . . . I then killed my wife."

That was all right; the detectives had what they needed from my father. "Okay," Edmonds asked him, "what do you think should happen now?"

"I thinking, um, I go to the electric chair or . . . or somebody kill myself. I mean I have to pay for what I do to your country . . ."

"Do you feel guilty?"

"I feel guilty, and I'm ready to receive anything and everything you guys to do, I mean this country to me. I don't feel like I want to try to not being guilty when I know that I'm guilty."

"Is there anything else that you can think of that you want to tell me right now?"

Yes, he said, it was the drugs and the drug dealers who were responsible for the murders. "Uh, what I want to say is that I want . . . I want people that sell drugs around Sonoma areas is getting arrested, or something like this thing I do happen to somebody else."

As the jet approached the Sonoma County airport, yet another horde of media was waiting. And there was more: A crowd of angry citizens was gathering outside the jail.

Even more so here than in San Diego, the VCI team was concerned that someone would try to kill my father. So they told the pilot to taxi to the sheriff's department helicopter hangar. With deputies holding the press back 120 feet, but in full view, Dave Edmonds stepped out of the jet to "accept the prisoner" from Brown. As the cameras recorded the event, my father climbed down, this time with his wrists cuffed in front of him.

He was then trundled into a white van, which pulled away behind the hangar. There, out of sight of the crowd, the convoy stopped momentarily and my father was rushed from the van into the backseat of the lead patrol car, where he was told to lie down. The convoy then pulled back into view as they continued on to the jail.

As they'd been warned, a crowd of roughly two hundred people had formed at the jail. Many of them chanted, "Kill him! Kill him!" as the convoy approached. Others waved signs saying SALCIDO DOESN'T DESERVE TO LIVE and YES ON CAPITAL PUNISHMENT.

With the mob focused on the white van, the patrol car with my father hidden in back drove past with no one the wiser. No one tried to attack the van.

Inside the jail, my father was taken to the booking room, where he was stripped naked. Every inch of his face and body was photographed—in part to record any injuries he might have received during his killing spree, but also so that the prosecutors could prove in court that my father had not been mistreated by either Mexican authorities or the Sonoma team, in case the defense tried to claim that his confession had been coerced.

They were smart precautions. A local public defender, Marteen Miller, was already trying to get himself appointed as Dad's representative. With his swept-back silver hair, perpetual tan, and snakeskin cowboy boots, Miller looked like he'd stepped out of a TV law show. He had a taste for the spotlight and for the kinds of high-profile cases that would bring him media attention.

When news came of my father's arrest, Miller immediately asked a judge to approve his traveling to Mexico. The judge denied his request, but that didn't stop Miller from telling the media that he wanted to check on my dad's physical condition. He noted that my father had made a lot of "incriminating statements" to the Mexican authorities, and he hinted that the statements might have been forced. He suggested that my father should undergo "brain scans" to see if some sort of physical defect had caused him to snap. Given the unusual nature of the case, he even wondered aloud whether provisions of the U.S. Constitution—such as the *Miranda* warnings—applied to a suspect arrested in another country for a crime in the United States. Until that issue was resolved, he suggested, it was unclear whether my father's statements would even be admissible in court.

After he was booked, my father was given his own cell in the women's section of the jail, to prevent any of the male prisoners from attacking him. He was also placed on suicide watch to prevent him from cheating justice.

As he watched my father being photographed, Mike Brown noticed that he seemed as nonchalant as he had during his airborne confession. It was clear to the detective that his prisoner was enjoying all the fuss. My father was a speck of a man who had never amounted to anything in his whole life. This was his shot at fame, and he was soaking it all up. Even if the rest of the world was horrified by what he had done, at least he had their attention.

After turning my father over to his jailers, the Sonoma County team returned to their desks to finish their reports. Emotionally exhausted, they were grateful for the congratulations cards that awaited them in their office, including one from the district attorney's office and another from the kids at the Dunbar school, thanking them for "making us feel safe again."

Inviting Arturo Zorrilla to join them, the team then decided to get a drink in downtown Santa Rosa. As they headed out the door, Brown saw Randi Rossmann standing nearby. He didn't think much of the rest of the media, which had treated the murders and investigation like a circus. But most of the *Press Democrat* reporters, like Chris Smith and particularly Rossmann, had done their jobs professionally and with sensitivity. She had asked tough questions and worked twelve- to fourteen-hour days to keep ahead of breaking news, but that was her job, and they could respect that.

Brown asked the others if they minded bringing Rossmann along. When no one objected, the reporter found herself sitting in a crowded restaurant booth with six drained but happy detectives. As the beer flowed and the stories poured out of the men, she was impressed by how each of them had supplied his piece to the puzzle. *A real team*, she thought.

The party was winding down when Dave Sederholm raised his glass. "We did it for Carmina," he said.

Mike Brown's mind flashed back to the sight of a surgeon with his fingers in my throat. "We couldn't do it for the others," he agreed, "so we did it for Carmina."

Twenty-one

Early on the morning of September 17, 1990, a line formed outside the thick wooden doors of Courtroom 2F of the San Mateo County Courthouse. The trial had been moved to San Mateo after my father's lawyers were granted a change-of-venue motion due to the publicity in Sonoma County.

It was a small courtroom without much room for spectators, so when the bailiff unlocked the doors the press scrambled to find a spot, competing with citizen spectators and courthouse personnel for every seat. Seated at the prosecution table was Peter Bumerts, the Sonoma County chief deputy district attorney, and his cocounsel, deputy district attorney Ken Gnoss. Detective Dave Edmonds sat next to them.

Across the aisle, public defenders Marteen Miller and Bill Marioni chatted nonchalantly on one side of my father; on the other sat his Spanish-language interpreter. Clean-shaven, with a conservative haircut, my father was dressed in a new gray business suit provided for him by the taxpayers. (Like most defense attorneys in major criminal trials, his attorneys had demanded that he be allowed to appear in civilian clothes rather than a prison jumpsuit—which, they contend, can imply guilt to impressionable jurors.)

His brown skin had faded in prison from lack of sunlight; under the courtroom's fluorescent lights it looked almost as gray as his suit.

In the first spectator pew behind the defense table sat Mary Stuart, a law-student intern working for the public defender's office, who had been assigned to act as the liaison between my father and his defense team. Mary, who visited him daily, had grown concerned that my father was despondent and seemed suicidal. But his depressed state hadn't stopped him from corresponding with several women who, for whatever reasons, wanted to develop a personal relationship with him. At least one had even professed her love to the media and said she hoped they could marry someday.

Otherwise, my father had few supporters. Ever since he was brought back from Mexico, he'd been kept in isolation from the other prisoners who likely would have tried to kill him for what he'd done to children. And as he was being transported to Redwood City for his trial, one of the deputies escorting him pointed out San Quentin State Prison—the California maximum-security facility that housed more than 290 condemned men on death row. "See there," one of the deputies is rumored to have said. "That's going to be your new home."

In the nearly seventeen months since my father murdered seven innocent people, there had been long weeks of waiting and brief moments of high drama.

At a pretrial hearing in May 1989, around the time I was released from the hospital, my father pleaded not guilty to the charges against him. Then, during a preliminary hearing in September, he was formerly charged with seven counts of first-degree murder "under special circumstances"— making him eligible for the death penalty—as well as the attempted murders of me and the Buttis. The defense won its motion to change venues the following March, arguing that my father could not possibly receive a fair trial for a crime the sheriff had publicly called the "most heinous crime in county history."

The demand for a change of venue came shortly after a long piece in *Glamour* magazine, revisiting what writer Shirley Streshinsky called "a cautionary tale of the collision of innocence and machismo, of inchoate yearnings and the American dream turned nightmare" in the "achingly beautiful wine country" of Sonoma County. The story rehashed the facts while featuring new quotes from former neighbors and friends of the victims, some of whose relationships with the deceased and roles in the events in April 1989 seemed to have expanded in the intervening months.

The writer dredged up my father's claim that my mother was having an affair with Tracey Toovey, though she reported that it was dismissed by both Toovey's friends and family, as well as friends of my mom. Appearing in a magazine filled with ads for modeling schools and fashion-design colleges, the story emphasized Mom's dreams of modeling and the possibility that they may have helped drive my father to lash out at her.

Toward the end of the article, the writer noted that my father was spending his time in prison folding cigarette papers into flowers that he said were for me. But I think the paper flowers were part of a conscious effort by my dad to "act crazy." His jailers reported that he sometimes sat in his cell using crayons to draw pictures of me—and that he claimed that I had visited him in his cell to tell him stories and asked him to draw for me.

That August, at another pretrial hearing, deputy coroner Greg Berry was on the stand to discuss the autopsy results when my father stood up in the courtroom and shouted, "I tell you they're not dead!" He pointed a finger at Berry and yelled, "Liar!" before being subdued by the guards.

My father's lawyers had already made it clear that his mental state—perhaps pushed over the edge by drugs and alcohol—would be his defense at the trial. Such an outburst seemed like an obvious way to drive that point home.

The judge in the case was Reginald Littrell, the presiding judge of Sierra County Superior Court. Lanky, soft-spoken, and laid-back, Littrell had been asked to take on the trial when no judges were available from Sonoma or San Mateo counties. The prosecutor, Peter Bumerts, was widely regarded as the best trial lawyer and strategist in an excellent district attorney's office.

Bumerts opened his case by telling the jurors that my father had begun his "journey of death and destruction" after learning that he was not Sofia's father. Brooding over that long-held secret, he said, my father had returned home on the morning of April 14 and became enraged when he discovered that his wife was gone, leaving their three children alone.

Crime by crime, Bumerts described the murder scenes to the jury: the Petaluma dump where my father slashed my throat and those of my sisters; Cotati, where he waited until my grandfather left his home to murder Grandma because he believed that she knew that my mom had been pregnant by another man when she married my dad. Anticipating the defense's main argument, Bumerts told the jury that my father may have been using cocaine and alcohol the night before the murders, but he was nevertheless "thinking clearly" when he committed the crimes. My father's confession would show that he had planned the killings deliberately, the prosecutor said, and that "with cool efficiency, he eliminated his family."

As Bumerts pointed out, it took more than two hours to drive from his home in Boyes Hot Springs to the dump, where he slit our throats; on to Cotati, where he murdered Grandma, Ruth, and Maria; back to his home to shoot Mom; out to Grand Cru winery, where he gunned down Tracey Toovey; and finally to the Kunde Estate, where he shot Ken Butti. That was more than enough time to plot where to go next and whom to kill—and more than enough time to have cooled down and stopped himself.

With that in mind, Bumerts asked the jury to return guilty verdicts for seven counts of first-degree murder, as well as three more guilty verdicts for the attempted murder of Ken and Teri Butti and me, his daughter.

Throughout Bumerts's twenty-minute opening, my father showed little emotion as he listened to the attorney, accompanied by the low droning of the interpreter. Shortly after Marteen Miller began the case for the defense, however, Dad began to cry—and he kept it up. He wept as Miller argued that events throughout his life had conspired to turn him into a murderer; he dabbed at his eyes as the public defender talked about how he'd intended to kill himself along with his family.

To Miller and his defense team, keeping my father off death row was all that really mattered. Obviously, there was no argument that Dad was innocent, that someone else had committed the crimes. The evidence against him was monumental, and he'd confessed. But the public defender thought he had a good shot at helping Ramón avoid the gas chamber—starting with the makeup of the jury. None of the eleven women and four men was a fan of the death penalty; in fact, during jury selection half of them had indicated that they were more likely to lean toward a life sentence, even if the defendant was found guilty of first-degree murder. It took a unanimous verdict to sentence a criminal to death; all Miller would need was one dissenting juror to save Ramón from the executioner, either during the trial itself or during the sentencing phase.

On the morning of the murders, Miller claimed, my father was suffering from psychotic depression, aggravated by the cocaine and alcohol he'd consumed. In that condition, he argued, Dad could not have formed "the intent and deliberation necessary" to be guilty of first-degree murder. Instead, Miller said, he should be found guilty of second-degree murder or even voluntary manslaughter—neither of which carried a death sentence.

Faced with the brutality of Ramón's crimes and his incontrovertible guilt, Miller was grasping for an emotional appeal that might sway at least one juror. He began with a surprise: the disclosure that my father had had not two wives who gave birth to other men's children, but three.

Dad's marriage to Debra Ann Whitten had been widely reported. But few were aware of his first marriage in Mexico, or knew that his first wife had also given birth to a child that was not his.

Miller claimed that my father had suffered from mental illness since childhood. By 1989, he argued, that instability, combined with his mounting personal problems—the revelation of Sofia's parentage, Debra's child-support demands, his own job issues—caused him to sink into depression. Stir in a two-day cocaine-and-alcohol binge, the lawyer said, and by the morning of April 14, 1989, my father was no longer able to think clearly about his actions.

In my father's confession, Miller pointed out, he said that he'd talked about suicide with Angela, whom the attorney labeled "a religious cultist." Quoting his client, he said, "She told me couple of times, 'Why not kill ourselves and not live in this world?'"

In this delusional state, Miller said, my father decided that if he and my mother were going to die, then their children should die along with them. But not out of anger, he claimed. "He loved his children. They were an extension of him."

The defense was not begging for mercy, Miller told the jurors. But he was asking them to base their decision on the legal definition of what constituted first-degree murder, which Ramón could form. Aware of the horrific crime-scene photographs and testimony the jurors would see and hear during the prosecution case, he urged them to wait until they'd heard all the evidence before making up their minds.

* * *

The prosecution case took ten days, beginning with a parade of witnesses. The first was Tim Smith, who was still haunted by what he'd seen the day he carried me up the embankment, away from my dead sisters.

Grandpa was sworn in, mostly to identify objects from his house, such as the .22-caliber handgun Ramón stole and used to kill Angela and Tracey Toovey. As Grandpa recalled kissing Maria good-bye before he left for work that morning, he broke down and sobbed.

Catherine Toovey also took the stand, despite objections from the defense that she was being called solely to evoke an emotional response from the jury. She'd already broken down once, during a pretrial hearing, when she was accidentally shown a photograph from her husband's autopsy. This time, she calmly testified that her husband had told her that my father was having issues at work, but that "it wasn't [Tracey's] job to fire him." And therefore there was no reason for my dad to be angry with him.

Perhaps the most dramatic testimony came from Dr. Dennis MacLeod, who told the jury how I survived for thirty-six hours after having my throat slashed "from jawbone to jawbone." If I hadn't sat up the entire time, he told the jury, with my chin propped on my chest, I would have suffocated or bled to death. He talked about how doctors discovered that I'd eaten pebbles when I got hungry during my ordeal. I was suffering from emotional trauma and clinical shock when I arrived at the emergency room, he said, and would have soon died if I had not been found.

Besides the cut to my neck, MacLeod described one other injury—a small cut on my ring finger. It was a defensive wound, the surgeon said, consistent with a three-year-old trying to defend herself from her father.

The parade of prosecution witnesses continued. The Buttis described Ramón's cool detachment, as well as the blood on his arms. A neighbor testified that my mother was planning to get an annulment. Debbie Ghilotti talked about seeing Mom at the Wells Fargo ATM at 5:30 A.M. And some of the men who were with my dad the night before the murders agreed that he'd consumed cocaine and alcohol—though not in the quantities his lawyer was claiming, and not so much that he wasn't thinking clearly.

A psychologist also testified that Ramón's crimes were organized and planned. "The acts," he said, were "inconsistent with someone whose mental functions are impaired by drugs and alcohol."

On the day of deputy coroner Greg Berry's emotional testimony, the *Press Democrat* sent columnist Chris Smith to write about the courtroom scene. Smith was a young man who planned on having his own kids, and he was revolted by the crimes. He hated the fact that the case seemed to have changed his community for the worse. Doors that had once been unlocked were bolted shut when Salcido was at large—and they remained that way after his capture. Sonoma County would never again be quite as idyllic.

The column he'd write after his day at court reflected the reaction of the community. He interviewed Linda Dvorscak, a forty-year-old San Mateo woman who'd been first in line that morning to get a seat in the courtroom. A regular in the spectator gallery, Dvorscak had come prepared for the long day with a paperback book, a bag lunch, and this time, her mother. "I'll be honest with you," she told Smith. "I know people who have taken a large amount of drugs and drunk alcohol, and they didn't go out and kill people." An older woman from Menlo Park showed up wearing dark glasses and a straw hat as a disguise. She liked to attend murder trials, especially high-profile ones. "I'm interested in humanity," she said. "I would like to write a story sometimes on why people do things like this. There are probably a lot of potential Ramón Salcidos running around." She refused to give Smith her name. "You know why? My relatives are not into this sort of thing," she confessed. "They think it's sort of bizarre."

Some were more bizarre than others. On the day he was

scheduled to testify, Detective Mike Brown was standing outside the courtroom during a recess talking with Peter Bumerts when he noticed a woman standing off to the side watching them. She was dressed all in black, including a floppy black hat with black veil—as if she was in mourning. After Bumerts went back inside, the woman approached the detective.

"Are you going to testify?" she asked.

Mike had no idea who she was, or what business it was of hers what he was doing. "What are you talking about?" he asked.

"I'm in love with Ramón," she replied.

Without a word, Brown turned and walked into the courtroom. She followed him in and sat through his testimony.

Just another nutcase, Mike thought when he looked back and saw her watching him. He knew about women like this one—drawn to publicity at any cost, looking for attention by latching on to monsters like my dad.

The most contentious part of the trial involved the crimescene photographs. The prosecution wanted them all in; my father's attorneys fought to keep them out.

Marteen Miller argued that the images would so inflame the jurors that they wouldn't be able to follow the law. In particular, he said, the photos showing the bodies of my aunts Ruth and Maria should be withheld because the prosecution wanted to use them to imply that the girls had been sexually assaulted—even though his client hadn't been charged with those crimes. Judge Littrell denied Miller's motions during pretrial hearings but told the defense attorney he could renew his objections at trial.

By the second day of the trial, Littrell had reviewed the photographs and decided that some of the photos could be shown to the jury but not others. He allowed blowups showing the bodies of my mom, my grandma, and my aunt Ruth, but he prohibited prosecutors from using the photograph of eight-year-old Maria.

The photo of Ruth showed my aunt lying facedown in a pool of blood, with her nightgown pulled up to her chest, her legs spread, and her blood-soaked panties lying at her feet. When the crime-scene technician who took the shot started talking about finding a bloody handprint on Ruth's right buttock, Miller leaped to his feet to demand a mistrial.

After the judge excused the jury from the courtroom, Miller complained that Bumerts was trying to convince the jury that my father had sexually molested Ruth. "He has a good case already, and he has enough evidence without this," he insisted, turning on Bumerts. "If you've got it, why don't you charge it?"

Miller was trying to lay groundwork for a later appeal, and the prosecutors knew it. They hadn't charged Salcido with sexual assault, not because they didn't think he'd committed those crimes as well, but because they didn't want to distract the jury from the murder charges by making a circumstantial case for sexual assault. There was plenty of concrete, physical evidence to convict him of the murders and put him on death row. Making the case for sexual assault would only cloud the issue.

The judge knew all this, too. He didn't even wait for Bumerts to respond before dismissing Miller's demand for a mistrial.

So the photographs remained in full view on September 28 as the jurors listened to the tape of my father's matter-of-fact confession.

> *"You were mad because you could not find your wife?"*
> *"Yes."*
> *"So you decided to kill your three children?"*
> *"And kill myself, yeah."*
>
> *"I walk in front of her. I don't say nothing. I just turn her around and cut the throat."*
> *"Did she say anything to you?"*

"No, sir."
"Did you touch her body after she fell down?"
"No, sir. I . . . I . . . I just move her out of my way."

*"I walk in my home. I wanted to tell my wife that I
already killed my daughters and, uh, my mother-in-
law and her sisters, and then we can kill ourself."*
*"She was trying to call the police when I shoot her
right in the head."*
*"I said, 'I'm gonna kill you.' He said, 'What'd I do
to you?' And I said, 'Because you was trying to fire
me a couple times on the job.' I said, 'I'm gonna kill
you' and I shoot him."*

*"Okay, Ramón, I know this is hard, but we found
bloody handprints on Ruth's butt."*
"Yeah."
"Why are there bloody handprints on her butt?"
*"I don't . . . I don't remember, sir. I don't do noth-
ing to her. I would like to help you but I . . . I don't
remembered I do. I don't know any prints or something I can said that it was me."*

The prosecution wrapped up its case on October 2 with
testimony from Dr. Boyd Stephens, the San Francisco medical examiner, who described the injuries my father had inflicted on each victim—including the defensive wounds
they suffered in fighting for their lives.

Before his defense team had a chance to begin its case, my
father threw them a curveball: He demanded that he testify
on his own behalf. His lawyers were desperate to avoid such
a move, because it would open the door for the prosecutor to
cross-examine him as well. They couldn't stop him if he
insisted on testifying, but they knew it would do him more
harm than good.

Miller appealed to the judge to prevent my father from

taking the stand, describing him as a "poor, disturbed, pathetic individual," whose motives for testifying were unclear. "I suppose he wants to say he didn't do it," the lawyer said; his client was in a "state of pathological denial. It's the only way he can survive."

As proof of his client's mental state, Miller claimed that my father had been writing letters to my sisters as if they were still alive. Miller said he planned to use psychological experts to prove that Ramón was in such a confused state that he was incapable of planning the murders or weighing the consequences of his actions. I'm not sure why, but eventually the idea of testifying was dropped.

The trial resumed on October 9. My father's attorneys called a parade of his friends, acquaintances, and former employers to the stand, mostly as character witnesses.

One of his former employers at Grand Cru testified that he was an excellent employee and that his behavior on the job began to deteriorate only after he was served with the child-support demands. Some of his friends in the Mexican community described him as likeable and funny—he'd even been nicknamed "the Joker"—and said that he loved his wife and children. But their recollections were called into question when they had to admit under cross-examination that he had also brandished a gun from time to time and threatened violence for those who "got out of line."

In fact, many of the witnesses on my father's behalf seemed to contradict themselves. They said he drank and snorted cocaine on the night before the murders, but that he didn't appear "sloppy drunk." One man testified that he loved his wife and children, "especially Carmina," and that he never saw his friend being physically abusive toward Angela. But then the witness turned around and said that Mom and Dad used to argue about his "chasing around" at night, and that on occasion he mistreated her. "I told him he couldn't treat women in the United States like they do in Mexico," the witness said.

The defense also called several "expert witnesses" to try to establish an explanation for my father's behavior. Alex Saragoza, an associate professor of Chicano studies at the University of California-Berkeley, testified that Dad didn't fit in well with his own culture. He claimed that my father didn't make friends easily with other Mexican immigrants (though several had already testified on his behalf) and that he preferred Anglo bars to Mexican bars. He pointed out that my father was boastful about Mom's beauty but resented her modeling ambitions and her independent streak. When my father began to suspect that my mother was cheating on him, the professor noted, culturally he should have confronted her and the men. Instead he let his anger build up inside.

The real key to the defense case, however, was my father's mental state—and this meant calling a host of witnesses to describe my father as mentally unstable. Miller began by calling Norman Ross, a Catholic deacon who visited my dad in jail after his return from Mexico. The deacon said that my father had shown him photographs of our family and insisted, "They're not dead. They're alive." When Ramón asked for Holy Communion, Ross said he refused because my father "didn't appear rational."

Miller's team called half a dozen experts covering a variety of issues—from the violence associated with cocaine use to the contention that my father had suffered a "brief temporary psychotic episode" on the day of the murders. Like Salcido's friends, though, these experts didn't always agree—even with their own findings. The psychiatrist called to establish the "temporary psychotic episode" theory said he wouldn't "bet my life" on his diagnosis. Another psychiatrist described my dad as having "egotistical, grandiose fantasies" about himself, a preexisting mental disorder that was exacerbated by cocaine and his personal problems. Yet both psychiatrists gave the impression that Dad might have been feeding them what he thought they wanted him to say. "It was frustrating dealing with Mr. Salcido," one said. "I found it difficult to find clear evidence of a mental disorder that would explain what happened."

My father even showed a deep-seated suspicion and hostility toward his own attorneys "and me," said a psychiatrist. He tended to "flare up" when confronted, and kept track of the injustices he felt he'd suffered, "which he carries around and reads off like a litany of saints."

It took nearly five hours to present the closing arguments in my father's trial.

In his summation, Peter Bumerts pointed out that my father had blamed everyone but himself for the murders he had committed. Child-support laws. Cocaine dealers. Mom, for being unfaithful and not being home with their children that morning. Grandma, for supposedly hiding the truth about Sofia. Sofia herself, simply for being another man's daughter. He blamed Ruth and Maria for witnessing their mother's murder. And my mother for trying to call the police. Bumerts said that my father had "thought out each one of these murders and set out to accomplish them. Who cares how much cocaine he had if it didn't affect his behavior?" he asked the jury. "It's time he took responsibility."

Marteen Miller's defense argument also turned on the question of responsibility. He argued that my father was guilty only of voluntary manslaughter, because his ability to reason and understand what he was doing had been blurred by cocaine and alcohol, sending him into a delusional, psychotic depression. He'd killed Sofia and Teresa, and tried to kill me, because he thought we would all meet again in heaven.

After they finished, it took nearly four days of deliberations for the jury to reach a verdict. Dressed in a gray pinstripe suit, my father looked almost uninterested as the eight women and four men on the jury filed into the courtroom. Nor did he react when the clerk read the verdicts: guilty on six counts of first-degree murder, one of second-degree murder, and two of attempted murder, for the attacks on Ken Butti and me. The only charge the jury rejected was for the attempted murder of Teri Butti. They reached the second-degree verdict for the murder of my aunt Maria, they later said, because they didn't think my father had intended to kill her until she wandered out of the bedroom and saw what he was doing to her sister.

"What this means for the victims and their families is, one chapter of this nightmare can be put to rest," Bumerts told the press afterward. Still, Pastor Rich Gantenbein said, the verdict came at a high price. "This part is done," he noted. "But this is not going to end it by any means."

Despite the verdict, Detective Mike Brown was in no mood to celebrate. "It's a sad end to a sad story," he told the press. "No one should feel happy about it. It was a tragedy from start to finish." He knew, by then, that I had found a new home. He hoped it was with a family who loved me. And he prayed that no harm would ever come to me again.

Twenty-two

The penalty phase of my father's trial was marked by a series of dramatic moments.

In reviewing the evidence that had convicted my father, Bumerts listed a series of "aggravating factors" the jury should consider—including the fact that my father committed several of his crimes to cover up other crimes, such as murdering Ruth to prevent her from calling the police.

He also introduced one new piece of evidence: the photograph of my aunt Maria on her back with her knees up in the air. Miller had managed to keep the picture out of the trial itself, but now Bumerts argued that the picture demonstrated the callousness with which my dad killed his youngest sister-in-law—another potential "aggravating factor"—and this time the judge agreed to allow the jury to see it. However, when the prosecutor showed it to the jurors, the judge reminded them that there had been no evidence at trial that Maria had been sexually assaulted. "And you should not speculate along those lines."

The defense team countered by calling my father's family to testify. His mother, Valentina Borjorquez Seja

Armendariz, and two of her sons, my uncles Arnaldo and Leopoldo, flew from Mexico to San Francisco, where they were interviewed by the press before their courtroom appearance.

My paternal grandmother said that her son was sorry for what he did and had repented. "He's asked for my forgiveness," she said, "and as his mother, naturally, I have forgiven him." But his crimes weighed on her heavily, she told the reporters. "It's hard for me to believe that he was found guilty. The wings of my heart have fallen."

On the witness stand, she described the phone call she'd received on that terrible day, April 14, 1989. Dabbing at her tears, she told the court interpreter that my father had said only that he'd killed his wife. "He said he left the children with a friend and they were okay." She never asked her son if he had killed any other people, or what he did to their bodies, or why he murdered his family. Nor had her son ever told her. Even when he showed up in Los Mochis, and they cried together all night over my mother's murder, he had said nothing about the children. She had learned of their deaths only from the media and the police.

"Can you imagine anything worse that a son could do?" Peter Bumerts asked when it was his turn to cross-examine Valentina.

The fifty-year-old woman listened to the translation, and then her face fell apart. "No," she said, sobbing.

Before her appearance, my uncles had told the press they wanted only one other thing: to know my whereabouts. "My mother wants to see her," Leopoldo explained. "She wants to hold her and touch her."

Now, after taking the stand, Grandma Valentina told reporters that she had brought a doll from Mexico but had no way of giving it to me. "I would tell her I love her very much," she pleaded.

But no one could tell her where I was living. I was lost to them.

* * *

Both Peter Bumerts and Marteen Miller made emotional closing arguments. Normally reserved and mild-mannered, Bumerts grew angry as he reminded the jury how each of my father's victims had been attacked, and of how he'd left me to die with my sisters in a garbage dump. My father had uttered "no word of sorrow, nor word of regret" for his crimes. Instead, he'd revealed his true nature by beginning an affair from his jail cell with a Los Angeles woman less than four months after slaughtering his family.

As his voice cracked, Bumerts reminded the jurors of the pictures of the victims and their families in happier times, and then of the pictures of the crime scenes. "Compare those first photographs with this . . . and this . . . and this," he insisted, laying out the horrible images one at a time, ending with a photo of me lying in a hospital bed, a bandage around my throat that held a tracheotomy tube in place.

"You must announce to Ramón Salcido," Bumerts demanded, "that his conduct is so inhumane that you repudiate it, and impose upon him the ultimate penalty."

Miller tried to counter with his own righteous anger. "To put this poor, sick, pathetic, disturbed individual to death is not justice," he said, scowling. "It's vengeance, vengeance, vengeance." Hoping to persuade at least a single juror to hold out against the death penalty, he pleaded with them to "stand firm" and not allow their fellow jurors to bully them into voting for the death penalty. He even made a desperate, left-field attempt to accuse Bumerts of seeking the death penalty for personal "political gain."

Defense cocounsel Bill Marioni also took a shot at appealing to the jurors, trying to give them a different way of looking at life in prison. "In spite of the horribleness of these crimes, death is not the appropriate penalty," he argued. "There is no shadow of doubt he will die in prison. The only question is who is going to decide when. Will it be you or will it be God?"

What neither the attorneys nor Judge Littrell nor anyone

else said aloud in that courtroom was that even if the jury condemned my father to death, it was impossible to know when—or if—that sentence would ever be carried out. The State of California had not executed a single prisoner since 1967.

On Friday, November 16, 1990, after three days of deliberation, the jury voted unanimously for the death penalty. My father again showed no reaction when the verdict was read, even as one of the jurors openly wept.

But the verdict would not be final until it was confirmed by the judge. First, the judge allowed my grandpa Richards, who had been a quiet presence through most of the trial, to speak. He begged Judge Littrell to carry out the jury's decision. And let justice be swift, he said, sobbing. "Why drag this thing out for years? He admitted he did it."

Before pronouncing on the verdict, Judge Littrell reviewed a presentencing report on my father written by deputy probation officer Angela E. Meyer. There was little in this report to persuade him to reverse the decision.

There is little doubt that Ramón Salcido was an alcoholic and that he used cocaine habitually as well, and that at the time, his judgment may have been impaired by these substances. There is also no doubt that his substance abuse at least exacerbated his personality, family and financial problems. However, he was able to cope reasonably well under the circumstances, mostly because his wife assumed the responsibility for keeping the family affairs in order throughout their marriage.

It is acknowledged that the defendant was under stress because his employment was in jeopardy, and because the discovery of his previous marriage made the dissolution of his marriage to Angela Salcido imminent. The financial strain of his unwelcome child-support obligation would certainly have made the prospect of supporting another ex-wife and child distasteful, especially in view of the self-indulgent habit which he maintained. To continue supporting these children would have required tremendous self-discipline and sacrifice, traits he had never cultivated. He had a very practical motive for wishing his family dead: His children threatened to become a heavy burden.

It has been pointed out that the defendant did not behave in a suicidal manner, contrary to his claimed intentions. He bandaged his cut finger, stepping over the body of Marion Louise Richards to find a bandage. In his confessions, he admitted that escaping detection was a priority when he murdered his daughters. He had ample opportunity and certainly enough ammunition to shoot himself immediately after killing his wife. His escape indicates that he was a man who had reasonable expectations of evading authorities. Even his telephone call to his mother, in which he mentioned his intention to kill himself, seems to have been a successful manipulation of the emotions of a woman who he knew would come to his rescue. He could hardly expect his mother, who is a devout Catholic and whose cultural upbringing required her to be loyal before all else, to allow her son to commit suicide. She took the bait and Ramón Salcido took full advantage. If sudden religious fervor had prevented him from taking his own life, as his attorney suggests, one would think that he would have been moved to see a priest upon his arrival at his mother's home, which he did not do. Instead he went to the train station to take a train to Guadalajara, where he could have changed his identity and easily have been lost in the big city. Later, while awaiting trial, he complained that his rights were not adequately protected, an unlikely complaint from a man who supposedly wants to die.

Every human being is deserving of some compassion, but Ramón Salcido has yet to reveal his humanity. He killed children and was unmoved by their desperate struggle to defend themselves. His sexual misconduct with the dead or dying Maria and Ruth Richards is abhorrent. The transition between the acts of cutting the throats of young girls and the lascivious pleasure of exposing their genitals is unimaginable.

Regardless of whether the court imposes the death penalty or grants the defendant a sentence of life without possibility of parole, it is certain that Ramón Salcido will have many years to reflect on his crimes. As Angela Salcido's father pointed out, the children of the victims will have to live with unresolved grief for a long time. One can barely imagine the emotional suffering of Carmina Salcido who, as she reaches maturity, will have to come to terms with the memories of her father's acts as well as the loss of her mother, sisters, aunts and grandmother. If the defendant ever matures enough to think beyond his own needs, and if his arrogance ever crumbles with age, he may someday find it within himself to feel remorse for the suffering he inflicted on his victims and the part he played in the destruction of three families.

Before announcing his decision, Judge Littrell asked my father if he had anything to say. But even now, with everything at stake, he could not bring himself to say aloud that he had murdered seven innocent people and tried to kill two others. Or even to say he was sorry.

"I ask everyone to forgive me for the things that I have done," he mumbled in the same monotone as his confession. "I want to express that I repent for the things that have happened to the family that I loved the most, and for all the grief and pain I have caused."

Repentance is not the same as regret. Asking for forgiveness is not the same as apologizing. Asking for forgiveness is trying to find a way out of trouble.

Judge Littrell found nothing in my father's statements to alter the jury's decision. The sentence, he said, would be death.

Afterward, Peter Bumerts was asked if he thought that Ramón was sincere in his statement. "I think we saw a sincere outpouring of emotions by Mr. Richards today—and that was the only sincere outpouring."

Years later I asked Detective Mike Brown to come with me to visit the cemetery where my family is buried. On the way there, we stopped to get red and white carnations. I separated the bouquet and put flowers on each grave. Even so many years later, when it comes to my father, Mike has a hard time controlling his emotions. "He still doesn't get it," he said of Ramón. "He wouldn't get it if he saw those graves."

Twenty-three

Ten days after my father murdered my family, I turned three years old.

That I had survived was a matter of luck, or divine intervention, according to my doctors. They say that simply moving my head could have easily reopened the wound, yet I sat up and crawled—even stood and walked a few feet—before I was scooped up by Tim Smith and carried to the top of the embankment in the Petaluma dump.

After the surgery, I remember waking up in my hospital room. I was aware of people walking in and out. I felt something sticking out of my throat—it was my tracheotomy tube—and when I reached over to pull it out the nurses rushed over to stop me. They put my arms in restraints, and as soon as they did I started flipping out. They must have given me a sedative, because moments later I slipped back into darkness.

I don't remember much about my time in the hospital, except that my grandpa was around a lot more than he'd ever been before. I hadn't been all that close to him before the murders, but now he was there right beside me, bringing me coloring books and stickers, and for a little while I felt a lot of love.

I do remember him trying to explain why my mother and sisters weren't around. I didn't understand the idea of death; I thought it meant they were somewhere else. I wondered why I wasn't allowed to see them.

Ten days later, I was doing so well that the doctors were able to remove my intravenous feeding tube in time for my birthday. They even let me have birthday cake and ice cream. I wasn't talking yet—the tracheotomy tube was still in my throat—but I was whispering up a storm with my nurses and Grandpa.

By that time the hospital had received thousands of toys for me, and the nurses wrapped up several of them to give me for my birthday. I unwrapped more toys on that one day than I'd received in my whole life until then. My favorite was a lavender tricycle. So many toys and stuffed animals arrived that the hospital asked people to stop sending them and instead donate to the trust funds set up for me and my grandpa as well as the Toovey family.

Most of the letters and postcards for me contained simple birthday wishes. As I look back now, though, I see that not all of them finished with a happy thought.

"Please consider moving this little girl out of the state of California, changing her name, dying her hair, and setting up a new life for her," one man advised my grandfather on a birthday card that otherwise wished me "much fun in all you do." "If her father only gets 2nd Degree—which I think is sick—he'll be after her," he continued. "They'll let him out on parole for some awful reason, or maybe just because the jail is too crowded."

Most of the cards contained warmer wishes. One college student sent a donation and wrote to say she was praying for me, but that I was going to need all the help I could get. "Little Carmina will have a difficult road ahead of her. It will be a road that must be paved with compassion, under-standing, and a love like no other. She will need to find the courage to accept what has happened and to go on with her life."

Some found creative ways to help. One local musician, Jim Williams, recorded a song he wrote called "God Protect the Children" and donated the proceeds from the record to the trust funds.

When six-year-old Aaron Alexander heard about me on the evening news, he told his mother that he wanted to give me his favorite Care Bear stuffed animal—Brave Heart Lion, the character who protected the others from danger. His mother took him to the hospital, slipping in through a side entrance to avoid the press and handing the toy to the front desk. "For her protection," Aaron said.

While my father was still at large, I was guarded by as many as ten deputies and police officers, as well as three hospital security officers. After his capture, a deputy and a security guard were stationed outside my door—only now it was to keep out well-wishers and the media. "If we didn't have security, she would have hundreds of visitors a day," hospital spokeswoman Mary Frost told the *Press Democrat*. "It's just important that she's not subjected to a lot of strangers."

A few special visitors were allowed in, among them Detective Randy Biehler. Although he had been assigned to the Cotati crime scene, and there was no professional reason for him to see me, he later told me he needed some living connection to the victims, some affirmation of life.

Seeing me with my throat bandaged was heart-wrenching, he said, but knowing I was alive seemed to soften the horror.

From the start I was the darling of the nurses, who got used to me wheeling up and down the hall on my lavender tricycle and visiting them at their stations.

Dave Lopez, a big, burly security officer who was working at the hospital the day I was brought in, was with me often in the weeks that followed. His favorite assignment was to escort me on walks around the hospital grounds or up to the roof, where I could ride my tricycle in the fresh air.

As the weeks passed, the media moved on to other stories. In early May the *Press Democrat* ran a front-page story by Randi Rossmann updating readers on my condition, accompanied by photographs taken by a hospital staff member. There I was in OshKosh overalls, a blouse, lacy socks, running shoes, and pigtails, sitting next to a stuffed panda bear that was as big as I was and laughing uproariously at something just off camera. The only clear sign of what I'd been through was the barely discernible bandage covering the scar around my throat.

One of my surgeons, Dr. Ralph Keill, said I was expected to fully recover from the throat injury. I could even get cosmetic surgery someday to repair the scar. "She's acting like a normal three-year-old," he said. "She plays, she pouts; she has temper tantrums."

When Rossmann asked if I'd been asking for my mother, Keill said he wasn't aware of it. He said I seemed happy just to be alive.

On May 10, just shy of a month after I was brought in on a gurney, I was released from the hospital. The nurses on the floor cried when I left. Even big Dave Lopez cried, though first he went and found a spot where no one would see him.

My hospital bills totaled about $24,000, but they were covered entirely by Medi-Cal and the Sonoma County Victim Assistance Center. And, though I couldn't have understood it at the time, the trust fund set up for my welfare would eventually total nearly $200,000—a nest egg I might need someday, for therapy or college or to start a business.

Yet nothing would ever come easy.

Two days after the murders, my grandfather had gotten a call from the California Department of Social Services informing him that a custody hearing had been scheduled to determine where to place me after I got out of the hospital. The hearing was scheduled for Tuesday, April 18, the day before the funerals, and just four days after the murders. *You have a right to attend,* the voice on the other end said—

"I just lost my whole family," Grandpa replied in disbelief. "I don't know what I'm doing tomorrow, much less what to do with my granddaughter."

The woman was unsympathetic. The hearing was going to take place; he could attend or not.

Grandpa didn't know what to do. He called a friend he knew at the agency and asked if the hearing could be postponed, but she was only able to get it delayed one day, to the day of the funeral. That just left him numb—too drained to fight about it, much less attend. On the day he buried his wife, his daughters, and two granddaughters, the California Department of Social Services got a judge to declare me a ward of the state.

If he wanted me, Grandpa would have to go to court and get me back.

Until he did, I was placed in a foster home with a woman who had nursing training and could take care of my tracheotomy tube until it could be removed. That made sense, but it didn't change Grandpa's desire for custody. He'd been coming to see me several times a week since the funerals, playing hide-and-seek with me on the floor or in the park, sitting with me and reading me stories. Sometimes he'd slip me a piece of candy I wasn't supposed to have, asking the nurses, "What's the harm?"

Still, Grandpa wasn't sure what he would do with me if he got custody. He was an emotional wreck himself and spent his evenings alone crying. Sometimes, when he looked at me, he would see my mother's face and choke up. He worried that he might not be much use to me. But he didn't want me to remain a ward of the state or go to someone neither of us knew.

Eventually, the judge ruled in Grandpa's favor and granted him custody. The question then became what to do next. Though he'd grown somewhat stronger emotionally as the weeks went by, he had no idea how to raise a three-year-old girl on his own. Bringing up the kids had always been Grandma's job, while he went out and earned a paycheck.

And the truth is, he wasn't coping very well. He could muster the stamina to play for a couple of hours, but he didn't know if he had the energy to give me the love and support I would need over the long haul.

Ultimately, Grandpa decided that the best thing for both of us would be to put me up for adoption. It wouldn't be hard to find a loving family; offers had been flooding in since the day I'd been found alive. But there was one challenge: Grandpa wanted me raised in the same way he'd brought up his own children, as ultraconservative Catholics and followers of Tradition, Family and Property. That way he'd know I was being taught good moral values and that my soul would be safe. He figured that he could stay in contact with my adoptive family and me, and therefore wouldn't lose me forever.

When Grandpa put the word out among the TFP membership that he was looking for a new home for his granddaughter, he got a swift response. But finding the right family turned out to be a long, tough, and emotionally taxing chore.

One woman who came to visit looked like my mother, especially the way she wore her hair. When I saw her, I pointed and said, "Mommy."

"Your mommy's in heaven," Grandpa said. He was still trying to explain what death meant, and I was still clinging to the idea that my mother and sisters would be returning.

"No, Mommy's right there," I insisted.

The woman seemed to enjoy being called Mommy, but Grandpa kept looking.

At one point, he thought he'd found the right home, with a TFP family in good standing in northern California. He and I even lived with them for a time. But keeping up with my energy and sense of adventure was a challenge. I was recovering quickly from my wounds, and I loved exploring the family's backyard. One day, while my potential new mom was working in the garden in another part of the yard, I came across a mushroom and took a bite of it. I then ran across the yard to show the woman the tasty morsel. "Look what I found!"

The woman was horrified. My tasty mushroom was a poisonous toadstool. Before long I was vomiting black and on my way to the hospital to have my stomach pumped.

Things didn't work out with that family; I was too much for them to handle. I didn't get along with their biological child, and I was a bit too strong-willed and hungry for attention. My grandpa didn't like the woman, and they argued constantly. They decided it wasn't a good fit.

There was another possibility with a family of twelve who lived on a farm in Kansas. Grandpa and a social worker from the California Department of Social Services went out for a visit, but the social worker nixed that after one of the boys locked his younger sister in a rabbit hutch while they were there. I was still healing; I didn't need to be stuffed into an animal pen.

Grandpa was starting to wonder if he'd ever find a good situation for me. Then, late one night, he thought of the Swindells, a prominent TFP couple who lived on a big piece of rural property in the midwest. In their early middle age, the Swindells were one of the most respected TFP couples in the country, held up to others as the model of a perfect Catholic marriage. Grandpa had met them while attending TFP seminars, and he knew that they'd adopted children in the past, along with raising their own.

Grandpa called Clyde Swindell and told him about his predicament. "Would you adopt Carmina?" he asked.

Mr. Swindell didn't hesitate—or even bother to ask Mrs. Swindell. "Absolutely," he said. Only after he got off the phone did he tell his wife and youngest daughter, Elaine, that he'd just agreed to adopt another child.

A short time later the people of my hometown learned—through a brief paragraph in the newspapers and on television broadcasts—that the little girl who survived the Salcido murders had found a home with a family in the rural midwest.

The people of Sonoma County, and those around the world who'd followed my story, would move on with their lives. My father's trial would begin and end. Some would forget all but the basic details of that dark time, but many others would always wonder what had become of me. They would hope that I'd found a loving family, and that with time and tenderness, the horror of what I had been through would fade. But as far as they knew, I was lost to them forever.

Looking back on my grandpa's decision today, knowing all that has happened since, it's hard to convince myself that there wasn't some other way. Life could have taken me on any number of paths at that point. The one I was thrust down wasn't the one I would have chosen. My uncles were angry at my grandfather for not keeping me. They still are. But it was his decision, and I try to see it as he did—through the eyes of a man who'd just lost everything and wasn't sure he had enough strength to share his life with a needy little girl.

What's done is done. I don't have much family, so there's not much sense in being angry at those I have left.

Twenty-four

Mrs. Swindell and Elaine flew to California to pick me up. When we landed at the airport, Mr. Swindell was there to meet us.

"Here's your new father," Mrs. Swindell said, trying to hand me to him. I looked at this big, bald, potbellied guy—at fifty-something, he was much older than my real father—and froze.

"No, he's not my daddy," I said.

"Yes, he is," she barked. "Give him a hug!"

Mrs. Swindell's voice was so harsh it shocked me, and I allowed myself to be thrust into Mr. Swindell's arms. I couldn't even look at him. It was an awkward moment, I think, for both of us—made all the more tense by Mrs. Swindell's telling me to "hug your new father."

Eventually, the Swindells convinced me to call them Mother and Father, though they forbade me to use more informal terms, such as Mama or Mommy or Papa. I knew they weren't my parents, but I had nowhere else to go.

They changed my name, too. Deciding I should be known by my middle name, my adoptive parents now said I was Cecilia Ursula Mary Rose de Carmel Swindell. Once, when a friend of the Swindells asked my name, I replied, "They used to call me Mina." A surprised look crossed Mrs. Swindell's face before she recovered, cleared her throat, and corrected me. "No, no, your name is Cecilia. It always has been."

It was the first step in my adopted parents' plan to separate me from the past and bring me into the fold of Tradition, Property and Family.

To its critics, TFP may have been a right-wing religious cult. But its members viewed themselves as the vanguard of Western Christian civilization, standing firm against liberalism, communism, and modernism. Its original supporters in Brazil and then other Latin American countries were the wealthy landowners and businessmen. The liberal mandates of the Vatican II reform had shifted the Catholic Church's power in Latin America from high-ranking bishops and cardinals, who had supported the wealthy since the 1500s, to local priests who tended to side with the poor, and even to some leftist land reform and equality movements. TFP had then spread from Latin America as an anticommunist, and antiliberal, movement.

Many in both Latin America and the United States have accused TFP of brainwashing its followers, especially young men. TFP denies those allegations. But it makes no apologies for its belief that the world's masses would be better off under the leadership of an elite class, even in democratic nations such as the United States. According to the group's own literature:

> TFP promotes the values of Christianity, and opposes liberal and egalitarian ideas, policies, and trends in both society as a whole and in the Catholic Church. . . .
>
> In addition to supporting all official Catholic teaching, the group also argues for the need for authentic elites in society that raise, above all, the moral tone of general society, as witnessed by one of Corrêa de

Oliveira's most available works, "Nobility & Analogous Traditional Elites in the Allocutions of Pius XII."

In this book, Corrêa de Oliveira seeks to balance the notion of "preferential option for the poor" [that characterizes] some modern liberal Catholic social thinking, with support for the natural elite that exists in all societies.

In another work, *Revolution and Counter-Revolution,* Corrêa de Oliveira maintained that the modern world had undergone three phases of "gnostic and egalitarian revolution," each of which had undermined the church and social order: the Renaissance (including the "Protestant pseudo-reformation"); the Enlightenment and the French Revolution, which had ushered in modern political liberalism; and the communist revolution. Today, he argued, marked a final phase in which the church and Christian civilization risked being eradicated by the forces of "radical egalitarianism and neo-paganism"—that is, by those who believed that all human beings were created equal.

That was the theological side of TFP. In American daily life, however, TFP members concerned themselves with more familiar right-wing causes. They showed up at anti-abortion rallies, picketed abortion clinics, and protested against "liberal ideas" such as gay rights, as well as art and entertainment they considered offensive or sinful. Although the general public didn't always know who they were, they led the protests against films such as 1985's *Hail Mary* and Martin Scorsese's 1988 *The Last Temptation of Christ.*

In many ways, TFP members seemed no more than a throwback to a more conservative time. Like my mom and her sisters when they were growing up, TFP women didn't wear pants or makeup and dressed to hide their bodies. Men wore suits and ties in social settings; jeans and denim were prohibited altogether. (TFP contended that Levi Strauss was a communist, and that the purpose of denim was to make everyone look alike.)

Young men and women from TFP didn't date in the modern sense; rather, they met through their parents under closely supervised circumstances. Even then, marriage and childbearing were discouraged. Instead, young men were encouraged to join the priesthood and young women to join a convent. This sinful world needed more priests and nuns, the leaders of TFP believed, not more children.

In the TFP world, the man was the head of the household. Women were often described as "companions" for their men, but a better term might have been *willing servants*. They were expected to stay home and take care of the house and children after their husbands went off to work, to know their place, and never to argue with their lord and master.

By the same token, children were expected to be quiet, obedient, and helpful to their parents. Though some boys were sent to TFP schools, most TFP children were home-schooled and generally sheltered from other children, who were likely to taint them with the evils of television, secular literature, and rock and roll.

The TFP leadership's calls for restoring ancient monarchies and the "elite classes" trickled down in the form of distinctly medieval trappings. They hung elaborate coats of arms in their homes, attended protest rallies wearing red capes and carrying huge Crusader-style banners, and gave their children long, antiquated names like Cecilia Ursula Mary Rose de Carmel Swindell.

The Swindells had three children of their own, and had adopted one boy, before I came along. Only Elaine was still living at home when I arrived.

They lived in a rural part of the country, in a rambling two-story house perched atop a hill and surrounded by acres of pasture and woodlands. Their house was forty-five minutes from the nearest town for shopping and more than two hours from the nearest big city, and that was how Clyde Swindell wanted it; when he'd gone looking for a homestead for his family, he told the real estate agent he wanted to be "a rifle shot away from any neighbors."

A burly former marine, Clyde Swindell sold electrical equipment and traveled around the country on sales calls, sometimes with his wife and children. He'd taken out a sizable loan to start the business and purchase the house, though the business had never quite taken off the way he'd hoped and money was tight.

Betty Swindell stayed at home with the children, never venturing out except to shop for food, clothing, and other necessities. They'd gained considerable attention as a model TFP couple, hailed at conventions and in newsletters as people to look up to and emulate. Though they weren't rich, their reputation in the layered social strata of the TFP put them on much the same level as wealthier families.

I didn't arrive in their home penniless; the media had widely reported on the size of my trust fund, contributed to by people from all over the world. Some of the money had been sent to both Grandpa and me, so he kept part and gave the rest to the Swindells to hold on to for me.

Looking back, I see early signs that my life wasn't going to be a fairy tale. When the Swindells drove to California to pick up the trust fund check, Grandpa offered to let them stay at his home. "Are you crazy?" they replied. "Your place won't be safe. Some of Ramón's friends are probably watching you. We'll meet you at a restaurant."

And there were other signs of trouble. One of the conditions of my adoption, laid down by California's Department of Social Services, was that the Swindells were required to take me to a pediatric psychologist to help me deal with the trauma of what had happened. But the Swindells weren't happy about it—especially when Mrs. Swindell was told she had to wait in another room while I talked to the psychologist alone.

The first time it happened she argued with the psychologist, though eventually she gave in. But she didn't give up trying. Every time we went, she complained that she should be with me. She wanted to know what I was saying and what the psychologist was telling me. And when I finished she would hustle me out of there as fast as she could—and demand to know everything we said.

In spite of the grilling by Mrs. Swindell, I enjoyed the sessions with the psychologist. Most of the time the Swindells kept me cooped up in the house with no one to play with but Elaine, who was quite a bit older. They only took me on those trips to the psychologist because they had to, but at least it got me out of the house and allowed me to see a little more of the world.

The psychologist helped me find the self-esteem I needed. She'd tell me how pretty I looked and how smart I was. I was only four when I went to live with the Swindells, but Mrs. Swindell started early telling me that looking in the mirror was vanity and a sin. The psychologist reassured me that it was okay.

At one of the sessions, the psychologist asked me what I thought of the deaths of my mother and sisters. I wasn't quite sure how to answer; even more than a year after the fact, I still didn't have a good grasp of what death meant. I still thought the others had gone somewhere—and left me behind, which I resented.

In these early years, the Swindells wouldn't talk about my parents. But I was supposed to pray for my sisters, aunts, and grandma. I didn't understand where heaven was. I just knew I couldn't visit them there.

The psychologist was also the only one who ever asked what I thought about my father. She showed me a clay figure, which she said represented my dad; then she put it in front of a toy jail and asked me if I thought he should be in that jail. But I didn't understand the concept of prison, so I just shrugged.

Then she tried a different tack. Had my father done something bad? she asked me. People who did bad things were put in jail so that they couldn't hurt more people. That was something I could understand. Yes, he had done something bad. I picked up the clay figure and put it in the jail.

Eventually, a day came when the psychologist explained

that we wouldn't be meeting anymore. I was doing fine and didn't need to see her. But she seemed uncomfortable just turning me over to my new parents. Picking up a toy telephone, she took my hand and looked in my eyes.

"If your new mommy and daddy ever hit you or yell at you," she told me, "or do something or tell you to do something that you don't think is right, or hurt you, pick up the telephone and dial 911."

Twenty-five

Life with the Swindells was lonely and stifling, espe-cially for a child as gregarious and active as I was. In Sonoma I'd had my sisters and aunts to play with, as well as the other children in the neighborhood. We'd gone on pic-nics and trips to the beach and spent plenty of time playing in the park. Now all of that had been ripped away from me, replaced with a sterile, isolated existence, under the strict observation of my obsessively religious adoptive parents.

The Swindells' property was about two-thirds pasture; the other third was a forest of oak, elm, hickory, wild persim-mon, and black walnut trees. The only people we socialized with were other Tradition, Family and Property members—and the closest TFP families were two hours away in one direction or five hours in the opposite. I rarely even laid eyes on other people except on those infrequent visits, or on Mr. Swindell's business trips, or when we went to TFP conven-tions. Even waving to the occasional car passing on the road below our property was forbidden.

My isolation increased when I was five years old and Elaine left home to work in a nursing home two hours away.

I lost the only person I had regular contact with besides the Swindells, and the only one remotely close to my age. The sole break in my hours of loneliness came when Mrs. Swindell would take me shopping. These trips were the only time she left the property without her husband, and they were hardly social occasions. But they got me out of the house and off the property, and that was a welcome relief.

Most of my days were spent following Mrs. Swindell around the house, learning to be a proper Catholic woman. Any sort of preening or primping was considered vanity, a sin. Certainly Mrs. Swindell, who wore formless dresses over her plump body and kept her silver hair pinned up in a severe French twist, was never guilty of that. When we did go out, she had me wear cute little dresses with pinafores, ruffles, and little flowers attached. At home I wore jumpers and "play" dresses.

I had arrived at the Swindells' with boxes of the stuffed animals, toys, and clothing I'd received in the hospital. But my adoptive parents had thrown most of it away—especially "forbidden" items like pants and Barbie dolls. Most of my "acceptable" clothing was given to me by other, wealthier TFP families, who also donated food to our family.

When I reached school age, I was kept home and taught—haphazardly—by Mrs. Swindell. I didn't begin to learn to read until age seven, and even then I wasn't allowed to read most secular children's books. My reading material consisted of the Bible, religious histories published by the TFP, and books about nature. Even my coloring books were full of religious imagery: no Cinderella or Snow White for little Cecilia.

One of my few creative outlets was music. There was always classical music playing in the Swindell house, from Gregorian chants to operas and symphonies by Mozart or Vivaldi. And they had a piano. Like any child, I liked pounding on the keys with no real purpose—until we went to a piano recital and something clicked in my head. I came home and started experimenting, and in a very short time, much to everyone's surprise, I started playing chords, and then parts of compositions I'd heard on the record player.

By the age of five, I could play whole pieces on the piano after hearing them several times through and then practicing until my fingers played the song I was hearing in my head. And I could sing opera. I'd listen to one of the Swindells' recordings of Pavarotti, and soon I was singing along. I didn't understand the Italian words, but I intuitively got the music.

Music was one of the few interests I had that the Swindells indulged. Mr. Swindell often asked me to play piano before dinner, and they proudly asked me to perform for guests. But even music couldn't cure my loneliness. I was living in a bubble, protected from the world, but also denied the pleasures of being a child.

Even on the rare occasions when I played with other TFP children, I had to be careful what I said about "the tragedy," especially when asked about the scar on my throat.

Most people knew enough not to say anything about it. They probably already knew the story, and Mrs. Swindell made it clear that it was not to be talked about.

Once, though, on a visit to another family's home, I was playing with their daughter in her bedroom when she asked me about the scar. So I told her what I knew. "Stay right here," she said. "I'll be back!" Then she ran out and told the adults what I'd said. I got a severe scolding from the Swindells and was told never to talk about it again.

Every year, however, on April 14, the anniversary of "the tragedy," Mrs. Swindell would cook a special meal, and the Swindells and I would gather at the dinner table and observe the occasion together. The table would be set nicely, with candles and all, and Mrs. Swindell would set out photographs of my sisters, my aunts, and my grandmother. "They are all saints in heaven now," she would say. And every year they would ask me to tell them what I remembered about what happened to me. That's probably one reason I remember it all so well today.

But there were no photographs of my parents; in fact, when I was young they never referred to my mother at all. Only when I was older would Mrs. Swindell mention her—and then only to say that she had sinned by sneaking out to see my father, and brought "the tragedy" on our family. My mother wasn't in heaven with the others, she insisted; if she was lucky, she might be sitting in purgatory, awaiting her final dispensation. On the rare occasions when they talked about my father, it was to say that he was possessed by a demon and would go straight to hell when he died.

The Swindells were determined to wipe out my past. Once, when someone who had known my family in Sonoma saw me at a TFP conference, they called out to me: "Carmina!"

I turned, momentarily confused; I hadn't heard that name since I was four years old. But Mrs. Swindell interceded. "Carmina died a long time ago," she sternly informed the stranger. "Cecilia is the miracle who lived!"

After Elaine left, my only companions at the Swindells' were the horses, cows, and other animals that lived on the neighbors' property. The horses would trot over to the fence to let me pet them, and often I sang to the cows, who gathered around me like an audience. Besides music, my only creative outlet was drawing; I would sit for hours drawing horses. Only years later would I learn that I shared that love with my mother.

I did have one favorite animal of my own—a lamb named Lilly. Every day I would let her out and we'd romp around together, leaping into the air, hiding around trees, and butting heads. From her I learned that people and lambs are alike in one important way: We need company. Lambs are used to being in a flock; single lambs are likely to die young. I was like a lonely lamb, pining away for the family and friends who once surrounded me.

Without any real friends to play with, I started looking around for imaginary ones to share my adventures. I started by talking to my dolls and stuffed animals, but they never talked back, which was disappointing. So by the time I was five or so, I started to surround myself with pretend friends. Some of them were older, like my sister Sofia, but others were my age or as young as baby Teresa. They had their own lives and their own families, and they weren't always around, but sometimes four or five of us would be there together.

The magic of these imaginary friends was that they could be with me wherever I went. If I was playing, or doing the dishes, or studying, or in the bath, they'd be there with me, carrying on conversations. I talked out loud to them, which drove Mrs. Swindell crazy. "Why don't you talk to your sisters, or God and the angels and the saints in heaven?" she'd ask me. But my sisters weren't there in the kitchen or my bedroom with me. They had left me to be alone.

The Swindells didn't go for heraldry as much as my grandparents had. But they did have a large medieval-style broadsword hanging on a wall at the front entrance, and a statue of the Infant of Prague on a table. And they had even more religious statues, crucifixes, and paintings than my grandparents had—including a life-sized outdoor statue of Our Lady of the Sea.

The Swindells slept in separate rooms. Mr. Swindell occupied the basement, which was fully equipped with a fireplace, refrigerator, stove, sink, full bath, and bedroom. The family television was down there, too; on Saturdays he watched golf there, and on other days we watched TFP videos and good "wholesome" movies like *The Song of Bernadette, Joan of Arc,* and *A Man for All Seasons.*

There were three bedrooms upstairs: "Mother's room," Elaine's room, and my own room down the hall, with a full-sized bed. The house had nice views from its picture windows, especially the living room, which looked out over a pretty valley. On the other side of the living room was the main dining room, dominated by a long wooden table that could have held a medieval feast and sometimes did.

The Swindells were big on entertaining visiting TFP members, especially VIPs in the organization and the wealthier and more influential members. They set the table as if for visiting royalty, with crystal stemware, silver knives, two forks, and three spoons—each with a purpose and place next to the fine china plates. At an early age I learned to fold the linen napkins in a variety of fanciful shapes, such as flowers or birds, as well as how to serve the guests and clear the table as they finished each course. Everything was top-notch, from the wine and liquor to the food, all of it made from scratch.

As classical music played in the background, the Swindells and their guests—all of them part of the TFP "elite classes"—would discuss Dr. Corrêa de Oliveira's latest teachings and lament the downfall of Western civilization. I sat quietly at the table or hovered nearby, absorbing their talk of "revolutionaries"—the immoral sinners who were doomed to hell—and the TFP "counterrevolutionaries" who thought that civilization had been going to hell—literally—for centuries.

I tried to be a good Catholic girl, like Saint Bernadette, writing down the little fervent prayers I began making up around the age of six or seven.

O my God Bless me and give me faith!
Protect me and keep me from all evil, Amen.

As I got older, the prayers grew longer and more intense, if sometimes misspelled:

O most sweet Mother Mary I ask of thee
from the botum of my hart
to help me at this time of need give me the graces
to do what thou wasts [*wants*] of me.
Sweet Jesus be my love.

What I didn't tell the Swindells was that I prayed not only for my sisters and aunts and grandmother but also for my mom. And sometimes even for my dad's conversion.

I was conflicted about Ramón. Sometimes I imagined ways that he should be put to death—run over by a tractor, or hung up over a dump so that the birds would peck at his eyes, flies covering him as they'd covered my sisters. Yet another part of me believed in the Christian principles I was taught and prayed that my father would convert and ask for forgiveness so that his soul could be saved. I imagined that I'd see him again someday and that he'd be contrite and I would forgive him as Jesus would have wanted.

But these weren't things I could talk to the Swindells about.

On the outside, the Swindells embodied the perfect TFP family. But the image they presented to TFP luminaries and other associates wasn't the reality at home.

Mr. Swindell liked to drink—a lot. He'd get home and start making drinks for himself and his wife, usually Jim Beam with water and ice, though Sundays were reserved for gin and tonics. Even when TFP guests were visiting, he'd end up drunk, talking faster and louder, until he'd finally nod off in the living room.

There were times when all this drinking could be funny—like when he'd forget himself and curse, which would set Mrs. Swindell off on a hellfire-and-brimstone tirade. But there were also times when Mrs. Swindell would get so drunk that she couldn't walk and I'd have to help her get to bed.

The Swindells believed in "spare the rod and spoil the child," and many a wooden spoon was broken on my bare bottom. But I was not the sort of child easily beaten into submission; I'd scream at the top of my lungs, hoping they would ease up. If I "mouthed off," or was otherwise disrespectful, they would pour Tabasco sauce onto my tongue or insert a bar of soap into my mouth and make me keep it there until Mrs. Swindell said I could take it out. In the years since, I've tried to keep my sense of humor about it. I like to say I learned early in life that a mouthful of Fels Naptha is better than bitter old Safeguard.

The Swindells discovered that it wouldn't be easy to break my stubborn streak. One day, when Mr. Swindell demanded that I pick up my toys, I reached back to what the psychologist had told me. "No!" I shouted, picking up my toy telephone. "I'm calling the police and reporting you!" That was the day I was given my first severe spanking with a large wooden paddle. My toy phone was taken away for good. And I wasn't allowed to answer the real phone until I was fifteen years old.

The Swindells showed little understanding or patience for my emotional outbursts. When I acted out, Mrs. Swindell would accuse me of being possessed by a demon, "like your father." They even talked about finding a priest to conduct an exorcism. While it never came to that, Mrs. Swindell began waking me up in the morning by throwing "holy water" in my face.

Long before I was old enough to do anything about it, I started thinking about escaping from the Swindells. I'd dream of climbing behind the wheel of a car and driving off as fast as it would go.

Even if I could have pulled off such an escape, though, the problem was always the same: I had no place to go. I was lost to the people of Sonoma and lost to my unknown family in Mexico. I saw my mom's brothers, who were now working for the TFP offshoot America Needs Fatima, once in the first year, but that was it. Later I learned that Lewis and then Robert had left the organization; after that, they were no longer welcome in the Swindell home.

My grandpa was allowed to visit, but he never felt welcome—only tolerated—in the Swindells' home, so he came just once a year. I enjoyed his visits and couldn't understand why he didn't come more often—a complaint the Swindells were only too happy to exploit.

"See? He doesn't care about you," Mrs. Swindell would say.

Of course, Grandpa had a way of pushing their buttons. He loved taking pictures of me, even though he knew my new family didn't like it; Mr. Swindell used to warn him not to take any photographs or videos of "Cecilia" because they didn't want anyone from my past to know where I was living. And sometimes Grandpa would forget and call me Carmina, which always brought the same response from Mrs. Swindell: "Carmina died a long time ago."

As time passed, Grandpa grew more and more concerned about me. I didn't seem to have any playmates, and the Swindells didn't seem to be making much of an attempt to educate me. My grandma Louise had been a good home-school teacher for my mother and her siblings, but my studies with Mrs. Swindell seemed sporadic and limited. Doubts were eating away at Grandpa's conscience about whether giving me up for adoption had been the right decision after all.

At the time, it must have seemed like the only choice. He had cried for two years after the murders, even after he moved to southern California following my adoption, as if changing his address could change the past. For a while it would seem like he might finally be moving on, but then he'd hear a child in the supermarket who sounded like Ruth or Maria or one of his grandchildren and he'd start sobbing again. Even coming to visit me was heartbreaking because I reminded him so much of Angela as a young girl.

Grandpa knew there was something wrong with the way I was being raised now. At one point he even asked my former social worker in California if there was any way to reverse the adoption process. But she shut him down quickly, reminding him that he'd given up his rights when he offered me to the Swindells.

In their campaign to sever the ties between me and my grandfather, the Swindells didn't even invite him to the most important religious moment of my young life: my First Holy Communion.

In the TFP community a First Communion in such a model family as the Swindells was a major event, and the organization wanted to make a splash. They offered to arrange a special ceremony in New York City and to coordinate it with the release of a new TFP book, *The Nobility*. The Swindells and I were put up in the nicest hotel in the city, paid for by their wealthy TFP patrons. The night before the big event, I was wandering the hotel hallways in my white Communion dress when I looked up—and there was Grandpa.

He was as shocked to see me as I was to see him. He had come to New York for the book release; he had no idea I was having my First Communion the next day. He wasn't even staying at the same hotel; he didn't have that kind of money. He just happened to be checking in with some friends when he saw me.

The next day I would give my first confession and receive the blessed sacrament of the Eucharist. My First Communion would signify that I had reached "the age of reason," that I was old enough to participate in the sacramental life of the Roman Catholic Church. After my baptism, there was no more important day in my spiritual life; it was a day when all of my family should have gathered to celebrate.

Yet my grandfather had been purposely left out.

In the morning he showed up at the Swindells' lavish suite bearing presents for me. I waited to open them until after he left, but as soon as he was gone I happily opened the box and pulled out a small, heart-shaped locket and rosary beads.

Mr. Swindell glanced at the locket. "Cheap," he said with a sneer. "Probably plastic."

I looked at my presents. With Mr. Swindell's words in my ears, I threw them into the trash can.

Before I could receive the Eucharist, I had to go to confession. I wasn't sure exactly what I needed to confess, but I'd been told I shouldn't take Communion without confessing *all* of my sins, or I'd risk eternal damnation. So I made a list.

"What do you have there?" the priest asked when I got into the confession booth.

"I wrote down my sins," I explained.

The priest seemed amused. "Don't you know what you've done wrong?"

Not really, I thought, but I nodded. "Yes."

"Then give me your list and confess," the priest replied with a chuckle. When I finished, he told me, "Say five Our Fathers for penance."

Afterward, I saw Grandpa approaching. At first he was smiling, but as he drew closer, he saw that I was holding a fancier set of rosary beads given to me by Elaine.

"Where are the presents I gave you?"

"They were plastic," I replied. "Mr. Swindell said so. I threw them away."

Shocked and hurt, Grandpa confronted Mr. Swindell. Why hadn't he been told about my Communion? Why would the Swindells say such things about the presents he'd rushed out to get his granddaughter on a moment's notice?

But Mr. Swindell brushed him off. Grandpa didn't have any rights, he said.

After that day, Grandpa felt even less welcome at the Swindells' house. Yet he never stopped visiting once a year, and he never failed to send me a present on my birthday and Christmas. Then, one day, Mrs. Swindell told me to write Grandpa and tell him that, instead of presents, I wanted him to send money.

After that, the presents slowed and eventually stopped. And if he sent money, I never saw any of it.

Twenty-six

Just four years after my father's rampage, Sonoma County residents were terrorized by another horrific crime that would draw intense media scrutiny from around the world. On October 1, 1993, twelve-year-old Polly Klaas was kidnapped at knifepoint from her mother's home in Petaluma.

Polly, along with two of her friends who were staying with her overnight, were accosted in her bedroom by a man at about 10:30 P.M. He tied up the two friends, told them to count to a thousand, and then fled into the night with his sobbing victim.

The story struck home with families around the country. If a child could be abducted from her room while her mother and younger sister slept down the hall, how could anyone feel safe?

The people in Petaluma and surrounding communities banded together and formed the Polly Klaas Search Center. Men, women, and children came by the dozens to do what they could—answer phones, stuff envelopes, create PR packages, and help manage the nearly four thousand volunteers who offered their services.

The ground search for Polly covered more than a thousand square miles of orchards, vineyards, fields, and forests, as bloodhounds were brought in and psychics called to offer their help. The air search covered another three thousand square miles. In a technological innovation, three-dimensional CAD maps of the search areas were developed. Television shows like *America's Most Wanted* and *20/20* broadcast dramatic re-creations of the crime and appealed to the nation for help, as Polly's dad and mother tearfully begged whoever took her to "please just give her back."

There had been another change in those four years: The Internet, barely in its infancy in 1989, now offered a way to distribute digital photos of the missing girl, composite drawings of her kidnapper, and details of the crime to millions of computer users all over the world.

In the end, however, even the Internet made no difference. On November 30, police arrested Richard Allen Davis, whose palm print had been found in Polly's bedroom. Four days later, he led police to her body off Highway 101 near Cloverdale in northern Sonoma County. Raped and then strangled, she had been buried in a shallow grave with her miniskirt pulled up above her waist and her legs spread apart.

Davis was a career criminal with a record dating back to the 1960s that included burglary, assault, robbery, kidnapping, and rape. Due to all the publicity, his trial was moved from Sonoma County to San Jose. In July 1996 he was convicted of first-degree murder and four special circumstances—kidnapping, robbery, burglary, and a lewd act on a child—and on August 5 a jury recommended a sentence of death.

As the verdict was read, Davis stood and gave the finger to the spectators in the courtroom, including Polly's family. Later, at his formal sentencing, Davis claimed that before he killed her, Polly said, "Just don't do me like my dad," implying that Klaas's father was a child molester. Marc Klaas lunged at the grinning killer but was held back by deputies.

Judge Thomas Hastings then pronounced the death sentence, saying, "Mr. Davis, this is always a traumatic and emotional decision for a judge. You made it very easy today by your conduct." Davis was then sent to San Quentin, where he joined my father and several hundred others on death row.

Despite the obvious differences between crimes and the criminals, many in Sonoma County were reminded of the murders my father had committed seven years before.

Dr. Linda Beatie, the anesthesiologist who been in the emergency room when I was brought in, lived only a few blocks from the house where Polly was abducted. Suddenly it was as if an old nightmare had crept back into her sleep. She'd never forgotten me or her fear of Ramón. For years, she had talked about that day in the emergency room to anyone who would listen, as if still trying to purge the horror she'd felt when she realized that she held my life in her hands. After a while, even her family and friends told her they were tired of hearing the story, that she should stop dwelling on the past.

But she couldn't. Some years after she heard I'd been adopted, she started taking an evening photography class in Sonoma. She hadn't thought about it when she signed up for the class, but she would have to drive past the Petaluma dump on her way there. Only when she reached the turnoff for the dump that first day, realized where she was, and glanced over did her mind leap back in time—to the image of me smiling as I reached for the Polaroid photograph. Every time she drove by after that, she looked again and remembered me that way, the image superimposed on the dump site like a double exposure.

The day Polly was abducted was also Lieutenant Mike Brown's twentieth anniversary with the Sonoma County Sheriff's Department. He was now in charge of the entire detective bureau, with six investigative units and two clerical-support units under his command.

Mike's only involvement in the Klaas investigation was meeting with his good friend Captain David Long of the Petaluma Police Department, which had jurisdiction, to discuss how the sheriff's department could help. Then, after her body was found, Mike was present at the morgue when her remains were delivered in a white plastic body bag. But he didn't attend the autopsy—there was no investigative reason for him to do so, and he'd seen far too many autopsies and far too many dead kids.

Just the presence of Polly's remains, he told me later, reminded him of the Salcido case more than he would have liked—especially of Ruth, who was almost the same age as Polly when she was murdered, and of her body lying in a pool of blood.

Mike had watched the massive local reaction to the Klaas case and believed that it was in part due to the murders of my family. Our story had played out so quickly that there was no time to launch a volunteer effort before we were found in the Petaluma dump. When Polly was abducted, the volunteers mobilized in the hope that they might save her—or at least locate her body and bring her abductor to justice.

Twenty years of police work had taken its toll on Mike; he clung to the positive stories, such as mine, and on particularly rough days he made sure he told Arlyn and his boys how much he loved them.

On the evening Polly's body was recovered, he went home and looked up as he often did at a particular hillside in the lush green valley where he lived. Some years before, a retired lieutenant from the San Francisco Police Department had crafted a large cross—fifty feet tall and thirty-five feet across—out of rocks and boulders painted white in a hillside meadow that could be seen from the highway. Though local kids sometimes rolled the stones down the hill, the lieutenant always rolled them back into place.

Mike didn't know the man who created the cross, but he felt sure that he built it as a way to cope with what he'd seen during his days in law enforcement. That cross gave Mike hope. At least one other cop had found a way to survive his career, and he would find a way to survive his.

He also hoped I had found a way not just to survive but to thrive. He liked to believe I was growing up strong and healthy, that I was happy and loved. And that perhaps I'd been able to forget what he could not.

Twenty-seven

Every time we left the Swindells' property, I was reminded just how isolated we were from the "normal" world. And it wasn't just physical distance; it was as if we were living in a totally different time. More and more, as I grew older, I noticed the looks Mrs. Swindell and I would get when we went out shopping in our long dresses and long, old-fashioned hairdos. "Are you Amish?" people would ask. "What religion are you?"

In the corners of my eyes, I saw other teenagers nod and smirk at us to their friends. Like my mother when she was my age, I noticed everything the other girls wore. I saw how they did their hair, wore their makeup. I saw them having fun. I saw them with boys. And I wanted all of that so badly.

But the Swindells had made it clear that boys were off-limits—long before I could have had any serious thoughts about them. Once, when I was about four years old, we were visiting one of the Swindells' daughters when we kids started a game of hide-and-seek. Thrilled just to have someone to play with, I hid under the covers of a bed with one of the other kids—a six-year-old boy.

Unfortunately, the person who found us was Mrs. Swindell. She pulled me out from beneath the covers by my hair and started shrieking and slapping me, demanding to know what we were doing in bed together. I was too young to know what she was talking about and I had no idea why she'd gotten so mad.

It would be years before I understood.

But life with the Swindells wasn't always horrible. Religious holidays like Christmas and Easter, as well as birthdays, were celebrated with lots of presents and treats. However, Mrs. Swindell would even use those days as a way of controlling me. "Look at everything we've done for you," she'd say. "Look at what we bought."

There were other times—when the Swindells and I would settle down to watch one of the approved movies on television, or when we were setting out on a family trip—that I could imagine we were a happy family. Music was always a common ground for us. Since the age of eight I'd been asking for a violin, and when I was fifteen the Swindells bought me one. By now I was playing half a dozen instruments and singing along with opera recordings and "sacred songs" like "Ave Maria."

Music was an outlet for my feelings. For some reason I couldn't learn to read music, but all I needed was to hear a piece several times before I could mimic it on an instrument or with my voice. I composed, too, songs that were expressions of my mood at the time, never to be repeated. If the Swindells wanted to know how I was feeling, all they had to do was listen to what I was playing. It was the only time they praised me for something I enjoyed doing.

Yet these periods of peace never lasted long. And the hardest part was that even during such times, I never felt loved. It was as if I was a project—they were responsible for training me, and often were disappointed in my progress.

The older I got, the more abusive and repressive my home situation became. Mr. Swindell's blowups could be terrifying, but he rarely hit me, perhaps out of fear of what I might tell someone. But Mrs. Swindell had no such compunctions, and she could carry a grudge or remember a mistake I made for months, or even years.

When I was younger, Mrs. Swindell had spanked me with a wooden paddle or wooden spoons. By the age of ten I'd become "too mature" to spank, so Mrs. Swindell took to slapping my face, pulling my hair, throwing things, and screaming.

I would take it—for a while, for as long as I could. Then I'd resort to my "evil eye," a look so venomous that Mrs. Swindell would yell, "Get that look off your face before I slap it off!" But it also seemed to make her nervous, enough that she'd back off.

The physical abuse continued until one day, when I was in my early teens, I told Mrs. Swindell that if she hit me again, I'd hit her back. After that, though, she ramped up my regular dose of verbal and emotional abuse, as if to compensate. Sometimes she gave me the silent treatment, going an entire day without saying a word to me. But her real weapon was the guilt trip she laid on me constantly, punctuated with criticism and insults.

You're lazy, she told me. *You're a liar. You can't be trusted.*

I was never quite sure which way to turn. If I did something wrong, I'd try to apologize, but Mrs. Swindell would say with a sneer, "Sorry? All you're going to do is do it again. Sorry doesn't mean anything coming from you!" So the next time I *wouldn't* apologize, knowing it would only make matters worse—and get scolded for my sinful "pride and arrogance." I could never get it right.

When she really wanted to hurt me, Mrs. Swindell would use my mom and dad against me. If I acted willful, she'd say, "You're going to end up like your mother." If I "flirted" with a boy on a shopping trip—which might include something as harmless as returning a smile—she'd accuse me of acting indecently and having impure thoughts. "It was because your mother was disobedient and sinful that she met your father and brought his evil into the family." She seemed to blame my mother as much as my father for what had happened, and I, of course, was never told the truth.

The remarks hurt, but I refused to let Mrs. Swindell see how much. I yelled back at her, however I saved my tears for when I went to bed. That's when I'd think of my father and scream at him in my mind. *Why me? I hate you for leaving me here alone. Keeping me alive is worse than killing me!*

Still, I refused to give in. I found ways to cope with the steady stream of criticism, the boredom, and the loneliness.

I spent as much time as I could outside, away from Mrs. Swindell. Among the few secular books the Swindells allowed in the house was a collection of nature books on trees and North American birds. I wandered the property with the books and learned the name of every kind of tree on it—the birch, white oak, hawthorn, walnut, dogwood, and Judas— and I could identify every bird species in that part of the country. The Swindells noticed my interest in nature and bought me a big book on butterflies; soon I had a collection of every variety that migrated across the valley.

Each fall the black walnut trees would drop their nuts on the ground, and the local kids, mostly from farm families, would go "walnutting," collecting the nuts and bringing them to a local feed store to be hulled and weighed. Each pound earned its collector ten cents. One year I collected eighty dollars' worth.

Still, such activities couldn't fill in the lonely times; they couldn't substitute for having people I could really talk to, in whom I could confide my thoughts and dreams. I had no teachers, no school counselors, no friends who hadn't been indoctrinated in the teachings of TFP, and even my TFP friends I rarely saw. I was allowed to have female TFP pen pals, but they seemed to think that their only choice for the future was to join a cloistered convent and "marry" Jesus.

So I began entertaining the idea of joining a convent, too. As a young girl I'd been fascinated by the Carmelite Sisters of the Divine Heart of Jesus, an order that helped in the nursing home where Elaine had worked. Later, Henrique

Fragelli, an executive with TFP in America, introduced the Swindells and me to an order of discalced (that is, barefoot) Carmelite nuns in the nearest city. Having been taught for most of my life that the world needed fewer marriages and more nuns and priests, I couldn't help wondering if I'd be happier in a convent. I didn't seem to have a lot of other options, and I knew so little about the secular world.

Grandpa still visited once a year, and several times he asked the Swindells to let me come live with him for a little while. They, of course, refused. When he'd get ready to leave after a visit, I would lean into his car, so they couldn't hear me, and ask him to take me with him. But he couldn't. He'd given up that right.

When I asked the Swindells why I couldn't visit my grandpa, they said they were worried he'd expose me to the world they were protecting me from. In recent years Grandpa had been distancing himself from TFP, and the Swindells felt he wasn't to be trusted. They said he'd probably try to make money by selling my story. "And he'd get it all," they warned. "You wouldn't see any of it yourself."

I still had my pretend friends to help me ward off the loneliness. In my mind they had grown up with me, and now they were living lives like any normal teenagers. They even started to date and to talk about the future. I listened in as if I was overhearing people talking about a wonderful, exotic land I knew I would never see.

At first my pretend friends had all been girls. But as I got older they were joined by boys—starting with Ryan, who just happened to share the name of a neighbor boy I sometimes saw from a distance caring for his family's goats.

When Mrs. Swindell learned that some boys had joined my pretend friends, and that they and the older girls had started dating, she told me to stop talking to them. "You're too old to have pretend friends anymore," she complained. "God made angels and saints to talk to. You don't need pretend friends."

I shrugged her off. Angels weren't people, and saints were

dead. My pretend friends were real to me. I could see them. Hear them. And they understood me. Most of them had nicer families than mine, but theirs weren't always perfect. If I got into trouble with Mrs. Swindell, they'd commiserate. There was nothing they could do about my situation, but they could support me and offer advice. They knew what I meant when I said I wanted to run away—If only I'd had someplace to go.

For the most part, I was the leader when my pretend friends and I went on our various adventures. But sometimes one of them would come up with an idea, and I was happy to follow along. One game we all loved was wandering the Swindells' property as modern knights, "defenders of the faith" against all evil. I made a suit of armor and a shield out of cardboard and used a stick for a sword. I patrolled "the kingdom" for hours at a time, using a rake handle to brandish a homemade banner showing Saint James's Cross. I climbed atop a three-foot stump on the property and pretended to be Joan of Arc, battling the heretical Protestants from England and dying in exquisite martyrdom.

That idea—martyrdom—seemed so romantic. The TFP literature told me that for the time being the counterrevolution was a spiritual resistance against evil, but that someday it would become a real, physical battle. And that was fine with me. I looked forward to being able to lash out and strike down my adversaries—or be struck down in the process. It couldn't be worse than the life I was living.

Worst of all, I felt haunted. Always.

My pretend friends weren't the only otherworldly presence in my life. Ever since the tragedy, I had sometimes caught movement out of the corner of my eye. When I was alone, dark shadows, with shape but no substance, lurked on the edge of my sight. But when I looked directly at them they'd disappear around a corner—or into thin air. I remember once noticing something in my peripheral vision at the far end of the hallway. It moved from one bedroom to another. It was so real that I was sure it was Mrs. Swindell. But when I went to investigate, no one was there.

Some of these visions appeared as small creatures—such as rats—or even as small people. The one that frightened me the most was a thin, faunlike shadow with legs like a goat and the upper body of a man. But some were merely indistinct, but purposeful, shapes. They'd startle me, and for a moment a bolt of fear would stop me before I could take a deep breath and move on.

As I grew older, I began to worry about what these shadows meant. What if the same evil that overtook my father had unfinished business with me?

As disturbing as the moving shadows were, darker still were the nightmares I began having at about the age of ten. All of them involved my attacking Mrs. Swindell. In one dream, I took a knife and stabbed her over and over. In another, I twisted her head until her neck broke. I didn't know how to feel about the dreams. I hated her, but I wondered: *Would I really do something like that? Could I do something like that? After what my father had done?*

Years later I told a psychologist about the dreams. I was relieved to learn that they were a natural response to what I was going through with the Swindells—an outlet for all the anger I was carrying inside me.

I never actually came close to harming Mrs. Swindell, or anyone else. But I do remember looking at her one day when she was yelling at me and thinking that she needed to stop or something bad might happen. Today, I see horror movies where people mistreat their kids until they become mass murderers, and I understand how it might happen. A person can only take so much.

Alone with my aging parents, I saw the future as bleak—until I made a series of discoveries. When I was thirteen or so, the Swindells assigned me to clean the garage. I didn't mind; the family cat lived in the garage, so I had her for company, and it was a chance to get away from Mrs. Swindell.

As I dug around, I opened up a box and discovered that it was filled with books: *My Friend Flicka*, *The Adventures of Sherlock Holmes*, and *The Little Colonel* series, about a young southern girl who is given that nickname because of her demanding ways.

I knew the books were "of the world," and that the Swindells would take them away if they saw that I had them, so when no one was watching I smuggled them to my room. Then, when the others had gone to sleep, I turned on my night-light and read them, imagining myself as the heroine riding free on my horse Flicka. Or using deductive reasoning like Sherlock Holmes and tracking down the deadly hound of the Baskervilles.

Over the next few months I opened other boxes—and made even more important discoveries, which would someday launch me on a quest to regain my past.

One box I found contained years' worth of letters my uncles had written me—letters I'd never been allowed to read. Another box contained information about family I didn't even know I had—my grandma's family in northern California and my father's in Mexico.

Another box was full of little porcelain and crystal figurines, and as I looked at them I realized that they had belonged to my aunts. I found birth announcements, photographs of my sisters, even a "baby's first tooth." Still another was full of drawings signed Angela Richards, most of them of horses. I barely remembered my real mother, and yet in that moment I felt an immediate connection to this artistic young woman—an innocent victim whom the Swindells had always portrayed as little more than a disobedient whore.

The most shocking discovery I made, however, was a box filled with newspaper and magazine clippings from 1989 and 1990.

Even into my teenage years, the Swindells had kept up the practice of holding a special dinner on the anniversary of the murders, followed by my recitation of what had happened. I'd always told the story as if I was remembering a dream. Yet here was proof that my memories were all based in reality, often to exacting detail.

The clippings told me more about the life my mom had lived. She, too, had been raised in a strict, religious household, with no friends, no dates, no proms, no sleepover nights or gossip about boys. She, too, had longed for freedom—and gone on long walks looking for it, much as I did with my pretend friends on the Swindell property. In those yellowed clippings I read about my mother's dreams of a modeling career, and learned that she had planned to take me with her to a photo shoot on the day of the murders because I was the child who looked most like her.

The more I read about my mother, the more I identified with her. She might have been looking for something more than a dead-end existence with an abusive husband, but she had also been a good mother and loved me and my sisters. She was no whore, no sinner who had somehow brought tragedy down on her family. The Swindells had lied.

Through the articles, I also learned that I'd arrived at the Swindells' with a large amount of money in my trust account, which they'd never mentioned. I wondered what had become of it, and whether it would be handed over to me someday.

I pulled the boxes upstairs and asked the Swindells about them. But Mrs. Swindell took the boxes and put them up in a closet, never to be seen again—except one day when I snuck back into them and removed my mother's paintings of horses.

Finding the boxes made me want to learn more about the world beyond the Swindells. At night I would sneak downstairs to turn on the television. Until then, my TV experience had been limited to TFP-approved films like *The Song*

of Bernadette and, after one of the Swindells' sons convinced his parents on a visit home that there was nothing
wrong with it, *The Sound of Music.*

Now, however, I was getting an education. I learned about
the world from late-night movies, soap operas, and reruns of
The Jerry Springer Show. I learned about dating and relationships from reality television and talk shows. And I
learned about romance and passion from a box of Harlequin
novels I found in the basement. Every now and then a piece
of contraband would show up in the mailbox at the end of
the driveway—a catalog from Victoria's Secret, or a misde-
livered women's magazine—and I would sneak it past Mrs.
Swindell to hide it under my bed for later reading. Late at
night, I'd admire the pictures of half-naked men and women
on their pages and imagine the wonderful, free lives they
must lead.

I had quite a stash going, until one day Mrs. Swindell
found it during one of her periodic "inspections." I had no
privacy—not even a *right* to privacy, as she often pointed
out. Now, discovering that I was curious about fashion—
and the opposite sex—she felt vindicated. "Liar! Sneak!"
she shouted. "You can't fool anyone!" I was "impure," and
that trumped almost anything. Being impure meant you'd
committed a mortal sin, and if you died in a state of mortal
sin, you went straight to hell—no ifs, ands, or purgatories.

Still, that didn't stop me from gathering more treasures.
Or Mrs. Swindell from regularly tossing my room and be-
rating me for what she found.

In 1999 I got another eye-opener about the world I was
missing. The Carmelite Sisters of the Divine Heart of Jesus
bought me a ticket to go with them to see Pope John Paul II,
who was appearing in St. Louis. It would mean staying over
two nights with a non-TFP Catholic family, and the Swindells were none too happy about letting me go—they had
never let me out of their sight for even a single night. But
rejecting the offer would have been a public statement of
defiance, and that wouldn't have looked good. The Swin-

dells might have been critical of the pope—as most TFP families were of modern popes—but they were still prominent in the national Catholic community.

I had assumed that all Catholics were pretty much alike. But my host family listened to modern music on the radio; their teenagers, who belonged to a Catholic youth group, seemed as normal as the teens I saw when I was out shopping with Mrs. Swindell. And the women wore pants!

Going to see the Holy Father was like going to a big party. There were Christian rock groups and Christian rap artists, their music blaring from immense speakers to pump up the crowd. I returned to the Swindell household with an entirely different viewpoint on what it meant to be Catholic.

One aspect of my worldly education was actually encouraged by the Swindells, though they later regretted it. They wouldn't allow me to get a job outside the house, but when I was sixteen they were more than happy to farm me out as a telemarketer for TFP, hawking books and contacting people who had "left the church" and trying to persuade them to return. I was paid eight dollars an hour—not a cent of which I ever saw, as it went straight into the Swindells' account.

But there was one side benefit. During one of my telemarketing sessions, I accidentally dialed the wrong 800 number and was connected to a fantasy telephone-sex line. I listened in amazement to what the woman on the other end of the line was saying. Then I wrote down other 800 numbers and continued my sex education.

My fun came to an end, though, when I accidentally left the list of telephone numbers in my bathrobe. Mrs. Swindell found them the next time she did the laundry, and she was still screaming at me at four o'clock the next morning. "Oh my God, what are your holy sisters in heaven thinking? They must be disgusted. So evil!"

And then, not for the first time, she used the occasion to compare me to my father. "You're no better than him," she said, seething. "Maybe you should go live with him in his cell."

What was I supposed to do? It wasn't as if I could talk to Mrs. Swindell about things like sex, or boys, or the emotions that sometimes roiled around in me. Since the age of twelve, I'd floated in and out of depressions, sometimes finding myself in a place so deep and dark that I contemplated suicide.

The first time I got my period, I had no idea what was going on because no one had ever explained it might happen. I didn't dare tell Mrs. Swindell, but she discovered my secret when she found a stain on one of my dresses and asked me about it. She then explained what it meant in as few words as possible, as if we should both be ashamed.

Sometimes I dreamed of being rescued by a knight in shining armor—or at least a nice boy with a car. He'd confront the Swindells with his love for me, and if they didn't give us their blessing, he'd just carry me off to live happily ever after. But most of the time I despaired of finding a happy ending. In other TFP families, I'd seen women in their thirties or forties still living with their parents. And I knew that somehow I had to escape the Swindells before I became one of those spinsters living at home forever. But there was only one way I knew to accomplish that.

In search of freedom, I joined a convent.

Twenty-eight

Despite the Swindells' negative example, I never lost touch with my own spirituality. I had always felt close to Jesus Christ, and especially moved by the Passion. He had died in the eyes of humans, yet his death wasn't what it had appeared to be. In a sense, I felt I understood something of what Christ had gone through. I, too, had nearly died but continued to live.

Much of my interest in becoming a nun was sparked by Father David, a TFP-friendly priest my family knew. Father David spoke eloquently about the intimacy a nun has with Jesus Christ as her spouse, savior, and lover, and soon I was consumed with desire to join a convent. One of my TFP pen pals, Catherine Lee, was also thinking of joining the discalced Carmelite order, and we wrote back and forth about it. If I wasn't going to be allowed to meet boys or get married, and I wanted to avoid spending the rest of my life growing old with the Swindells, it seemed like my only option.

But the greatest influence on my decision to join was the reverend mother of the Carmelite order, with whom I had begun communicating in my teens. Because the order was cloistered, our personal contact was limited to sending letters and talking through a screen in the convent mailroom. But even that posed a problem. Mrs. Swindell insisted on reading aloud every letter that passed to or from the house; there was no such thing as privacy in that household. She even tried to claim that under some circumstances a mother should be allowed to accompany her child into the confessional booth. She said it was to make sure I confessed to everything, but I'm sure it was really out of concern about what I might say.

When I did write letters, Mrs. Swindell insisted that my spelling and penmanship be perfect. One little error and she'd make me start over; she also censored what I said. It all made communication difficult and so tiresome that I sometimes didn't bother. In any event, I could never have told the reverend mother everything I wanted to in my letters. If I had dared talk about some aspects of my upbringing, Mrs. Swindell might have cut off my mailing privileges altogether.

But I was able to talk with the reverend mother, and I did so often, sometimes for an hour or more. That's where I was able to tell her about myself—about my childhood, about the murders in Sonoma, and about what I called my "life in hell" with the Swindells.

Without any sense of what I was discussing with the reverend mother, the Swindells were happy when they learned I was planning to join the convent. But they also used the knowledge against me. Whenever Mrs. Swindell discovered one of my secret stashes of books or magazines, for instance, she'd warn me: "If you want to be a nun, we better start seeing a change in your behavior now. Or I might have to tell the reverend mother you shouldn't be allowed to join."

But I wasn't the only one who was capable of offending the Swindells. When they found out the Carmelites celebrated the *Novus Ordo*—the New Order Mass, in English instead of Latin—they hit the roof. "How can you go there and accept this sacrilegious blasphemy?" they scolded. But I turned it around on them. Joining an order with no Latin Mass would be a big sacrifice for me, I told them—but maybe my suffering, along with my prayers, would eventually cause the nuns to bring the Latin Mass back. I was playing their trumpet, using their own tools against them, but they took the bait.

The usual age for joining was seventeen, but I was fifteen when I first tried to gain admittance to the order. The reverend mother even championed my cause to the bishop when he visited the convent that Easter, and arranged for me to meet him in the visiting room after Mass. But the day didn't end as I had hoped.

When I knelt to ask his permission to join, he said, "This is not the day or the time." This bishop was known for his wry sense of humor, so the reverend mother and the other nuns assumed he was joking, and they laughed in response. "Oh, please, come on," the reverend mother said. But the bishop turned beet red. "No, Reverend Mother, I mean it," he said. Everybody was silent; they didn't know what else to say.

I cried all the way home. When I walked in the door, the phone was ringing. It was the reverend mother calling to apologize. I was devastated, but I reassured her that I was fine. I set my sights on joining when I reached seventeen. By then, I knew, neither the bishop nor the Swindells could stand in my way.

In fact, the only person who could have possibly stood in my way was me. Although I felt a spiritual connection to God and to the Carmelite nuns, I had to talk myself into being willing to live as a cloistered nun for the rest of my life.

My years of solitude—of having only myself for a confidante—had made me pretty introspective, so I knew my main objective in joining a convent was to escape from the Swindells. But even though I could have left them when I reached the age of majority, I knew I'd have no place to go. I had never been trained for life on my own. Other than telemarketing for TFP and walnutting on the Swindells' land, I had no job experience. My education, such as it was, had essentially stopped at the eighth grade. I had no high school diploma and no plans for future education; TFP women didn't go to college.

In a convent, I knew I would have a place and a purpose. Yet in my heart I still wanted a normal life, and I knew I was tricking myself—not just the Swindells—into believing I actually wanted to become a nun.

The truth of this hit me when I was sixteen and the family was watching *The Sound of Music* together. In the movie, the heroine, Maria, has convinced herself that she wants to be a nun, despite her love for more worldly things like music and hiking and romance. Others—including the reverend mother in the movie—recognized this, too. So when Maria falls in love with Captain Von Trapp, and his kids, the reverend mother tells her she's not cut out to be a nun. She had had to climb every mountain, ford every stream, follow every rainbow, till she found her dream.

Of course, I identified with Maria. During the points in the movie when it was obvious that she wasn't meant to be a nun—such as when she fell in love with the captain—I had to look away from the screen, certain that if the Swindells had seen my face, they'd have known that I, too, was wrong for the sisterhood.

As it was, the Swindells constantly challenged my commitment. I kept hiding contraband in my room, inviting another round of recriminations and threats every time Mrs. Swindell found something new. "Hypocrite!" she'd yell. "Liar! You're a fake! I should tell the reverend mother about what I found! The truth will come out, and if they don't see it right away, they'll learn soon enough who you really are."

Finally, on April 24, 2003, I turned seventeen—old

enough to join the convent on my own. By then, though, I had a new problem. Though I'd been accepted by the nearby Carmelite order Henrique Fragelli had introduced me to, now there was another prospect on the horizon: a Carmelite convent out west that was a direct descendant of convents established in sixteenth-century Spain by Saint Teresa of Ávila.

This convent, my friend Catherine informed me, was much more conservative than the one I had aspired to join. Their nuns were cloistered, discalced, and wore the traditional habit; they also celebrated Mass in Latin—and were well regarded by TFP.

I didn't like the sound of this. I liked the reverend mother at the convent I knew. But soon I was getting a lot of pressure from the Swindells, as well as TFP officials and priests associated with TFP, to consider this new convent. Though Father David was friendly with the first convent, he told me he thought the new option was better. Another priest put it more directly: If I joined a convent that didn't have a Latin Mass, I would be joining the side of evil. "May God help you," he said, if I went that route.

At last I agreed to visit the second convent. The Swindells were delighted and offered to drive me there to meet the reverend mother and see the grounds. The contrast between the two convents was enormous. Where the convent I'd been accepted to was located in a modest building in an urban setting, the new convent was breathtakingly large and beautiful, set on a hill surrounded by acres of rolling pasturelands. The chapel itself was a work of art, with a large domed roof and big stained-glass windows.

There were several other girls visiting that day, and we spoke to the reverend mother, a gracious, charming woman from Mexico, and the novice mistress, whose main purpose was to teach and watch out for the novices. They both seemed to radiate personal peace—and that was something I wanted, too. By the time I left, I had made my decision: I wanted to join this convent as soon as possible.

Of course, it wasn't that easy. The convent normally didn't accept applicants that quickly. So I wrote a letter to Father David appealing for his help. To explain why I was so anxious to make the move, I told him about some aspects of my life with the Swindells that I'd never revealed to anyone else—secrets I wanted to forget.

Before I could send the letter, however, Mr. Swindell insisted on reading it himself. I refused to hand it over, knowing full well that once he read it he would never let me send it. I held my ground, insisting that a letter to a priest deserved the same privacy as a confession. "It's none of your business," I told him.

"Don't give me that 'none of your business,'" he barked, demanding the letter.

Then, to my surprise, Mrs. Swindell suddenly took my side. "She's right," she said. "It's private."

Mr. Swindell scowled. "This place is becoming communistic," he said. But the letter got sent—unread and uncensored by the Swindells.

After reading the letter, Father David put in a good word for me at the convent. And on Good Friday I got the news: I'd been accepted to join that May.

That left me with one difficult task: writing to the reverend mother at the original convent where I'd been accepted to let her know. I explained that the other convent had a Latin Mass and that the Swindells wanted me to go there. "It's how I was raised," I wrote simply. I was relieved when she wrote back to say that she and the other nuns were disappointed but that she understood my decision. "God bless you," she wrote. "We'll always be here for you, and you will be in our prayers." She signed it with love.

With that, I accepted that my path was set. I would spend the rest of my life shut off from the outside world. I prepared to leave my home in the midwest and put the past behind me. A week before I was to leave, however, my past reminded me that it wasn't through with me.

I was sitting at the kitchen table when I saw one of those

dark shadows that had haunted me since childhood. It darted swiftly across the floor and crawled up my dress before I could move. I could see it squirming beneath the cloth like a snake. Frightened speechless, I froze for a moment. Then, carefully, I reached for the spot where it was writhing—and it disappeared.

I sat there, trying to catch my breath, and prayed that the shadows of the past would not be able to follow me onto the sacred ground of a convent.

Twenty-nine

On the weekend I joined the order as a postulant, a crowd of well-wishers gathered at the convent to mark the occasion. Most of them were family friends from TFP, but my grandfather was also there to see me off.

However, my new life began on a troubling note. That Friday night, the night before the ceremony, Grandpa and some family friends joined us at a restaurant for my last meal outside the convent walls. I was looking forward to the dinner, though I wasn't quite sure what I should have. Strictly observant Catholics don't eat meat on Fridays, and I was about to enter a life where eating meat was a rare privilege, usually reserved for nuns who were ill and needed the protein—and even then only with the local bishop's approval.

As I looked over the menu, a meat-loaf entrée caught my eye. I wasn't sure it was a good idea, but I was surprised when the others said they were sure this one last exception would be all right. So I ordered the meat loaf, and we all had a lovely dinner before heading back to our rooms to rest up before the big day.

Then, at four o'clock in the morning, I woke up with extreme pain in my stomach and started vomiting. I was up the rest of the night, doubling over and throwing up every hour, and by the time of the ceremony I was exhausted. At the lunch afterward they served lasagna, which is usually my favorite meal. But I couldn't eat a bite.

My family and friends assumed it was just a case of nerves; girls entering the convent are often emotionally distraught on that first day, knowing they may never see their families again. But that couldn't have been it for me; after all, I was looking forward to getting away from my "family."

My symptoms lasted for a week, long after all the visitors were gone. Finally, the novice mistress called a doctor, who diagnosed my reaction as a case of food poisoning and recommended a diet of Jell-O and Gatorade until I recovered.

Life in a Carmelite order had not changed much in several centuries. Aspiring nuns enter the order as postulants, a sort of trial/probationary stage; after that they become novices, and finally professed nuns. We dressed the same way Saint Teresa's original postulants had some five hundred years earlier, in simple loose brown dresses with brown capes around the neck and over the shoulders to a little below the elbow. We wore veils that covered our hair and were tied at the back. We were taught to walk with our hands clasped in front of us beneath our capes, with only our faces uncovered. The less skin we showed, the better.

Like the other postulants, I slept in a small cell, about ten feet by twenty, with a single small window and plain white walls unadorned except by a crucifix and a painting of the Virgin Mary. The only furniture was my bed, which consisted of two wooden planks laid across two sawhorses and covered with a two-inch-thick mattress of blankets sewn together.

The convent itself was divided into the chapel, different wings with cells for the postulants, novices, and professed nuns, two recreation rooms, a laundry, sewing room, food-storage room, kitchen, and dining room. Outside were two large gardens. The sisters raised chickens for eggs, sheep and llamas for wool, and a cow for milk.

It was an austere life. No television. No movies. Books were allowed—mostly religious ones, but the library also contained a copy of J. R. R. Tolkien's *Lord of the Rings,* C. S. Lewis's *Chronicles of Narnia,* and the Sherlock Holmes mysteries. We were allowed to correspond with our families by letter, but not with friends, other than to thank them for their letters.

A typical day began at four o'clock in the morning, when we rose for meditation—a less structured version of communing with God than a traditional prayer—for an hour. After that we attended Mass, ate breakfast, and began our chores, such as sweeping the halls, doing laundry, and feeding the animals. Then there were prayers until lunch and an hourlong siesta, followed by more prayers and meditation before dinner. After eating, we had an hour for "recreation" at 6 P.M., and then we prayed until ten before going to bed.

Except for singing in the choir and the hour of recreation, our lives were conducted in silence. Most recreation consisted of folding laundry, sewing, or making little "third-level" religious relics, such as taking a piece of cloth that had been touched to the bones of a saint and laminating it to a holy card. These would be sold in the convent gift store or given to family and friends. But there were lighter moments. During recreation hours, the postulants, novices, and sisters were free to chat and laugh as we told stories from "out in the world." And sometimes, during the winter, we got in some sledding—and even managed an honest-to-goodness snowball fight.

A Carmelite's life is one of prayer, offered up for reparation, sacrifice, and the saving of souls. As I had planned, I prayed for the genuine conversion of my father.

I had read that some saints had willingly sacrificed their own eternal happiness—spending time in hell—in order to save a loved one who was otherwise damned. I told God that

I would be willing to make that same sacrifice if my father would do what was necessary for his own salvation.

I believed that prayer was the strongest possible statement of hope. It may be that we can never really know the reasons for any change in the world—whether it happens because of God's will or simply because we want something enough that our minds make it happen. The only thing that mattered to me was that it happened.

Although our lives were spent in contemplation, prayer, and chores, I saw that most of the women in the convent were happy. While they might pass one another in the hallways without speaking, they did so with smiles on their faces; they were very close to one another, a true spiritual community. They were at peace. I hoped that I could find such contentment myself, and that I now had a home where I could live out my life in peace.

Yet, from the very beginning, my body and my mind conspired with my past against me. My food-poisoning episode marked the start of a long, arduous year battling health problems. Several weeks before entering the convent, I'd had my wisdom teeth removed, and my gums had become infected; it took six trips to see a dentist and finally an oral surgeon before the problem was fixed. Each time I was accompanied by the novice mistress. It was a lot to ask of a cloistered nun who was trying to avoid dealing with the outside world, and I felt bad for dragging her out into it.

But no sooner were my teeth fixed than my allergies began acting up. I'd always suffered from seasonal allergies, but that spring and summer they struck with a vengeance, triggered by pollen from the surrounding farms. I had such severe asthma attacks that several times I had to be taken to the local hospital emergency room for Benadryl shots; once they even had to call an ambulance for me.

My body seemed to be breaking down in new ways all the time. As soon as I'd get one issue under control, a new one would come along to take its place. Other than the allergies, I'd been a tough, healthy kid, but constant kneeling on concrete floors to pray caused my knees to swell and become inflamed. I tried to ignore the pain, but it became so intense that the reverend mother noticed me hobbling around and once again a doctor was consulted. He prescribed antibiotics and ordered me to stay off my knees.

Yet for all of my physical ailments, it was my mind that doomed my life as a nun.

The dark shadows had followed me to the convent. They didn't seem able to enter the building itself, but that didn't matter. I would catch glimpses of them as they passed like clouds across my window or the glass doors of the convent, reminding me that they were waiting for me out in the world.

Were the shadows a manifestation of evil? A psychological response to the trauma I'd endured since childhood? Or my brain's metaphor for dark memories? I couldn't say. But there was one shadow that truly troubled me—a deepening shade of depression, which began to overtake me toward the end of my first year in the convent.

In this new, peaceful setting, all those years of suppressing what had happened when I was a girl—and the years of abuse and neglect with the Swindells that followed—caught up to me. Ever since the tragedy, I had never been able to take silence. I had always made sure I had some kind of noise to distract my mind, to dilute my anger and sadness. The Swindells always had music playing, and when there was no one to talk to, I talked out loud to myself and my pretend friends. It helped me to block out what was going on inside my head.

At the convent, I was happiest when I was allowed to care for the sheep, taking them to the fields to graze and then bringing them back in. With all that silence, I welcomed the distraction of a physical purpose. But the life of a cloistered nun is meant to be spent in religious contemplation, indoors and in seclusion. And the reverend mother let me know that was expected of me, too.

Yet living in silence, alone with my thoughts, was like having a volcano going off in my mind, bubbling and erupting within me all day long.

It didn't come over me all at once, but a little at a time. At first it seemed almost inconsequential. One of the sisters would ask me to perform some simple task, or to pick up after myself, and I'd forget to do it. Then I'd forget the next time, too.

I didn't know what was happening to me, just that I wasn't happy. I felt lethargic, unable to think straight. I remember feeling frustrated, as though I was always in a black hole. My mind played tricks on me. I wanted to die, and the very thought of it ate away at me.

Several more times I had to be taken to the hospital, disoriented and hyperventilating, suffering from panic attacks. I'd get lost trying to find my way back to my cell, or go wandering outside in the pouring rain as lightning stabbed the ground around the convent.

The other sisters noticed my behavior, and they worried about me. The reverend mother and novice mistress did what they could, even inviting psychologists and psychiatrists to the convent to talk to me. The shrinks diagnosed me as suffering from clinical depression and prescribed antidepressants. And, for a time, I felt better and began to think my troubles were over. But then the pendulum would swing back the other way, and I found myself even farther down than I had been before.

I prayed for help and hoped to find salvation in religion. Inside the chapel, I would stare up at a beautiful golden statue of a dove that held the Blessed Sacrament, suspended in the air on the nuns' side of the chapel. Contemplating what it represented brought me some comfort, but it never lasted long, and I grew more bitter with each passing week.

As my depression deepened, I felt myself withdrawing from spirituality, feeling abandoned by God the way I had felt abandoned by my mother and sisters. Some days I even refused to receive Holy Communion.

* * *

Health issues delayed my entrance into the ranks of novices until near the end of my first year in the convent. But in February 2004 I was accepted to receive the holy habit of a novice in April. I was no longer Sister Cecilia; from that point on I would be known as Sister Mariam of Jesus Crucified.

Aware of my history, the sisters at the convent had chosen the name carefully. Mariam Baouardy, later known as "the Little Arab," was born in 1846 in Galilee, Palestine, to a Christian family of the Melkite Greek-Catholic Rite. Orphaned at two years of age, Mariam was raised by an uncle in Alexandria, Egypt. But when she refused to marry a man selected for her by her adoptive parents—preferring to remain a virgin and dedicate her life to Jesus—Mariam's uncle flew into a rage. Though she was scolded and beaten, she refused to change her mind. Her uncle then began treating her as a servant, assigning her the most menial and degrading chores.

Isolated from her family, "desolate" and lonely, Mariam talked over her woes with a young Muslim servant who suggested that she convert to Islam. He also suggested that the two of them could be together as man and wife. When she realized his intentions, Mariam replied, "Muslim, no, never! I am a daughter of the Catholic Apostolic Church, and I hope by the grace of God to persevere until death in my religion, which is the only true one."

Enraged by her rejection, the young man kicked her to the floor, then drew his sword and slashed her throat. Believing she was dead, he dumped her body in an alley. Years later, she would tell her novice mistress at a convent in Marseilles that a nun dressed in a blue habit found her and stitched the wound in her throat; then, after delivering her to a monastery to recover, the nun—whom she believed to be the Virgin Mary—disappeared.

At age twenty-one Mariam entered a Carmelite convent and took the name Sister Mary of Jesus Crucified. But her troubles were not over; at one point she was possessed by a demonic spirit for forty days, persevering and ridding herself of its presence through her faith. Her reward was that reserved for the most privileged of humans: she was fixed with stigmata—the marks of the wounds suffered by Jesus. She also experienced levitations, facial radiance, the ability to prophesize, and possession by a good angel.

After helping to establish Carmelite missions in India and Bethlehem, Sister Mary of Jesus Crucified died after a fall at the age of thirty-two. In 1983, Pope John Paul II beatified her, and though she had not yet been formally canonized when I was accepted into the order, her elevation was expected soon.

I was transfixed by the story of my namesake. There were the obvious reasons—we had both had our throats slashed; had both suffered near-death experiences; had both endured isolation and abuse at the hands of our adoptive families; had both been troubled by depression (or "desolation," as Mariam put it), and had both had our experiences with "dark spirits." Yet Mariam had conquered her past and found peace within her faith and the Carmelite order. So, despite the mixed feelings I had been having about my spirituality, her story inspired me to look forward to the Day of the Clothing, when I would receive my habit and become a novice.

Before that day, postulants go on a ten-day retreat, in which they spend all their time at the convent in solitude and silence—no eating with the other sisters, no recreation hours spent chatting and laughing. The purpose of the retreat is to allow the postulant to prepare and cleanse herself for the next step in her religious life. It is supposed to be a time of reflection and meditation.

I spent most of my retreat in my cell or on the occasional walk outside alone. Other sisters had described their retreat as relaxing and healing, but for me the silence was filled with agony—with bad memories and accusatory voices from my past. *Maybe, if I'd been a better daughter, my dad wouldn't have become a killer. Maybe, if I'd walked out of the dump to get help, my sisters would still be alive. Maybe, if I hadn't been such a bad girl, my grandpa would have kept me, or the Swindells would have loved me.*

Instead of healing my soul, the silence only opened old wounds. Without even the relative distractions of life with the sisters, it was like being in solitary confinement in prison—alone with my thoughts and memories, with nothing between me and them. The anger and sadness and guilt I'd been trying to keep locked away now burst into the open.

The voice I heard most often in my head was Mrs. Swindell's, repeating like a broken record. *Lazy. Liar. Hypocrite. Can't be trusted. Just like your mother . . . responsible for what happened . . . for the evil. The nuns will find out the truth. They'll see right through you. You won't fool anyone for long.*

I began to agree with the voice. Yes, she was right. I couldn't be trusted. I was to blame for everything that had happened. Even the murders. Surely the reverend mother and novice mistress would see through me and cast me out. Then I truly would have nowhere left to go.

After this week of despair, I was told to make a general confession to prepare for the big day. My confessor was a priest with the Fraternity of Saint Peter, an order allowed by the Vatican to celebrate Mass in Latin. That day, for only the second time in my life, I told someone about my darkest secrets from my life in the midwest.

When I had shared my confidences with Father David, he was sympathetic, but he'd thought it was best to "move on" and put the past behind me. When this new priest heard me out, however, he bowed his head for a long moment. At last he sighed. Now he understood why I was having such difficulties at the convent. "You have to understand, none of this was your fault," he said kindly. "And you need to tell the reverend mother."

I took his advice and saw a look of understanding come upon the old woman's face. It all made sense now, the reverend mother said; I'd done what I had to do to survive.

The confession had several immediate effects. In one way, I felt relieved to be told I wasn't the guilty one. On the other hand, that knowledge gave me a strange feeling of powerlessness. I couldn't shake the feeling that if I *had* been responsible, spending my life in a convent, repenting and demonstrating remorse, would have been a true path to forgiveness and absolution. When it came to *someone else's* sins against me, on the other hand, there was nothing I could do—except to pray that they would repent and seek forgiveness.

And that raised another issue. Almost all of my life I'd been lied to, made to feel responsible for all the bad things that had happened to me and my family. Now that the priest and the reverend mother showed me that none of that was true, the relief I'd felt after confessing was replaced by anger . . . and curiosity. How much of what I'd been told about my family and my past was a lie?

On April 18, 2004, exactly one year after I entered the convent, I arrived at my Day of the Clothing. It was a happy day, full of anticipation. The darkness and confusion that had been hanging over my head seemed about to break at last. .

When a novice becomes professed, she is said to "marry" Jesus; by that token, the Day of the Clothing is her engagement party. The festivities began the night before. The other sisters kept me out of my cell so that they could decorate it with a small altar, a large crucifix on a table draped with burgundy-colored velvet, and a picture of Sister Mary of Jesus Crucified on the wall.

The next day I was given a crown of white and pink roses. A friend of the nuns on the outside ordered us all full meals from Red Lobster. Then the clothing ceremony finally arrived. I traded in my postulant's brown dress, cape, and veil for the full habit, including a cinch, or belt, with a long rosary, and the scapular, a sleeveless outer garment. My hair was shaved off and I was given a wimple—a cloth head-dress that covers the head and neck, a white veil—and sandals for my bare feet.

No vows are taken on the Day of the Clothing. That doesn't happen until three to five years later, when the novice becomes professed; then she promises to be faithful to the order and takes the vows of poverty, chastity, and obedience. But on that day I officially received my new name, Sister Mariam, and hoped that the change of clothing and name would also mean a change in happiness.

Within a week, however, I was being pulled back into the same struggle with depression. It came on gradually at first. I constantly needed rest and started missing the bell to wake up after the noon siesta. Then I'd miss the bell in the morning for prayers and meditation before Mass, a much worse offense. I was so drained that I was unable to function normally, and my lethargy troubled me emotionally, too.

By the end of July things had grown darker. The constant sound of Mrs. Swindell's voice in my head was now joined by outright hallucinations. I saw religious statues turn into black monsters and had to remove a painting of the Virgin Mary from my cell after it suddenly began changing shape, frightening me.

I spent all the time I could outdoors. The reverend mother allowed me to do this, knowing it helped me get away from my troubles. The animals had always been there for me, and here they were again. I spent time with a little Jack Russell terrier that showed up out of nowhere and romped around the fields with the sheep and llamas, and for a little while my fears and worries were tossed to the wind. But I couldn't always be outside, and I couldn't see how I would ever stay happy and rested between four walls.

The only indoor activity that made me happy was music. I played the organ for the convent, and sometimes my violin. I also was trained to make better use of my voice, which helped me fill the otherwise dangerous silences that surrounded me.

But nothing worked for long. Not music. Not being outdoors. Not the psychiatrists or each new antidepressant medication they prescribed. I found myself thinking more and more about suicide. When such moods threatened to overtake me, the reverend mother insisted that I call a suicide hot line.

Then, on the evening of August 8, I got up to get a glass of warm milk, which along with warm showers had been suggested by the mental-health experts. When I reached the dimly lit restaurant-style kitchen, I saw that the whole room had been cleaned and everything put away, except for a large knife that lay next to the sink.

Walking over, I reached out and picked up the knife. It was not in my nature to give up. I'd fought for life and happiness since the age of three, but I was sick and tired of it all. Suddenly, I was consumed with the urge to plunge the blade into my chest.

Then, out of the corner of my eye, I saw something dark move in the hallway outside the kitchen. This time, though, it wasn't a shadow. It was a nun in her black habit on her way to her room. Her appearance startled me—brought me back to my senses as if I'd been dreaming. I put the knife down and ran to tell the reverend mother what had happened. If that sister hadn't walked by at that moment, I said, I might have killed myself.

The reverend mother told me to call the suicide hot line again. The social worker asked me how I was feeling on a scale of one to ten, with ten being the worst.

"Nine," I said. I was ready to finish this horrible life I'd been given.

Calmly, the man asked me to hand the phone to the reverend mother. "You have to get her to a hospital immediately," he told her. "She needs to be under twenty-four-hour watch."

The reverend mother didn't hesitate. Once more the

novice mistress escorted me to the hospital, where I was admitted to the psychiatric ward. I'd worn my novitiate habit, but they stripped me of everything, including my rosary, the straight pins used to secure the tunic, and my belt—anything I could use to hurt myself. Then they put me in a room with glass on two sides and a night-light on at all times so that they could see me.

It took four days, but gradually I felt my sanity return. The psychiatrists adjusted my medications, explaining that recent studies suggested antidepressants might actually increase suicidal tendencies in some teenagers. The new medication they gave me seemed to work much better.

Perhaps more important, sound returned to my life. In the hospital I could actually talk to other patients, and interacting with them at group meetings I learned even more about the issues I was dealing with, as well as meeting people who faced their own challenges. I was also able to watch television and movies, and was encouraged to get as much rest as I wanted. And I wanted a lot.

I actually enjoyed my time on the ward—except on the afternoon of the third day, when a nurse called me to the phone. It was Mrs. Swindell. "Oh my God, Cecilia, what happened?" she said. I told her I'd been going through a major depression. And that I'd tried explaining it to her when I was twelve years old, but she didn't want to listen.

Then I told her about the things the doctors believed were behind my depression: the unaddressed trauma of what had happened in Sonoma; the emotional abuse I'd suffered at the Swindells'; the secrets I'd shared with no one but my doctors and the sisters and priests.

She exploded. "How *dare you* say such things! You're an impure little girl! It was all your own fault. And now you're trying to blame everybody else!" By the time she was done, I was in tears. I held the phone away from my ear, and even the nurses could hear her. Finally, I had enough. Sobbing, I turned to the nurses and said I wanted nothing more to do with the Swindells. One of the nurses gently took the phone from me and told me to go lie down. She would handle it from there.

On my sixth day at the ward, the reverend mother and the novice mistress came to visit. They brought me a box of chocolates and flowers. They sat down and we talked about how I was doing.

After a while I asked, "Am I going back?" My mental health was better, and I'd begun to think about returning to the convent. My new medications had stabilized my condition, and I had a new understanding of my issues and how to deal with them.

But it wasn't to be. With a sad face, the reverend mother said, "You can't come back. We did all we could for you, but our schedule and life isn't for you, dear. We will always be here if you decide later on to return to us. But we all agreed that you need to continue your healing, and we think that can be done best outside the convent."

I waited until they left, and then I burst into tears.

I was alone. Terrifyingly, completely alone.

Thirty

My sudden departure from the convent and admission to the psychiatric ward caused an uproar in TFP. But it had more to do with my accusations leveled at the Swindells than with any concern for my well-being.

After my mental health stabilized, I called the people in the TFP organization I considered friends, or at least those I thought might help. But I made the mistake of telling them what I'd told the two priests, the reverend mother and the novice mistress, and the psychiatrists at the psych ward. But no one in the group wanted to believe me. And even those who thought there might be something to it suggested that I was at least partly to blame.

I had no idea where I was going to go when the hospital released me. The Swindells invited me back to live with them, but to me that seemed like an attempt to keep me under wraps. I'd just be another TFP spinster with no voice, no freedom, and no future.

I considered calling Grandpa. But ever since I was three or four, the Swindells had been telling me he didn't care about me. He'd given me up for adoption; he'd only visited once a year. Even when I was at the convent, he wrote me only once or twice. I didn't think I even had a family anymore.

I was just eighteen years old, completely naïve about living in the world, and it looked like I was about to end up on the street. I had no friends. No money. Not even a high school diploma to help me get a job.

Then Father David called. He'd been the first one I'd told about the Swindells, and I had hoped that he might back me up. But he wasn't interested in dwelling on the past. He did tell me, however, that his sister owned a working ranch in Idaho that took in troubled teenage girls. Normally she didn't accept anyone over seventeen, and she charged fifteen hundred dollars a week. But he'd persuaded her to let me live there for now.

The ranch was billed as a residential treatment center "in the middle of God's Creation" for young Christian women with behavioral problems and addictions. These issues would be resolved on the ranch, according to their literature, by placing the girls in a "safe, loving environment," removed from the bad influences and peer pressure of modern life. They would be taught to coexist with other young women like themselves, as well as counselors, the ranch animals, and the Great Outdoors.

Father David only knew what he'd been told about the ranch—that it was a place for kids with drug and alcohol problems or extreme anger issues, hard-core girls whose parents couldn't handle them. But there were horses and mountains, and if everything worked out, there was a chance I could become a staff member. It sounded perfect.

I accepted the offer eagerly. The bishop at the local diocese even paid my plane fare. Eight days after my admission to the psychiatric ward, I landed at an airport in Idaho. I had everything I owned in the world with me—three cardboard boxes containing the few secular clothes I still owned, the letters I'd received at the convent, my own writings, some books, and my violin.

Father David's sister and her husband, Susan and Ray Holt, met me at the airport and loaded me into their car for the drive back to the God's Cowgirls Ranch. They said they were just hardworking rancher types; Susan was into horses, which excited me, while Ray handled the ranch business and took care of the equipment. They asked me a lot of questions about my past, and they seemed nice enough.

The ranch property was everything I imagined it would be. It stretched for miles in every direction, surrounded by mountains and occupied by beautiful horses. The living quarters seemed nice, too—simple log cabins with plenty of space around them.

Right away, though, there were hints that this wasn't going to be a vacation. Soon after we arrived, my three boxes were confiscated, taken to the owners' house "for safekeeping." They let me keep the large crucifix I'd brought to the convent, but little else. Their implication was that the other girls couldn't be trusted not to steal my things. But I soon realized that many of the rules—including a ban on jewelry and personal clothing—had another purpose: to create conformity.

I was introduced to the "team captains," or counselors. But I was surprised to notice that the introductions didn't extend as far as the other residents, seven girls who were sitting around outside the main cabin reading from a spiral-bound notebook.

Telling me to wait outside with the other girls, the Holts went inside one of the cabins with the counselors. Shy and socially awkward, I sat near several of the girls, wondering how to start a conversation. I hoped one of them would say something, but none of them seemed particularly interested in me. Finally, the silence was too much.

"So what's it like here?" I asked the girl nearest me.

All the girls glanced up when I spoke, then looked back down at their reading material without answering. So I asked if there were any rules I should be aware of.

Again the girls looked up and then back down. But the

one closest to me held up the thin binder she was studying and whispered, "Read the book."

I looked at the title: *God's Cowgirls Manual*. I started to say something again but was cut off.

"We're not supposed to talk," the other girl whispered.

Before I could ask any more questions, the cabin door opened and Mrs. Holt invited me inside. There I was told to strip out of my skirt and blouse; from that point on, I was only to wear the ranch "uniform"—blue jeans, T-shirts, special work boots, and, during cold weather, a hooded sweatshirt.

"Okay," I said. "Is there a room where I can change?"

"Just do it right here," Susan Holt replied.

Not knowing what else to do, I stripped down to my underwear. Nervous and embarrassed, I wondered what was next.

"What size pants are you?" one of the female counselors asked.

Four sets of jaws dropped when I said I didn't know. I'd never worn pants before. So they guessed.

"You need to take off your underwear, too," another woman said.

"What?" I didn't understand why I was being put through this. I was bashful about my body. Nudity was frowned upon in the Swindell house. I hadn't even bathed in front of Mrs. Swindell since early childhood, and the sisters at the convent showered in private.

"You can't have any clothes of your own—camp rules," replied the woman. "We'll provide your underwear, too."

"I've never undressed in front of anyone," I pleaded. "I just came from a *convent*!" But they gave me no choice.

After stripping down in front of the assembled counselors and putting on my new uniform, I was sent back outside, humiliated. I thought things couldn't get any worse. But I was wrong.

A couple of hours later, I asked a nearby counselor if I could use the bathroom. She smiled as if she'd just been asked to play a game, then ran inside one of the cabins and emerged with Mrs. Holt, who told the other team captains to call all the girls together.

When they'd gathered, Mrs. Holt announced, "Okay, everybody. We have a new team member who wants to use the bathroom, and we all know what happens." She turned to me. "It's time to initiate you to the ranch and how we do things here." Everyone's eyes turned to a five-gallon white bucket sitting next to a shed wall.

Only then did I understand what was required. I was going to have to urinate in the bucket in front of the others: seven girls, three team leaders, and the owner.

Later, I learned that the purpose of the bucket—as well as other humiliating experiences at the ranch—was to break a girl down so that the Holts and the counselors could "build her back up" their way. But that wasn't what I needed. I wasn't some angry kid with a drug or alcohol problem. I hadn't been in trouble with the law. I'd already *been* broken down. I needed a hand up.

There were some tough girls on the ranch. Violent, angry girls. Some of them had lived on the streets. Others had juvenile records. But none would prove tougher than me.

We were divided, or ranked, into four levels. Those in level one, like me, were usually new; we had few privileges and weren't trusted. At the top were the level-four girls; most of them had spent a long time at the ranch, had seen the errors of their ways, conformed their behavior, and thus enjoyed more privileges and trust.

All I needed to know to progress up the levels, I was told, was contained in the *God's Cowgirls Manual*. "While you're here," they'd say, "the manual is your Bible. Study it. No excuses."

The ranch was run by the manual's rules and regulations. Level ones, twos, and threes were not allowed to talk to one another unless an owner, counselor, or sometimes a level four was present to monitor the conversation. We were to complete our chores without exception. We were to do what we were told by the Holts, the counselors, and the higher-level girls, no questions asked. And we were to attend Mass every morning at a nearby Catholic church.

The food we were given was good and healthy. A breakfast of cream of wheat or oatmeal—except on the weekend, when there would be cereal with yogurt, or eggs—then for lunch a piece of fruit or occasionally a sandwich, followed by a hearty dinner that could range from hamburgers to Italian or Mexican cuisine. But it wasn't much, considering all the work we had to do. Our day began at 6 A.M., when we'd get up, brush our teeth, eat breakfast, and get ready to go to Mass. When we could, we cleaned and swept our sleeping cabins, or fed the animals, before we left.

Mass was at seven o'clock, and by eight we were back at the ranch to resume our chores. As Father David had told me, it was a working ranch and the girls were the workers. We fed the animals—though only level fours were allowed to pet them. We cleared rocks from fields, built fences, moved irrigation pipes, helped with the haying, and did any other ranch work that needed to be done.

At noon we returned to the main cabin for lunch. Then, after a short break, we went back to work—this time at a neighbor's ranch. At the end of each long day we returned to the Holts' for dinner, schoolwork, more chores, and then bed.

The level-three and -four girls were allowed to go to bed right after dinner. However, the level ones and twos, often nearly asleep on our feet, had to wait until the counselors had finished their paperwork at 10 P.M.

The general philosophy behind the ranch seemed to be to break us down—by working us to exhaustion and by intimidating or humiliating us if we were unable to keep up. There were no excuses for not pulling one's weight, and not much understanding or sympathy for those deep-rooted issues like my lingering depression.

The counselors piled so many chores on me that I was

scolded almost every day for not completing them—and then given even more chores the next day. It was a recipe for failure, and with each scolding my feelings of hopelessness only deepened.

Unfortunately, the Holts thought the best therapy for depression was to work me even harder. Exertion was better than medicine, they said. So instead of riding in the pickup truck to and from the fields, they made me run in front of the truck—sometimes for several miles. If I stumbled and fell, they'd honk the horn and yell, "Get up, drama queen!" Tears would well in my eyes, but I never let them see me cry.

I fought back by refusing to be intimidated and by committing small acts of rebellion. I drank a lot of water during the day to stay hydrated, which also meant going to the bathroom in the middle of the night. The problem was, the cabin door was rigged so that the lights went on when it was opened, waking everyone else—and requiring one of the level-three or -four girls to get up and go with me, because level ones weren't allowed to go to the bathroom without an escort. They told me to stop it, but I kept it up—so they bought me adult diapers and told me I'd have to wear them if I couldn't sleep through the night without waking them up.

The harder the Holts and the counselors tried to break me, the more I resisted. I was no rookie when it came to handling verbal abuse; I'd been dealing with it most of my life, letting cruel and angry words go in one ear and out the other, then crying later when no one could see or hear me. When it came to authority figures, I just smiled and shrugged when they said something mean, which irritated them even more.

As with the Swindells, not every moment at the ranch was torture. We sometimes got to watch movies, including all three of the *Lord of the Rings* trilogy in a Thanksgiving Day marathon. We even took a field trip to a retreat in North Dakota that also hosted members of a similar Christian boys' camp. It was the first time in my life I'd been able to socialize with "normal" teenage boys who weren't members of a TFP family. It was exciting and fun.

But the good times were few and far between. The thing I looked forward to most every week was visiting with the ranch psychologist, a young woman in her forties who was paid by the Holts to talk with each girl every Thursday. Finally, I had someone I could talk to on a regular basis about what I was going through and how my traumatic past was affecting me.

When I was first introduced at the ranch, I'd been asked to tell everyone a little about myself. As I told my story, looks of shock and sympathy appeared on the other girls' faces. As rough as some of them were, none of them had had their families murdered or their throats cut by their father. Many of them did have bad family lives, had even been abused, but no one else had been so isolated that she saw joining a convent as her only way out.

For a week or so after that, the other girls had treated me especially well. At weekly sessions, when we were encouraged to discuss one another's faults—in effect to "tattle" on one another—they laid off me.

The Holts and the counselors must have noticed that I was being treated differently, because one day they started insisting that the other girls stop letting me slide. "The past is the past," Mr. Holt said. "She's not here because of the past. You shouldn't treat her any differently than any other girl."

Nor were the Holts or counselors sympathetic when I tried to explain how my upbringing was causing my mood swings. They didn't believe a word we girls said—especially us level ones. Nothing I tried to tell the Holts or the counselors mattered; whatever I said, they thought I was lying. They'd take my words, chop them up and rearrange them, then say, "See? You're not making any sense. You totally contradicted yourself."

I wasn't surprised when I learned that the Holts were becoming friends with the Swindells, talking to them frequently by phone. In the entire time I was at the ranch, the only communication I was allowed to have with the outside world was a letter from Mrs. Swindell.

The only person who understood me was the psychologist. I told her everything that had happened to me. I hid nothing, including the fact that I didn't think the ranch was helping me. But there was little she could do about my circumstances; she just encouraged me to keep going, to keep improving myself.

Exactly what I was supposed to improve was the question. I hadn't been sent to the ranch because I'd done something wrong. I'd just come from a *convent,* after all. I'd spent my entire life isolated from the outside world. I'd never kissed a boy, never done drugs, never missed curfew or shown up at home drunk and belligerent. Yet here I was, being treated like I'd been convicted of a crime and sent to a prison farm.

I'd accepted the offer to go to the ranch because I had nowhere else to go. I'd hoped to have a home in the mountains, surrounded by vast fields where horses ran free. If I liked it, I thought I might someday be offered a job there, helping other young, traumatized women. At the very least, I hoped to find a comforting voice there, a place to heal, a place where the dark shadows of my past couldn't follow me. Instead it was another dead end.

But it wasn't the way I was treated that finally pushed me to make another change in my life. It was the mistreatment of one of the other girls. At twelve years of age, little Rachel was the youngest child at the ranch. She was angry and tough, with a wisecrack to answer just about any question or command, and she was already using drugs.

I identified with Rachel from the start. Like me, she'd been adopted, and much of her anger was directed at her adoptive parents. And like me, she resisted the ranch's efforts to break her.

Though she got into trouble constantly, Rachel's biggest transgression was stealing food. She never got enough to eat at regular mealtimes, nor could she seem to stop herself from sneaking into the pantry or refrigerator, no matter how much trouble it brought down on her thin shoulders.

I understood why she was hungry. Food at the convent had been plentiful, and with the sisters constantly encouraging me to eat, I'd gained a lot of weight there. But at the ranch we were kept on what was essentially a subsistence diet. Between that and all the work we did, I lost the pounds I'd gained at the convent. But Rachel was a growing girl, and all the work made her ravenous. She kept sneaking food, and she kept getting caught and punished.

At first Mrs. Holt and the counselors dealt with Rachel's behavior by taking away her few privileges; then they started adding more chores. When that didn't work, they made her run in front of the truck on the way to the fields—and, eventually, to run the two-mile length of the driveway—every morning before they'd pick her up in the van to go to church.

And still she stole food. So they put her on a "bland diet": cold cream of wheat in the morning, and boiled spinach or garbanzo beans, straight out of the can, the rest of the day. When that didn't work, they started locking her in a cabin by herself at night, cut off from everybody. Then, when she was sleeping, a counselor or one of the level-four girls would wake her every three or four hours by pouring cold water on her face. After that she'd have to get up and do push-ups or wall sits.

Finally, they'd had enough. At one of the weekly "tattle" meetings on "God's Cowgirls Day," the counselors asked the other girls if Rachel's food thefts affected them.

Yeah, the others said, they hurt everyone. I agreed with them; I didn't know our verdict was going to lead to anything more than another scolding for Rachel. But then the counselors told us all to head outside to a nearby hill, and said each of us had to return with a rock that symbolized how much Rachel's behavior hurt us.

Thinking this was just a bizarre symbolic gesture, I went to the hillside with the other girls and the counselors and returned with a rock. Mine wasn't very big, but some of the other girls brought small boulders they could hardly lift.

The counselors piled the rocks in the main cabin, where the meeting would take place. Then Mrs. Holt held up a large backpack. "The other girls are sick and tired of carrying your burden," she told Rachel. "From now on, you're going to carry it."

With that, she and the counselors filled the pack with as many rocks as it could hold. I took one look at the pack and knew that, as strong as I was at eighteen, even I would have had a hard time lifting it. But they said that until she changed her ways, Rachel would have to carry the pack—strapped to her front—wherever she went.

As Rachel looked at the pack and began to cry, the psychologist walked in. I often thought she disapproved of some of the methods used at the ranch, but she never said anything about it. Nor did she now, though the shock was clear on her face. Instead she just looked down at the floor and shook her head. "I'm leaving," she muttered. "Good luck, girls."

The next morning Rachel showed up wearing the pack as required. A collar was also placed around her neck, attached to a leash tied around the waist of one of the level-four girls. Then the older girl began to run in front of the truck with Rachel struggling to keep up. At one point the little girl stumbled and fell, crying out when she scraped her knees. But even as bloodstains appeared on her pants, she was forced to struggle back to her feet and keep running.

Later I tried to console her. I knew Rachel needed a friendly voice, and I thought maybe with a little counseling she might give in a bit, stop stealing, maybe go along with some of the rules. But one of the other girls saw me talking to Rachel without a counselor present and reported me. I was punished by being sent off on an hourlong run and forced to write "The Truth Shall Set You Free" 150 times every day for a week.

What was being done to the girls at that ranch amounted

to torture and abuse. And I'd had enough of that to last a lifetime. Three months after arriving at the ranch, I decided it was time to go.

It turned out that the Holts and the counselors were thinking along the same lines. I was called into the main office, where they told me that my attitude had kept me from "progressing" past level one. So now they were giving me an ultimatum: I could either start cooperating or leave. "You're eighteen," they said. "We really can't force you to stay." But it was December, they pointed out, and it was getting cold outside. If I left, I'd have to leave my ranch uniform behind; I could take only the possessions I could carry. Not only that, I'd have to walk; they wouldn't even give me a ride to the end of the driveway, much less the nearest town.

I think it was a test, and they expected me to cave in. They knew I had nowhere else to go, and no money to get me anywhere. But I was tired of the treatment and sickened by what happened to Rachel. I was determined to leave. But where would I go? I was in the same predicament I'd been in three months earlier.

Then, suddenly, I thought of Grandpa.

He only lived a few hours' drive away in Montana where he'd moved. "I want you to call my grandpa and ask him to come get me," I said.

The others looked shocked. "Well, if we do that," Mrs. Holt replied, "and he doesn't come for you tomorrow, you're out anyway."

I said I'd take my chances. And I stuck to my decision when they drew up a contract stating that if I left the ranch, I would be going without any money, with no clothes except what I'd brought, and I would not be given a ride. I signed it and left them to make the call.

The next day was a tense one. Hour after hour passed with no sign of my grandfather. What would happen if he didn't come?

Finally, at about five o'clock, I looked over at the ranch headquarters and saw a familiar car. Grandpa had arrived.

By the time I reached the building, the Holts had my possessions ready to go, including a stack of mail they'd received for me but never opened or given me. I hugged my grandfather gratefully, and we got into his car and drove off.

Soon we were headed to Montana, and I started talking my head off. As Grandpa and his second wife, Edna, listened, I chattered away as if I'd just discovered the gift of speech. The Swindells had kept me isolated, the convent had kept me silent, and the girls' ranch had tried to shut me up. Now I was making up for lost time.

Thirty-one

After my escape from the girls' ranch, Grandpa took me into his home in Montana. It was my very first taste of freedom.

Montana wouldn't be the final stop in my journey, but it was an important step along the way. It was where I got my first job outside the home, washing and grooming dogs, picking the trade up quickly, as if I'd been doing it for years. It was where I went to my first non-Christian rock concert, where I learned to use a computer and discovered the wonders of the Internet. It was where I got my first car and had my first car accident. It was where I smoked my first cigarette, where I kissed my first boy, and where he became my first lover. It all happened quickly, but I was trying to cram five years of adolescence into eight months.

In all the years I'd been away, I had never really been allowed to talk much to my grandfather. Now I was glad to get to know him at last, to hear him tell his story himself instead of the Swindells' version. He told me how he'd fought for custody of me, rather than abandoning me to the state—

or even to the custody of my father. (Despite everything he had done, my father's rights as a parent weren't automatically retracted.) Soon after my dad was captured, his defense lawyer, Marteen Miller, had stated publicly that he wouldn't interfere on behalf of his client with Grandpa's effort to gain custody. But then, apparently, Dad had had a change of heart and decided he wanted me to live with his relatives in Mexico. He filed for custody—forcing Grandpa to get a lawyer to battle both the state *and* Ramón.

My grieving grandfather then had to go to the courtroom and pass within five feet of my father. Grandpa was a little guy; he was terrified of my father, even as Dad sat there handcuffed and surrounded by large deputies. Through most of the hearing he avoided looking at my father, he told me now—but once, in an unguarded moment, he glanced up and into Ramón's eyes. My father didn't smile, he said, or scowl or nod or attempt to mouth any words. Instead he just stared at Grandpa, and that frightened him even more.

My own feelings about my grandfather were mixed. I loved him as my grandfather; I was filled with gratitude to him for rescuing me from the ranch, and now for all that I learned he'd done for me as a child. In a practical sense, I also understood that he felt putting me up for adoption was the best option. But I believe he could have made a better choice. He could have placed me with family, like Grandma Louise's relatives or my uncles. Or at least he could have looked beyond TFP, which I consider a cult, and tried to find a loving family to raise me. I resented the fact that he seemed to leave me behind when he left Sonoma County, abandoning me to fend for myself. He tried to explain his own emotional state, but his excuses didn't explain why he visited so seldom.

Grandpa did surprise me when he asked if I knew what had happened to the nearly $150,000 he said he'd given to the Swindells—my portion of the money from the trust fund that had been donated after the murders. I didn't; it had never been discussed. So I called Mrs. Swindell and asked her about the money.

There was a slight pause. Then she said, "It's gone." She said they'd spent it all on me. "We fed you, clothed you, gave you a roof over your head. You are so ungrateful!"

The story of the trust fund got me thinking again about an idea I first had when I found the newspaper clippings about the murders and had come back to many times in the years since: I wanted to go back to Sonoma County. And I wanted to know the truth about what happened to my family.

In 2005 I asked my grandfather whether he'd be willing to bring me back to Sonoma, and he agreed. We arrived in town in April, shortly after my nineteenth birthday. I hadn't been there since I was three years old, so Grandpa acted as my tour guide—though, as we approached my childhood home on Baines Avenue, my memory kicked in and I told him where to turn.

Obviously things had changed a lot in the little town of Sonoma since I'd last been there. But there was a spirit and a presence that would never change. I will always feel that family presence in Sonoma—like a ghost that's not at rest. I feel it every time I pass close by a place where someone was killed.

Driving from Sonoma to the Calvary Catholic Cemetery, we passed the Petaluma dump. There was nothing special about the turnoff; no memorial or roadside marker to say that I and my sisters were savagely attacked by my dad there. It's just a gravel road among the rolling hills leading to a ravine. Yet as we approached I felt as if I was being sucked in, and as we went by I felt something trying to prevent me from escaping.

Grandpa pointed it out, but he wouldn't stop. "We don't want to go there."

We did stop at the cemetery. I felt such peace there and wanted to stay. Finally Grandpa had to take me by the hand and say, "Let's go."

* * *

After about a year with my grandfather in Montana, I realized that I needed to continue my journey. Grandpa wasn't any more prepared to deal with an eighteen-year-old who was going through culture shock than he'd been to deal with a three-year-old child whose father had tried to kill her.

The tragedy still weighed heavily on him. He'd see me standing in the kitchen and forget and call me Angela. Then he'd cry when he realized his mistake. He had changed a lot from his days in Sonoma—among other things, he was no longer a member of TFP—but he was still pretty strict and conservative. After the initial glow of our reunion wore off, he and I fought a lot over my growing independence. I knew that it was time, once again, to move on.

It was around this time that I started using my birth name again. Carmina was the name my mother had given me, and it had been taken away—like my past and my trust fund—by the Swindells. Even my grandpa called me Cecilia. Using Carmina was a way to reclaim my past and my family, especially my mother, who loved me.

Ever since I visited Sonoma with Grandpa, I'd been thinking about the past. I knew the Swindells had lied to me about my mother's family. Now I wanted to find out the truth. So I jumped at an offer from my uncles Lewis and Robert to come live with them in the mobile home they shared in Sacramento, about an hour's drive northeast of Sonoma.

Both of them were angry with my grandfather for giving me up for adoption. And even more so when I told them how I'd been mistreated. "We knew something was wrong when you never responded to our letters or seemed to get our presents," said Lewis, the more talkative of the two. "After a while, we stopped sending things, figuring you probably weren't getting them." The two of them had visited me that first year, but after they left TFP they no longer felt welcome at the Swindells'—especially Lewis, who had married outside the church and then divorced. The Swindells said he was "on a downward spiral to hell."

For two bachelor uncles and their nineteen-year-old niece, out in the world for the first time, living together presented challenges. Yet we were family, something I'd once thought was lost to me forever. And they helped me get to know other family members as well, even taking me to southern Oregon to meet their mother's mother, my great-grandmother.

"Oh my gosh," the old woman greeted me warmly, "how we've been wondering about you all this time."

Freedom in my grandfather's little ranching town in Montana was one thing. Freedom in California's capital city was another. Going to the neighborhood gas station for candy or a snack seemed like an adventure. The wonders of Wal-Mart were within walking distance, and I even had a bicycle to tool around town on. For the first time in my life, I didn't have someone telling me what to do all the time. My uncles left me alone to adjust, which meant sleeping late, coming and going as I pleased, and turning in when I wanted to—though with a lot of grousing from Robert if I made too much noise at night.

I'd discovered computers and the Internet in Montana. Now I had just about free rein on my uncles' desktop—until one day Robert discovered that I'd been reading about witchcraft and the Wicca religion online. He flipped out until Lewis, the peacemaker, calmed him down and reminded him that, after so many years of oppression, I needed my space.

Much more interesting than reading about alternative religious cults, though, was the prospect of using the Internet to meet boys. For the most part, it was harmless fun. If I got a good feeling from someone I met online, I would agree to meet him at a local coffee shop. Sometimes that led to a second date, sometimes not. I knew that meeting men this way was risky, though I was probably a little naïve about the dangers. But I wasn't stupid: When one guy tried to get me to meet him late one night in a park, I knew better.

Not that I didn't make mistakes. One guy met me at a pizza joint and gave me a dozen roses. The flowers were a nice gesture, but it wasn't long before I starting getting a bad vibe, like he wasn't completely sane. I decided not to see him again, but he wouldn't leave me alone. He kept calling and sending me text messages and e-mails telling me how much he loved me and promising to get me anything I wanted. I tried to tell him it just wasn't going to work out, but that made no difference to him. At last I lied and told him that I had a new boyfriend and to "leave me the hell alone."

"I'm going to kill you," he messaged me back.

I threatened to call the police if he didn't stop. But he wrote back that his mother was a police officer, so he wouldn't get into any trouble.

Tired of being pushed around, I filed a police report. He didn't contact me again.

My uncles worried about me and the risks I was taking. But Lewis knew I had a lot of catching up to do—and that I wasn't going to listen if they simply told me not to do something. In fact, after what I'd been through with the Swindells and at the girls' ranch, it usually had the opposite effect. "She's going to make mistakes," he told his brother. "But she's strong. She's held her own this far. She'll survive."

Eventually, I got bored with just surviving. As I met new friends and talked about my life, many of them—after recovering from the shock—told me I ought to write a book about my experiences.

Before I could do that, though, I would have to learn what I didn't know.

I went to the library and started looking up old newspaper articles—the initial reporting on the murders and the coverage of my father's trials. Although this added a lot to what I'd learned from the clippings in the Swindells' garage, press clippings only went so far. I wanted to know more about my family and what happened to them from their neighbors and friends. But nobody in Sonoma even knew I existed anymore. The last thing they'd heard was that I'd been adopted by a "wealthy family" in the midwest.

In October 2005, I decided it was time to let them know I hadn't been lost forever. I knew that KRON, the San Jose TV channel, had covered the story pretty extensively at the time. So I called to see if they'd be interested in doing an update. The very next day, the station manager sent a crew, including reporter Don Knapp, up to Sacramento to interview me. For the next hour, as the camera rolled, Knapp led me through the story—and allowed himself to be led by me.

It was clear that he'd expected me to be some wigged-out victim, too unstable to tell my story reliably. After all, I'd told the station manager I could recall the horrible things my dad did to me and my sisters in great detail. How could anybody remember all that—from the age of three—without being at least a little crazy? But Knapp was easygoing, and with his guidance we soon developed a comfortable rapport. I felt competent, even confident, in holding up my end of the conversation. If he asked a question I was obviously uncomfortable answering, he backed off.

But there wasn't much I didn't talk about. I recalled everything I could about the day of the crimes, from watching my father slit my sisters' throats to his attack on me and my struggle to survive in the dump. I didn't go into much detail, but I did say that my life after leaving Sonoma had not been good. Still, I insisted that I was ready to move on, and mentioned that I was working on a book about my life. I said that I hoped that the interview would help put me in contact with people who had known my family.

The most surprising moment of the interview came near the end, when Knapp asked me what I was going to do next.

I said that I hoped to visit Ramón in San Quentin State

Prison. I looked into the camera and said that I'd forgiven him. I wanted to tell him so, face-to-face, in the near future. What I didn't say was that my forgiveness hinged on whether he would be truly remorseful and contrite—falling to his knees to beg my pardon for all the evil he had done to me and my family, as I'd imagined in my childhood.

Two days after the interview, "Carmina Salcido Returns to Sonoma" aired as the lead story on the evening news. I thought it would be featured, but I was surprised at the prominence and the time they gave it—nearly fifteen minutes of the thirty-minute newscast. And then they ran the entire thirty-five-minute interview the next morning.

The response was more than I ever hoped it would be. The people in the Bay Area, and especially Sonoma County, had not forgotten me, though they'd heard little or nothing of me for more than sixteen years. And they wanted to welcome me back.

The station's switchboard lit up as soon as the story aired. And they were flooded with e-mail messages for me; those that were deemed safe enough were passed on to me. (I used the name Goldendove as an e-mail address, in reference to the gilded bird that had hung in the convent chapel.)

One of those who saw the KRON interview was Chris Smith, the *Press Democrat* columnist. He'd never forgotten the Salcido murders, and like so many others he'd wondered what had become of me. As the *Press Democrat* noted in an earlier anniversary issue recounting the history of crimes in Sonoma County, the Polly Klaas kidnap-murder case may have had farther-reaching consequences—it was because of Richard Allen Davis that the California legislature had passed a three-strike law requiring that criminals convicted of three felonies be sentenced to life without parole. Yet for those people who had been in the county during my dad's killing spree—including journalists such as Smith and

Randi Rossmann—my father's crimes stood out as the end of an idyllic era for Sonoma.

A short time later, Smith asked to interview me himself. On the morning he was scheduled to meet me, he asked Rossmann if she wanted to go along. The Salcido and Klaas murders had been two of the biggest stories of her career, and she'd handled them well. But he also knew that Rossmann, who now had children of her own, had been greatly affected by the murders, as well as the other tragedies she covered over more than a dozen years. She had finally asked to get off the police beat after interviewing a mother and father whose daughter had just died in a car crash along with her husband and two young children. She didn't want to ask anyone else what it was like to lose a loved one and wait until they had finished crying for the answer. She would have been fascinated to meet me, she told Smith, but she declined. She was reluctant to revisit that part of her past.

The next day, when Smith's article appeared, it opened another floodgate of responses. Some wrote to say that they admired my "courage." Others wondered how I could possibly think about forgiving my father. Many wrote that they were saddened to hear that my life had been rough after leaving Sonoma but were glad that I'd returned. "Over the years we have wondered if you were happy and if all was well," one family wrote. "[We are] so sorry for your struggles since leaving Sonoma County. After what happened to you as a baby, nothing dark should have ever touched you again." Another woman told me that her daughter had been eight years old at the time of the murders. "Something changed for me after what happened to your family," she wrote. "You became all mothers' daughters that day."

Several e-mails arrived from people who had worked at Petaluma Volley Hospital when I was there—including David Lopez, the big security guard, who wrote to tell me about the role he'd played as my protector, and how he'd cried when I left the hospital.

When Dr. Linda Beatie read Smith's column, she wrote

to tell him about her own memories. He passed her letter on to me:

I was the anesthesiologist on call at Petaluma Valley Hospital that day when Carmina was brought in from the dump. People always say they remember a terrible experience as if it were yesterday. I think I do.

Afterward I told my story to anyone who would listen, about how I had to give anesthesia to Carmina so Dr. Dennis MacLeod could explore the neck wound, about how I was so afraid she would die during the induction after she had clung to life for two days while she lay in the dump. I talked about how the nurses took her picture for evidence with a Polaroid camera in the ER. I will never forget Carmina's smile for the camera.

Dr. Beatie also included a personal note for me:

It seems from what I read in the Press Democrat that your life has never been easy. Thanks for giving me this opportunity to tell you what happened that afternoon from my point of view. I hope you find happiness and peace.

Linda Beatie, M.D.

Pat Rile was working in her dress store when her son called to tell her that the daughter of her former student was about to appear on the evening news. She hadn't talked about Angela or the murders in years; she'd been terrified that my father would come after her if he ever got out of prison, and her husband discouraged her from talking about it. But her husband had died recently, and she decided to watch the broadcast.

When Pat saw the interview, she later told me, she was

struck by how much I resembled my mother—not just in looks, but in my laugh and the way I held myself before the camera. Tracking me down through Chris Smith, she told me she had saved two things for me from all those years ago, thinking that I might want them someday. One was the polka-dotted midriff blouse my mom had worn at the fashion show. The other was a videotape of the show, showing my mother walking the runway, talking to the other models, and laughing in the background.

It was the first time I had seen my mother except in a still photograph, or heard her talk and laugh, since I was three years old.

A couple of weeks after the TV interview, I received an e-mail in Spanish from someone in Los Mochis, Mexico—my uncle Jose Leopoldo "Polo" Salcido Borjorquez. I had to have it translated:

Hello Carmina Cecilia,

We hope to God that you are healthy and that God Our Lord will at least let us know that you are in good health. The people who are in contact with the Salcido family have informed us about your project and we are pleased for you to talk about it.

I want you to know that with all due respect to you and your whole family nobody not even your own father says anything to us nor do we talk with him about what happened in your family.

I met you when you were little and your family and your grandparents, and especially your mother Angela. She was always a wonderful person and I am sure that you are proud of her. She always loved you all, protected you, and struggled for a better life for all of you. I want you to know that I too feel badly and that I feel in a way committed to you for not being able to change the course of life.

Today is a great day because we think often of you and I would be grateful to you and would like it if you would permit us to see you.

We love you very much.
Polo Salcido

I could hardly believe the change in my fortunes. A year earlier, I'd been turned out of a convent, alone and afraid, and sent off to live in an environment of humiliation, degradation, and physical exhaustion. I considered myself an orphan, unwanted and unloved. Yet here I was now, living with my two caring uncles, back in touch with my grandfather and his wife's family—and yet another part of my family, in Mexico, was writing to say they loved me and wanted to see me.

It was more than I could have hoped for.

In 1999, Mike Brown was promoted to captain in charge of the Administration Division. Then, in 2006, after thirty-one years of serving his community, he retired. At the time, he was looking forward to forgetting the hundreds of homicides, and thousands of other violent crimes, he'd investigated in his career, turning his attention to restoring vintage cars and spending time with his wife, Arlyn. (She deserved it. A few years before, when he'd made captain—getting him off the streets and out of harm's way—she'd told him she could finally stop being afraid that someday he wouldn't come home.)

Chris Smith's article made Mike's day. For years he'd wondered how I was doing, almost absently saying a little prayer for me each time he did. The article answered some of the questions that he'd had, though not all of them, and some of what he read about the life I'd led troubled him. When he saw that I was thinking of writing a book, he thought about contacting me. But the thought dredged up unpleasant memories, and he hesitated for several weeks, unsure whether it was a good idea for him emotionally to go over that ground again. Finally, on November 7, he e-mailed me:

> *Hello Carmina,*
>
> *My name is Mike Brown. I was the sergeant in charge of the Violent Crimes Investigations Unit and the Crime Scene Investigations Unit and supervised the entire investigation regarding your family.*
>
> *I went to each and every crime scene and also went to Mexico to bring Ramón back to California to stand trial. I was also in the hospital emergency room while you were being treated by the doctors.*
>
> *Myself and my detectives worked very hard on this case and when we would get tired from lack of sleep or just overwhelmed by the nature of what had taken place, we kept encouraging each other by telling each other that we were "doing this for Carmina" as we could do nothing to help the others.*
>
> *I have recently retired from the Sheriff's Department after serving for 31 years. I don't know if you have any questions regarding the investigation but if you do, I'd be happy to sit down with you and try to answer them.*
>
> *I hope you have found some peace during your growing up years. You are very strong to have come in search of answers to this very painful part of your life. I have often wondered how you were doing and have prayed many times for your well being. I hope things are going well for you.*
>
> *May God always bless you,*
> *Mike Brown*

I wrote back several days later, gratefully accepting his offer to help. I told him I hoped my book would offer the lesson "that forgiveness is the strongest medicine for the victim and the murderer." I also thanked him for the work he'd done on the murders and for leading the other detectives in solving the case. "I understand that it must have been devastating for you all as well," I added.

I asked Mike if he knew how I could go about looking at the court records associated with my father's case, and he promised to look into the matter and call me with what he learned. "You have an extraordinary story to tell," he added. "Your message of forgiveness is almost beyond comprehension." Our bond began in those two e-mails, and it grew from there as I filled him in on the course of my life since 1989 and he answered my questions about the murders and the investigation.

When I got my appointment to look at the court records, Mike called ahead to make sure the worst of the photos were removed before I saw the file, and then went with me for moral support. We weren't allowed to photocopy any of the records, but we could take notes. Each of us transcribed half of deputy probation officer Angela E. Meyer's December 1990 report, with its bleak yet appropriate verdict on my father and his behavior: "Every human being is deserving of some compassion, but Ramón Salcido has yet to reveal his humanity. He killed children and was unmoved by their desperate struggle to defend themselves. His sexual misconduct with the dead or dying Maria and Ruth Richards is abhorrent."

As Mike and I continued our research, he was the soul of generosity. Arlyn and Mike took me into their home for several days, bought me lunches and dinners, took me shopping for clothes, gave me rides, and even brought me to the beach for an outing. They volunteered to pay for my tuition and books to enroll in a community college course to get my high school equivalency degree. Mike even looked into counseling for me through the Sonoma County Victim Assistance Center.

When I wanted to visit one of the nurses who had worked

at Petaluma Valley Hospital when I was there as a child, I asked him to drive me there. The woman prepared us all a breakfast, and then he sat quietly off to the side as we talked. Later that day he took me to the cemetery and stood by as I spent time alone with my family.

The more time passed, the more our relationship became like that of a father and daughter. I could talk with Mike about anything, from the murders and the years that followed, to the life I was trying to make for myself today—mistakes and all.

For the first time since childhood, I had found someone I could be myself with and who understood what I had been through in ways that no one else could have. And for that, I will always be grateful.

Thirty-two

Twilight settles like melancholy over the Valley of the Moon, muting the colors of the grapevines as the car pulls away from Mike Brown's house in Santa Rosa. The cruise back down Highway 12 toward Sonoma is somber. Sean Kingston is back on, playing another one of Carmina's favorite songs: "We've got little boys and little girls / Growing up on this sinful earth."

Mike Brown has been good for Carmina. As much as all the things he has done for her, she appreciates that he doesn't lecture her. "He doesn't say 'Do this' or 'Do that.' He says, 'Well, if I was in that position, this is what I would do.' All my life, people have told me what to do, and I learned to just tune them out. But I hear Captain Mike Brown. . . . I don't always follow his advice, at least not right away. But I always listen, and I usually agree—even if it takes me a little time to come around."

If only she'd had someone like him as a father, she muses, instead of Ramón Salcido. How different would her life have been? She thinks back on all the men in her life who should have looked after her. One tried to kill her. One gave *her away to strangers. One participated in her abuse, keeping her virtually isolated from the world and squandering money others donated for her future.*

Only one man she knew had ever come through for her: the detective who with his men had done everything they could to save her, and then to seek justice for her and her family.

Sometime after they met, she told him all of this in a letter.

Mike Brown responded: "It is the most beautiful letter that I have ever received."

I've tried as best as I can to deal with what I've been given. And that includes facing the last hurdle in my quest to come to terms with my past.

When I mentioned, in both the KRON story and my interview with Chris Smith, that I was hoping to meet with my father, the responses I received were many and varied. Mary Stuart wrote to tell me that, as a young clerk at the Public Defender's Office during my father's trial, she had had the job of visiting my father every day in jail. "I understand how you would want to see him and look him in the eye," she wrote me now. "I wonder if I would also be so brave (psychologically/emotionally I mean of course) if I were you." She offered to talk to me about her experiences before I went, and even to accompany me if I was looking for support.

Another e-mail, with the subject line "I knew your dad before you did," took me aback. "I have been thinking about all the things I wanted to say to you about your Dad," it read. "How I knew Ramón before he met your mother. He was a very nice young man. . . .

"But more important than anything I could say about him is what he would tell you about himself. His life in Mexico and why he came here. How he met your mother, and their life together. He would not lie to you, but only tell you the truth as he remembers it. We have talked over the years about many things. I pray you will give him a chance to tell it all to you in person."

This e-mail also urged me to get in contact with a woman who had "come to know Ramón since he has been in San Quentin," calling her "a wonderful sister in Christ." I could only assume this must be my father's "girlfriend." "I have kept in touch with [your father] all these years because he is more than just an acquaintance to me," the writer concluded. "I consider him a brother in Christ."

I couldn't believe that someone would actually write to tell me about my father's Christian virtues or urge me to meet his new girlfriend. Mike Brown warned me not to be swayed by such letters. "There are lots of strange people out there who are inexplicably drawn to associate with people on death row," he wrote me. "I think these people are suckers and easily led by lying convicts who will do and say anything to sway others into believing that they are really good people [in order] to try and get out of the ultimate punishment . . . and these naïve people just show up and eat it all up."

Mike knew I was planning to confront my father myself, and he reminded me that no mediator could pretend to heal the rift between us. "Only you will be able to decide for yourself if what Ramón tells you is the truth," he told me.

I had already reached the same conclusion. In my response, I told him I felt "there is always hope, but I am being careful and cautious, because remember I know a side of him that not many others knew . . . how he really treated my mom, Angela, and us children." I told Mike the truth—that I prayed for my father's soul every day—and that I hoped "for his sake that he is sincere in his remorse and conversion."

A few days after the KRON television interview aired, I received one other unexpected response: a letter from my father. He had seen the interview from his cell.

Dear Daughter Carmina Salcido:

Respectfully, I'd like to let you know that I watched the interview you gave to KRON Channel 4 news and my heart was filled with great relief and joy to know that you are taking steps to slowly overcome and to heal your physical, emotional and spiritual wounds I had inflicted on you when the terrible tragedy took place back in April 1989. Since the first day I learned about all what I did to you, I have done nothing but regret all of my wrongful acts. I pray daily to God up above for you and all the victims' families because no one in this world should ever go through what I put you all through.

All these years it has been for me nothing but pure hell. Not because I have been sentenced to death or for all what I have gone through myself with my imprisonment but because I didn't know how you and all the victims' families were holding on outside trying to deal and to overcome your own pain, grief and wounds. I have blamed no one other than myself for all what I put you, Carmina and all the victims' families through. To me, all this from time to time seems to be like a nightmare!

I would like to share lots more with you, but this time I just want to focus on what you requested from me on television when you said you would want to receive an apology from me. Well, I am going to take you at your word. Carmina, I do honestly regret all the pain I inflicted on your hearts. It has been very painful for me and honestly, my heart and prayers are with you all!

Carmina, I would apologize to you and to all the victims' families not once, twice but ten trillion times if this could be of some sort of small step for you all to find a little peace and healing in your hearts. If there is anything else I can do to help you with questions that you may want me to answer, please feel free to drop me a note at the above address or through any other means that you want me to respond, okay!

I would have sent you this apology letter to you from the day I learned you were in the hospital back in 1989, but I did not know how and no one from your attorneys or my attorneys know how this can be arranged. I only give a little history of your medical record, about your life as a child with me, etc. and my apology to your adopted parents' attorneys after your custody case was over. But, I must let you know that you have been in my heart and prayers all these years and I grieve and feel the pain with you over this terrible tragedy.

Thank you for publicly forgiving me for all what I put you through. Hearing this from you it really brings to me a little sanity and peace in my heart. It means the world to me! Thank you also for allowing me to bring back some awesome memories of both of us when you were my precious little girl. Seeing your face reminded me of your awesome laughter and our lives together before the tragedy. Your Grandmother Valentina recently went to be with the Lord. Before she passed away, she told me to please if I get in touch with you to let you know that she was very sorry for all what you and the victims' families went through and that she always loved you. I hope you forgive her and my family in Mexico too.

Take care of yourself and God Bless you today and forever!
Sincerely, your Dad, Ramón Salcido

The letter made me feel sick. Though my father seemed to apologize several times, he never did so very directly, and he filled the letter with *if*s and excuses: He would apologize *if* it meant a small step for us to find peace and healing in our hearts. He would have sent this apology back in 1989, *but* he didn't know how. His language seemed to distance himself from the murders, referring to "the first day I learned about all what I did to you." He even had the gall to suggest that I should forgive his family—who of course bore no responsibility for the murders he committed.

Worst of all, the letter kept coming back to the subject of *his own* suffering. "All these years it has been for me nothing but pure hell. . . . It has been very painful for me. . . . To me, all this from time to time seems to be like a nightmare!"

My father claimed he felt my pain. But I wasn't buying it.

I learned only later that my father had never really held himself accountable for the murders. In interviews he'd given to Spanish-language newsletters and other publications since going to prison, he had repeatedly lamented having "lost" everyone he loved the most, as if they'd been taken from him in some terrible accident—without ever mentioning that they were lost because he murdered them.

Ever since his trial, my father had been putting forth a portrait of himself as victim and martyr. Once, on a Christian prisoners website, he wrote: "After the police flew me back from Mexico to jail in Santa Rosa, a crowd gathered at the jail shouting, 'Kill him! Kill him!' It was a terrible tragedy and the whole world was shocked. I felt that all I wanted to do was die as I had lost all that I had ever loved." What "terrible tragedy" was he referring to—the murders, or the scorn he suffered at the hands of an outraged crowd?

From prison, my father professed to be a born-again Christian. He actually became a minister, claiming to have roughly three hundred followers on the outside, his girlfriend among them. He wrote sermons each week to be read to his congregation. And he supported his "prison ministry" with their donations and by selling art he created—mostly religious drawings—on a website called MurderAuction. com, which bills itself as a place where "the true crime enthusiast . . . can sell, buy, and view true crime artifacts," including prisoners' artwork.

My father has given several conflicting accounts of his

conversion. In one version, it happened shortly after his return from Mexico. "A little girl put a Bible in my cell. I read it and accepted Christ as my Savior," he wrote for the Christian inmate web page. "Then my heart was flooded with warm waves of forgiveness and true joy." But the story of the little girl wandering around the Sonoma County jail handing out Bibles—apparently with access to isolation cells—was only one version. In other versions, the "little girl" handed either a Bible or passages from the Bible to him as he made his way through the hostile crowd outside the jail—a story clearly modeled on the story of Jesus bearing his cross through the streets of Jerusalem. In still other versions, she handed him the Bible as he passed by the public on his way to a courtroom, or as he arrived at San Quentin.

As Mike Brown pointed out, all the versions were ludicrous: After his arrest, my father never got within arm's length of the public—including little girls with Bibles. Of course, being a pathological liar goes with being a murderous sociopath. And prison inmates who view themselves as victims are about as common as those who "find Jesus" behind prison walls, especially when faced with looming eternity. I take my father's little-girl story no more seriously than I do the occasional article he has written over the years decrying abortion as the taking of innocent lives, or urging people who have been wronged—presumably like himself—to "forget the anger and hate" before it gets them into trouble.

And yet this much was still true: Ever since I was a little girl at the Swindells' house, saying my prayers every night before I went to bed, I had thought about seeing my father again face-to-face. I wanted him to ask God to forgive him for the murders and the assaults. In so doing, I wanted him to save his soul. And I wanted him to fall to his knees and beg for my forgiveness—and maybe if I believed he was truly sorry, without making excuses or blaming others, I would be able to forgive him.

By early 2006, I had a new home—at least temporarily—on a ranch in a rural part of the county. After the owner, a woman who had known my mom, saw the KRON interview, she had contacted me with a business proposition. She had started a ranch for children who had been abused while they were in the foster-care system, she said, and she was planning to use her horses as therapy for these children. She told me that if I'd move from Sacramento to Sonoma to help her, she'd pay me fourteen dollars an hour, plus room and board. And I would get to work with the horses.

It sounded like a dream job—until I got there and learned that this woman hadn't actually started the ranch yet. She didn't actually own any horses, though a few had been left in her care on the property she was leasing. Nor did she have any money to pay me. In fact, her plan was to use me to help attract donations for the project. Once again, another adult in my life had disappointed me. I had thought achieving freedom would be like reaching the crest of a mountain and gazing out on the beautiful view. What I wasn't counting on was how much climbing I'd have to do to get there.

For the moment, though, I had nowhere else to go. All I could do was cool my heels and hope the woman would somehow find a way to get the ranch project going.

And that's how I ended up meeting my father.

One day, this woman and I were driving across the bridge to San Rafael when she pointed and said, "Oh, look—say hi to your dad." She was pointing to San Quentin State Prison, which sits on a peninsula in the San Francisco Bay.

Suddenly, I had a thought. I asked her to turn off the highway, and she drove me to the prison administration office. There I filled out an application to visit my father—and then went home to await word that he had approved it.

The approval came quickly. On a sunny day in February 2006, I drove to San Quentin State Prison to see the man who had murdered my family and left me for dead.

People often describe San Quentin as a scary place—a

monstrous building complete with barred windows, a fortress-like roofline, and a security tower. But I wasn't afraid of the building itself. I was nervous about meeting my father.

The last time I'd seen his face, it was twisted and angry, as if he was mad at me for fighting for my life. I remembered that moment as if it had happened just minutes before.

With security personnel everywhere I looked, I was led to the visitation area, which was essentially a large room divided into cages. Visitors enter one side of the cage and take a seat; prisoners enter the other side. Only a table stands between them.

Before I stepped inside, I turned to a guard and told him I had one request. "I don't want him to touch me at all," I said.

The guard nodded and passed on the instruction. Any attempt to touch me, he told Ramón, and he would forfeit his visiting rights until his execution.

My father nodded and sat down. He looked much the same as he had when I was a girl—a few pounds heavier, with salt-and-pepper hair instead of black, and no mustache. We faced each other across the table for a moment without saying anything. Then I decided to break the ice. "Well, let me start this way," I said. "I'm here on a mission to talk about what happened and forgive you for what you did back then. . . . I can't forget what you did, but I think I can forgive."

I left it unsaid that forgiveness was a two-way street. He would have to ask for it—from me and from God—to get it. But it would have to be his own idea, or it would be worthless.

If I expected my father to break down in tears and beg for forgiveness, I was disappointed. "You don't know how much this means to me," he said, with no more emotion than if I'd offered him a job. If anything, he seemed jovial as our visit went on—as long as we weren't talking about "the tragedy," a term both he and the Swindells used to refer to the slaughter of my family.

For the next two and a half hours we talked—or, I should

say, my father talked about himself. He talked about his life in Mexico and how he came to California. At one point he did ask me about how I was raised. But after listening to my answer for a few seconds he quickly returned to talking about his life and how bad things were for him in prison.

At another point in the visit, he sighed and brought up— not for the first time—how happy our family had been, how much in love he and my mother were. He made it sound as if nothing bad had ever happened in our family until that day—no fights, no drunken rants, no nights when he never came home.

"Wait a minute," I said. "I remember you and Mom having fights. In fact, I remember trying to break one up and getting punched by you." But he just changed the subject; I might as well have been talking about someone else.

I left the prison that afternoon in turmoil. I was happy I had taken that step, had faced my father for the first time, but I was angry, and sad, and confused about his obvious lack of anything resembling remorse. He did say he was sorry about what happened, but he sounded like a disinterested third party talking about a train wreck. And he never admitted he'd done anything wrong. It was the drugs, and all the troubles that had been piling up on him, that were to blame for "the tragedy."

But what really struck me was that he kept talking about "the day I lost everything that meant the most to me." As if he'd played no part in what happened. As if *he* was the victim. Not me. Not my mom or sisters or any of the others. Just him.

It was all about him. And I was not about to forgive him for that.

After that visit, I had no intention of ever seeing my father again. He had not given me what I needed, nor did he leave me with any hope that he ever could. But he kept trying to establish a relationship. In March 2006 he sent me an e-mail (through his girlfriend) asking me to consider visiting him again.

When I showed it to Mike Brown, he confirmed my impression that both my father and his girlfriend were trying to build a new relationship with me, on the slim chance that it might help my father's standing with the courts. "They're clearly trying to get you to be sympathetic to him so you might have an influence in helping him escape the court's punishment," he wrote, "which means they're not very hopeful about any legal issues helping their cause. I'm glad that you are smart enough to see the plot and not be used by them. Like you said, it's still all about him."

More than a year passed before I decided to communicate with my father again. And it happened because I'd met a man just like him.

After moving away from the horse ranch, I was taken in for a while by Martha and Fred, a middle-aged couple I'd met through Pat Rile. But I couldn't stay with them forever, and soon I found myself out on the streets, looking for a place to live. Life on my own was harder than I'd expected. For a time I even lived out of an old van that had been given to me by a well-wisher.

Then I met Carlos. He was Mexican and in the country illegally. He was also a drug dealer. But he was the last man on earth the Swindells would have approved of, and perhaps for that reason, I fell in love with him.

But Carlos didn't return the love. He would go out late and stay out all night. If I asked where he went, he'd shrug and say it had to do with his drug business.

"Can I go with you?"

"No."

"Where have you been?"

"I can't tell you."

Or he'd come home and start yelling, accusing me of running around behind his back, even though I'd been home all night. Once, during a particularly heated argument, he pulled a knife on me. He accused me of cheating, which was bad enough. Then he said, "You're just like your mom. Ramón was right to do what he did."

It was the final straw. I was tired of being abused. Tired of wanting to trust someone and having them shove it right back in my face . . . or in my ribs. I held my arms out to my sides, giving him an easy shot at my heart, and told him to go ahead and use the knife. I wasn't afraid to die. After all, I'd been there before. *Kill me,* I thought. *See if I care.*

Carlos backed down. Later I called the police and had him arrested for threatening me with a weapon. I was done getting kicked in the teeth, and my father was about to find that out for himself.

During my brief time with Carlos, and at his urging, I started visiting Ramón again. Only now, with Carlos out of my life, I had a different purpose.

I was no longer interested in hearing Ramón beg for my forgiveness. Nor was I interested in saving his immortal soul.

What I cared about was filling in the holes in my memory—any stories I might get from him about happier times, about my short life with my mom and sisters. A trip to the beach. Playing in the yard and riding our tricycles. Visits to my grandparents. Tearing open the presents on our last Christmas Eve together. *Look at how cute they are. We can't be mad at them.* I had so few memories of my family, and no one to remind me.

So I kept returning to San Quentin. But it wasn't easy. On one of my visits, I showed up with my hair dyed platinum blond. I thought my father would be surprised, but he said he knew I'd dyed it before I came because he'd seen it on my MySpace page. I told him I didn't think death row prisoners had access to computers, but he winked and told me he was on a cleaning detail that allowed him to sneak onto a computer when no one was looking. I wasn't sure that was true, and Mike Brown agreed; he thought that was just my father's latest attempt to manipulate and control me. After all, Dad had once told me he knew everything I was doing in Sonoma—where I was working, who I was dating. He said his "paparazzi" were keeping an eye on me for him. He said it with a slight smile, but I recognized it as a threat—that he was capable of reaching beyond the walls of San Quentin.

Still, I wasn't sure I believed him about trawling the Internet—until some of my girlfriends started asking if I knew why someone with a San Quentin e-mail address was checking out their MySpace profiles. The next time I saw my father, I asked him about it. He admitted that he'd been on their MySpace pages—"looking for more kinky photographs of you."

I wanted to throw up. My father was coming on to me.

However, I wasn't going to let his behavior stop me from returning, from sticking with it until I had what I wanted from him. And he did answer my questions, such as telling me how we'd drive down the street with me at the wheel while he ducked to alarm the neighbors. And how I always wanted to ride on his motorcycle, even when my sisters ran away.

But I let him know about my memories, too—and not just the happy ones. Memories of him fighting with my mother, screaming at her. Of him coming home staggering drunk. Of his rages.

He only listened to what he wanted to hear. If he didn't like what I was saying, he ignored it or changed the subject. "If that's what you remember," he'd say, "I'm not going to argue with you."

Finally, the day before Mother's Day 2007, I had heard all I needed from Ramón Salcido. There were no more hollow places in my memory for him to fill. We had run out of things to say to each other. Even without Mother's Day around the corner, it would have been an emotionally taxing day. I had no place to stay, no money, no one to love. No family to go home to when I left San Quentin.

There was just one more thing to say to him. It was something I used to say before I cried myself to sleep in the Swindells' house. This time, though, I didn't say it quietly. "I wish you *had* killed me!" I yelled at him. "Because my life has been *hell* up to now."

I burst into tears. Until then I'd refused to break down in front of him, but that day I couldn't help it. I told him that the next morning I was going to the cemetery to leave roses at my mother's grave. "Thanks to you, I can't give them to her in person."

And what was my father's response? An apology? Asking at last for forgiveness and truly meaning it? No, just the same sentence he'd been repeating since we met, spoken in the same dull monotone. "I'd do anything to turn back the clock and make things different."

I left the interview room and drove away from the prison as fast as I could.

Others might believe my dad wasn't to blame for his crimes. Others might be fooled into calling him a changed man, a man of God. Let them think he'd been a good husband and a good father. That that one day was simply a "terrible tragedy."

He might have fooled other people—his girlfriend, those who supported his "ministry"—but I knew him for what he really was. An evil man. A dark shadow that had passed through my life. A monster.

That was the last time I went to see my father. There's no reason to go, nothing more I need to hear from him. I doubt I'll ever see him again—unless it's to attend his execution by lethal injection, the method that has replaced the gas chamber in California. I still haven't decided whether to attend. And if I do, I don't know whether it will be to comfort him or to represent the people he murdered. But any such decision is likely to still be many years away. When Ramón was sent to San Quentin in 1990, there were about three hundred condemned men on death row; now there are more than six hundred, and the State of California has shown little interest in speeding up the process.

When I look back at all my disappointments in life—at my experiences with my father, the Swindells, the Holts, Carlos, even my grandfather—I'm amazed that I can trust anybody. But then I think about the people who didn't let me down: my mom and my sisters, the Sonoma County District Attorney's Office, the Sonoma County Sheriff's Department, the detectives who worked so hard, the doctors and nurses who saved me, the nuns who did what they could, and especially Detective Mike Brown, who has saved me more than once.

In April 2007, I finally accepted an invitation to visit my father's family in Mexico. And from the moment I arrived in Los Mochis, I was treated like a long-lost treasure. Surrounded by uncles, aunts, and a myriad of cousins, I'd never felt as loved and wanted as I did during the month I stayed there.

I left Los Mochis fully intending to return someday—perhaps when I'm older, perhaps soon. It probably depends on what shape my life takes here in Sonoma.

For now, I am living in the moment. But I try not to close every door to my past. I still talk to Mrs. Swindell, though we have little to say to each other. I can only shake my head at what that trust fund money would mean to me now. The people who donated those funds had been trying to give me some hope, some chance of a future that my family could no longer provide. But I didn't even get a high school education out of it.

I've also heard that there have been a lot of changes at the God's Cowgirls Ranch: After someone complained to the state, real bathrooms have been built for the girls, and from their website it looks like they're taking a more sensitive approach—at least in their marketing.

I remain in Sonoma County, for now, and often visit the cemetery where my family lies together. Each time, the feeling of being at home and wanting to linger remains. It's as if my mom and sisters, my grandma, and my aunts are out there somewhere, not dead and gone forever. In fact, when I stand there in front of their graves, I feel as close to them as I can possibly be. I sometimes wonder if they're waiting for me.

When I left the ranch in Idaho, and then again when I returned to Sonoma, I thought I had reached the top of the mountain. There'd be no more heartache or struggle. But I know now that if I'm ever going to reach the summit and see that view, I'm going to have to put one foot in front of the other and keep climbing. Sometimes it feels like I've been walking such a long, long time. But I'm not lost, not anymore, and I'm going to get there.

Epilogue

In June 2008 the California State Supreme Court rejected Ramón Salcido's last appeal and upheld his death sentence. His lawyers had tried to argue that his transfer back to the United States in 1989 was in violation of Mexican law prohibiting extradition of its citizens to a jurisdiction where they may face the death penalty. After the court's decision, his lawyers announced that they would appeal to the U.S. Supreme Court.

A few days before the decision, Carmina received another letter from her father. He said he wanted to let her know that he appreciated receiving recent letters from her, "even if your words toward me are a little harsh and filled with grief and hate." He then rebuked her for "disrespecting your father" and cited several Bible verses intended to show her the error of her ways. He warned her that, if she continued to "hate and disrespect" him, then she would lose any chance for the "embrace of a father . . . love of a father . . . kiss of a father . . . and advice of a father," and that it would be "all your fault."

STEVE JACKSON

Acknowledgments

CARMINA SALCIDO

My love and thanks to the Reverend Mother Teresa (Madrecita) and Mother Mistress Agnes for all your love, understanding, prayers, and guidance. To my grandpa, Bob Richards, my utmost love and sympathy. I understand your loss, pain, and loneliness and will always love you. To my uncle Lewis, who was there for me in a really hard time in my life, when I was trying to learn what freedom meant; and to my uncles Robert and Gerald, whom I love and respect.

My heart-filled gratitude to retired Captain Mike Brown of the Sonoma County Sheriff's Department, for his dedication to finding and capturing my father. His kind support and advice when I returned to Sonoma, along with that of his lovely wife, Arlyn, mean more to me than I can express. Much appreciation to all the other detectives and officers who helped work on the case.

My thanks to Martha and Fred for their unselfish love, care, and friendship, as well as Donna and Mike for making me part of their family. And to Steve Jackson, my coauthor and companion in the making of this book. Without your talent, patience, and selflessness, this book would not have been written.

And to everyone else out there who prayed for me and re-membered me all of these years, thank you. It is my hope that this book will be an inspiration to anyone facing seem-ingly impossible obstacles. Never give up.

With love to Paul Wilson; much thanks for the good times we've had, hope we can go far in life together!

STEVE JACKSON

My adoration and thanks to my family, whose support and love I depend on; otherwise none of this would be pos-sible. And especially to my brother, Donald; you were the best big brother anyone could ever hope for, and I miss you every day. My thanks also to Michael Hamilburg, a superior agent and an even better human being; Calvert Morgan Jr., at HarperCollins, proof that behind every great book there is a great editor; Captain Mike Brown (ret.), for his invalu-able assistance, guidance, and friendship; and Detective Randy Biehler for his insights and help. Last but certainly not least, my thanks and respect to Carmina Salcido, a very brave young woman whose life story is, and I'm sure will continue to be, a lesson for all of us in what it means to per-severe despite all odds.